THE SECRETS MEN KEEP

THE SECRETS MEN KEEP

Stephen Arterburn

THOMAS NELSON
Since 1798

NASHVILLE DALLAS MEXICO CITY RIO DE JANEIRO BEIJING

Published in Nashville, Tennessee by Thomas Nelson. Thomas Nelson is a trademark of Thomas Nelson, Inc.

Stephen Arterburn published in association with Alive Communications, 7680 Goddard Street, Suite 200, Colorado Springs, CO 80920.

Thomas Nelson, Inc. titles may be purchased in bulk for educational, business, fund-raising, or sales promotional use. For information, please e-mail SpecialMarkets@ThomasNelson.com.

Cover Design: The DesignWorks Group, Inc.
Interior Design: Teresa Billingsley

ISBN: 9-781-59145-469-4 (hardcover)
ISBN: 9-781-59145-5424 (IE)
ISBN: 978-0-7852-8925-8

Printed in the United States of America
07 08 09 10 RRD 9 8 7 6 5 4 3 2

CONTENTS

INTRODUCTION

WHY MEN KEEP SECRETS

Secrets are not a bad thing. If they were, God wouldn't have them. There are some things that He keeps completely to Himself—"secret things," as the Bible calls them (Deuteronomy 29:29). He has other information that He reveals only to "his servants the prophets" (Amos 3:7). In fact, Proverbs 25:2 says, "It is the glory of God to conceal a matter."

If it's acceptable for God to conceal things, to have secrets, then why is it not completely acceptable for men to have secrets, "to conceal a matter"?

The difference between God keeping secrets and men keeping secrets reveals one of the core disparities between the two: motive. Being perfect and pure, God has reasons for keeping secrets that reflect His flawless character. Man, on the other hand, is not perfect or pure. Therefore, man's motives for doing *anything* are always suspect. Because of man's fallen human nature, we are, theologically speaking, guilty until proven innocent.

The bottom line is this (and every man knows it): most of the secrets men keep are held out of fear—the fear of embarrassment, shame, guilt, loss of respect, loss of stature and favor, repercussions, reparations, and the like. In other words, men mostly keep secrets for all the wrong reasons. Understandable reasons, but wrong nonetheless.

Not all of a man's secrets are sinful. For instance, it's no sin for a man to have done a less-than-adequate job of planning for retirement, to be a less-than-perfect communicator with his wife, or to be less than disciplined when it comes to keeping that spare tire from inflating around his gut. These aren't sins, but they are chinks in a man's personal armor, none which he is proud to reveal. He wishes he could tell someone besides God, to receive absolution and understanding from a band of brothers, but he can't. He either has no one to tell or is too ashamed to admit his flaws and failings to others. As a result, he stuffs them into a dark corner of his soul where they pick away at his self-image for a lifetime.

Other secrets are sins. And if a man finds it difficult to share his non-sinful secrets, how much harder is it for him to share his sinful ones?

Whether sinful or not, a man's secrets are covered up, walled off, and protected with a myriad of deflections that serve one purpose: to keep him feeling safe. Busy activity, sports obsessions, pride, preoccupations, work, male attitude, macho sex talk—these are just some of the guardrails that can surround a man's inner self. Yet secrets are anything but safe. In fact, they are the most dangerous forces within a man. Left unresolved, they can drag him into the gutter, or at least keep his mind headed in that direction. Secrets can consume a man's life. Think of the myriad of steps a man goes through to cover up an act of infidelity, indiscretion, or immorality. The secret becomes a dictator and a monster, directing and devouring his life. The man spends his days preparing meals (reasons and excuses) to feed the secret's ravenous demands and keep it at bay. Eventually, this skeleton in the cupboard becomes a master blackmailer, threatening to expose him for who he is.

Every man has secrets, some more than others. They are as much a part of the male makeup as those other facets that receive far more attention. Secrets are at a man's core, and they thrive as long as he keeps them out of sight and out of mind. Once in the shadows, they blend with desires, hopes, wishes, and dreams to form the foundation of a man's heart—the "real" him. And while he attempts to act upon what he believes to be true about himself, a man's secrets exist hidden in a parallel world yet influencing every act.

If you are a woman reading this, be assured that your man has hidden knowledge he will not offer up voluntarily. Whether or not his secrets are sin-based is certainly important, but that's not the focal concern. The main point is that you probably don't know your man as well as you think you do. There's no reason for that to cause despair, however, because the truth is that he hopes you will discover his secrets so you can save him from himself. Ultimately, he desires for you to help him become a transparent person, one who is completely known. (Secrets, like sins, have to be brought out in the open before change can occur.)

WEARING THE MASK

A good friend of mine recently married a wonderful woman who believed in him and his character. They had dated for more than two years, so she thought she knew the man to whom she was committing her life. All their friends were encouraging and supportive of their relationship and plans to marry.

My friend was considered to be quite a catch. He loved church, and he had an engaging personality and a laugh that could warm up a crowd in an instant. I thought he was one of the finest men I'd ever met and always enjoyed it when we ran into one another. His winsome ways, plentiful hugs, and smiling countenance left people feeling better about themselves. He was active in a men's encouragement group and a weekly Bible study, and he even saw a therapist on a regular basis as a means to greater maturity. I don't exaggerate when I say that my friend was a remarkable man, one any woman would be fortunate to have as a partner in life.

The couple's marriage ceremony was deeply meaningful as they exchanged vows of fidelity that included not only the physical part of life, but the mental and emotional as well. I was impressed. I had never heard vows that expressed such obvious forethought. As they drove away from the reception for a two-week honeymoon, I, along with all their friends, expected nothing but success for this couple.

With a setup like that, you know where I'm going: all was not as it seemed with my friend. Months later, he told me what a disappointment their honeymoon had been. They had refrained from sexual relationships prior to marriage, so he was anticipating the time of his life on their honeymoon. He fully expected all his past sexual hurts and wounds to be resolved in a cathartic relationship with his new bride.

But his bride could not deliver. She wanted to be all that he needed and desired, but his expectations were sorely unmet. For whatever reasons—her personality, stress and fatigue from the wedding, new-bride timidity—she fell short of his Aphrodite image of what a wife should be.

My friend had been previously married and had been divorced for several years prior to his new marriage. During that period (I came to find out) he engaged in sexual immorality with almost every woman he dated. Despite his active participation in all things Christian, he kept this immoral lifestyle a secret from everyone—even his therapist. I knew nothing of this until months after his new marriage. He viewed the hundreds of sexual encounters following his first divorce as temporary slipups that God would understand. He even rationalized sex outside marriage as a form of sexual healing from the wounds of his sexually-dry first marriage.

My friend's secret—one he refused to admit to himself, much less anyone else—was that he was a sex addict. His modus operandi was to feed his immature need for attention by attracting and seducing women with his charisma. Ultimately, his post-divorce life was a cycle of sexual pursuit and conquest. He needed to "own" the women he lured to affirm his own value— a process consummated by getting them into bed. He would later find out through therapy that he was trying to extract intimacy from these women to fill the vacuum left by his own distant and self-obsessed mother. The pain of never having real intimacy his entire life was temporarily relieved after each conquest, only to become unbearable soon after, which lead to another immoral act.

When he became engaged to his new wife he made it clear that he had been sexually active after his divorce, though he withheld the degree of his activity. His trusting fiancée assumed it had been a reaction to his divorce and that such activity would not be a problem in their marriage. His willingness to abstain from sex with her before marriage gave her a sense of power and confidence that she would be all he would ever need in the bedroom again.

Sadly, his marriage to this trusting woman was simply another act of ownership, unrealized by her. Once their relationship was consummated and the adrenaline rush was over (as it had been after all his previous conquests), he became as dissatisfied as ever. Though married, he was just as addicted to sex as he had been before marriage. His sexual dysfunction was the same after marriage as before. The change of "personnel" was like a drug addict switching from alcohol to Valium. His secret problem was still alive and well.

Things unraveled quickly after the couple returned from their honeymoon. They arrived home on a Friday to discover that her mother was ill in another city. They decided that she would go to assist her mother, while he would stay behind to help the church's youth pastor with a Saturday function and to attend an elders' meeting on Sunday. That meant he was alone for the weekend.

At the youth event he ran into a married woman, one of the most attractive women in the church, whom he had secretly had a crush on during his first marriage. The fact that she was married was of no consequence to him; his sex-drug addiction went into action and he began the conquest. Within a few weeks, he had wooed her into bed. But this time, the sex-drug left him dissatisfied and ashamed. He knew that he had blown a beautiful opportunity to create a marriage with a wonderful new wife.

He realized that only a pitifully sick person could start down a path of unfaithfulness the day after returning from his honeymoon. His shame and revulsion became great enough that he picked up the phone and called me seeking help. Once I learned his story I told him that he needed to humble himself in a public way and begin attending Sex Addicts Anonymous meetings. He agreed and I went with him.

He was a blubbering mess from the moment we walked in the door until the end of the meeting. Through his sobbing he told the group why he was there and what he had done, and was affirmed by the group for his desire to come clean and seek help. Within six months after being stabilized in therapy, he revealed his secrets to his wife. It was a devastating revelation, to put it mildly, for her to realize that her marriage was merely a means to meeting her husband's pathological needs. To her credit, she has stood beside him, and to this day they remain together. If they survive as a couple it will only be through a most painful process.

INQUIRING MINDS WANT TO KNOW

My friend's secrets are an example of the kind that are sinful and life-destroying. Of course, not all of men's secrets are like his; not all secrets are sick or pathological. But through my friendships with men over the years, talking with men who call in daily to my radio broadcast, and reflecting on my own personal life and experiences, I have concluded this: all men have secrets of some kind. Not a day goes by that a man doesn't think about something that no one knows but him—and that he often wishes he could at least talk about, if not deal with in a practical fashion. Men want to stop the static in their minds—the buzz that's there when they go to sleep and still present when they wake up. For some men the buzz is barely noticeable; for others it's a deafening roar. But for all men it's there.

When I came to understand that I wasn't the only man with secrets, my interests were piqued to discover what other men were thinking about that they weren't telling anyone else. I was intrigued by the secrets men felt they had to keep. To that end, my publisher and I hired survey and research firm Zoomerang to conduct the "Men's Life Satisfaction Survey" in late 2005, gathering answers to twenty-five questions from 3,600 (3,598 to be exact) randomly and anonymously selected men in the United States. In this book, I've devoted an entire chapter for each of those twenty-five questions.

Before we dive into the first of these queries, here are a few general factors to keep in mind:

- Less than 74 percent of the men were professing Christians.
- The remaining 26 percent were simply classified as "not Christian."
- Generally, the responses of the Christian and non-Christian men differed only slightly (within the margin of error on a survey this size, meaning a point or two outside the expected norm).
- The three issues on which the two groups differed most were:

  1. Ten percent more non-Christian than Christian men reported frequent and intense sexual fantasies.
  2. Nearly 8 percent more non-Christian men felt drawn to pornography in movies, magazines, and on the Internet.
  3. Nearly 7 percent more Christian than non-Christian men said they wanted to feel more cherished by their wives.

- Predictably, the largest discrepancy of all was on the question that asked men if they were bored with church and church activities. Twenty-three percent more non-Christian than Christian men admitted to feeling this way.
- For the remainder of the questions, the two groups were within 0 to 6 percentage points of each other—a startling fact in itself.

As you can see from the chapter and section titles in the Table of Contents, the survey covered a broad range of issues in a man's life: finances, career, family, feelings, spirituality, women, and sexuality. The goal was to probe as broadly as possible into what men are refusing to tell others.

In the chapters, I have correlated the survey results with other similar studies drawn from a variety of sources. I've then discussed the data and the topic from a man's perspective. Finally, I've concluded each chapter with some thoughts specifically for men (called "New Directions") and for couples (called "New Connections").

I did this because I believe both men and women will profit from reading this book. Men will discover that they are not the only ones who think the way they do, and women will come to a deeper understanding of how the men in their lives think—be that a husband, boyfriend, brother, uncle, father, grandfather, or friend. The goal of this book is breadth, not depth. It is an overview, not a study.

Let me also point out that this book is not an attempt to hang men's dirty laundry out in the open or drag skeletons out of their closets. After all, some of these secrets are mine too! Rather, the book is meant to be an exploration, a path of self discovery both for men and for the women who love them. And anytime we set out to discover more about ourselves, our first realization is that the process of self-discovery is one that never ends.

AN OPEN-BOOK TEST

The early part of my college experience was disastrous. I made many poor choices and, as a result, became so broken that when my life was transformed by God's grace my friends found it hard to believe. By the time I had graduated I'd decided to pursue a career in counseling to help others experience the same recovery I had.

I'll never forget one of my seminary professors who later helped confirm this decision. After going through the routine of introducing himself at the beginning of the term, he stunned our class by announcing that he would be an open book during the course. We were free to ask him *anything*; he had nothing to hide, no secrets to conceal. And if his personal life and experiences could be helpful, he pronounced, he was ready to share them.

I had never experienced such openness before. I had been raised in an environment where fudging the truth was normative and every revelation was calculated on a risk-reward basis. But I discovered over the course of that semester that my professor's offer was honest and authentic.

I had many secrets of my own. A life of sexual promiscuity had led to conceiving a child out of wedlock and paying to have it aborted. I was so sin-sick that I turned to God for relief and began a process of cleansing my soul from the detritus of a self-centered life. When I saw the power of openness, as modeled by my professor, I felt God calling me to be a "revealer"—to help people bring their issues to the light of God's forgiveness through books, radio, and television. If I would model honesty, I figured, then perhaps others might be encouraged to be honest as well. As a result, I have revealed things about my life through the years that other people and ministries spend great sums of money to cover up. Some people have criticized my openness, but more have appreciatively identified with my struggles, failings, and successes.

Even after years of being candid, working on this book has caused me to take a fresh look at secrets in my own life. Though there have been victories realized through being honest in the past, I have seen there are more battles yet to win. One day, after working through some of this material, I blurted out to my wife, "I am the most impatient person I know!" My impatience is often hurtful to her and to others, and has caused me to miss important moments of discovery and connection in life. It is a fault that gets me in over my head. I overcommit out of a need to justify my existence and, in so doing, put pressure on precious relationships. Impatience causes me to be impulsive, to play God instead of waiting on Him and His timetable.

Seeing this issue afresh has humbled me and caused me to ask for forgiveness from my wife and others. It's also made me realize how dependent I am on the grace of God. But that's typical of where the process of revealing secrets leads. It's not comfortable, but it is necessary. It's in the place of dealing with life's secret issues where transformation begins.

As 1 Peter 1:7 says, the heat of trials is what causes the impurities in our lives to float to the surface so they can be skimmed away. But who likes heat? Not me, and likely not you. Because of this, we avoid it and hold tight to our impurities, our secrets. Set a piece of gold ore in a lab dish at room temperature and it stays the same. But turn up the heat and it becomes something worth even more as the impurities are revealed.

Revealing impurities is one thing; skimming them off the surface is another. And dealing with secrets takes two levels of commitment for both processes: enduring the heat to reveal impurities, and removing those impurities once they are revealed.

My hope is that as you read this book you will have the same experience I have had. I pray that you'll become committed to dealing with secrets appropriately and to skimming the impurities off the top as they float to the surface. For those men who are married, you will ultimately need to involve your wife in the process. But keep in mind that you may need to meet with a trusted counselor or friend initially to discuss your issues and develop a strategy for life change. In every case, whether married or not, we must keep James 5:16 as the premise that underlies our actions: confessing our sins (our secrets) to one another (the appropriate people) and praying for God's restorative grace.

That process will look different for every man. In that regard, I recommend the life strategy of Oswald Chambers, the author of My Utmost for His Highest: "Trust God and do the next thing."[1] Whatever is necessary—intense therapy to close up lifelong wounds opened in childhood, or a quiet conversation and closure with your wife—is what must be done.

I hope you will join me in this process of self-discovery to become the man God created you to be: honest and whole, living a life that is a continual process of self-revelation leading to freedom.

SECTION 1

SECRETS ABOUT FINANCES, FAME, AND FAMILY

Chapter 1

FINANCIAL SECURITY:
NOW AND THEN

When the reporter arrived, Burt was raking leaves around the "For Sale" sign stuck in the middle of his front yard. Earlier that day Burt had received a phone call from the reporter asking if he would share his story. Burt agreed, the reporter wrote the story, and I read it.

Burt had worked for Enron. He had prepared for his retirement with Enron stock that had, at one point, been worth more than $2 million. Burt explained how his retirement fund made him feel free, like the man he had always wanted to be. When the time came, he would be able to maintain a decent lifestyle without financial worries. But within a few months it had all gone away as the story of Enron's failure became known. The reporter wanted to know what it was like for Burt now.

It was like being a fool, Burt had said. He had gone from confidence and pride in the provision and plans he had made to feeling like a fool for entrusting his future to Enron. At first he had been furious and wanted to fight like a man to the death. Then the depression hit and he wanted to die, or at least run. But he stayed, put his house up for sale, and started looking for a job. He explained that in addition to losing his house and his retirement, he had lost his manhood as well. Now all he had was anger, bitterness, sadness, and desperation. And a feeling that all of his hard work had been for nothing. It had all meant that much to him.

WHAT WE KNOW ABOUT MEN AND FINANCIAL SECURITY

Kiplinger's Personal Finance magazine published a list of thirteen "scary scenarios" related to personal finances. Number one on the list was "Not Saving Enough for Retirement," and number two was "Outliving Your Retirement Savings." Those are obviously the flip sides of the same coin, but they are different. The first has to do with the discipline of saving, beginning at an early age, while the second has to do with the sometimes daunting task of figuring out which will arrive first: the end of me or the end of money. Related to these two issues was number six on the list: illness requiring long-term care and the financial implications of such a scenario.[1]

The folks at *Kiplinger's* must have talked to some of the same people—at least some of the same men—we did. In our survey we found that this statement—"Men are fearful about financial security now and in retirement"— drew greater agreement than any other statement in our survey. Specifically, 68.3 percent of the 3,600 men surveyed agreed. (Of the Christian men surveyed, 69.1 percent agreed; of all other men surveyed, 66.2 percent agreed.)

What does this mean? In short, *more than two-thirds of all men live in fear of running out of money either now or in the future.*

WHAT FINANCIAL SECURITY MEANS TO MEN

Television producer Alan Eisenstock, in his book *Ten on Sunday: The Secret Life of Men*, tells about the experience of buying his and his wife's dream house in Santa Monica, California. In 1992, the couple lived through the Rodney King riots in L.A., which proved to be the last straw—they needed to move. They found a four-thousand-square-foot, six-bathroom house on several acres with a driveway wide enough for three-on-three basketball games. The asking price was seven figures, but the sellers came down and they signed a contract.

I'll let Mr. Eisenstock take it from here:

It's okay. I can afford it. I'm co-executive producer of a hot new sitcom [A League of Their Own] *and the money is rolling in, no end in sight.*

What I can't admit yet, what I don't actually know yet, at least not consciously, is that I am miserable.

It's not because of the two mortgages lashed to my back like two grand pianos. There is something deeper, a hole inside me, related to the midlife crisis I am facing and the numbing sense that, despite all the financial success I have achieved, I have, in fact, achieved nothing at all. The work I do, the television show I produce, and the more than one hundred television shows I have written and produced before, throb through my skull in a low-level hum, accompanied miraculously by an obscene amount of money that I receive every week, an amount that no one could possibly deserve. It's like some crazy game that I've gotten stuck in. I really don't want to do this, but I keep playing and they keep paying and I am scared to death to stop. Because if I stop, I'm afraid I will have to give up everything else in my life. I will have to live my life on spec.

After signing the contract to buy the house, Eisenstock and his wife, Bobbie, talk about his fears that they may be getting in over their heads:

"I think we should back out," Bobbie says, hard. "When in doubt, don't." Her motto.

"But you love the house."

"I do. But it's just a house."

Her eyes glimmer with the truth. I look deep into them and see no judgment. She is giving me permission to fail, the okay to walk away.

But I can't.

My upbringing and my gender will not allow me. I am bred to be the breadwinner. The man, damn it. I can't shake that. In the sixties, Ricky Nelson was my role model, but in the nineties I have become Ozzie. I am The Dad. Sire of two children, king of the castle, lord of the debt.

"Let's go for it."

Six months go by, during which they have the house remodeled (*. . . remodeling this house took a lot more money than we thought. Why is that? We had a budget. A drop-dead bottom-line number that we absolutely could not exceed, which we have now exceeded by seventy grand. How did that happen?*), and after which they move in.

They had been in the house only a short time when what happened to Job of old happened to Alan Eisenstock:

The next morning I get the word.

A League of Their Own *has been canceled after three episodes.*[2]

(Job, a man of great wealth, who experienced history's most famous financial reversal, said, "What I feared has come upon me; what I dreaded has happened to me" [Job 3:25].)

I hope you caught the part where he said his gender would not allow him to walk away. If you're a man, you get it. If you're a woman, you need to get it to understand your man. *Ozzie and Harriet* may have come and gone (Google it if you were born after 1970), but the ghost of Ozzie Nelson (and Ward Cleaver and Jim Anderson—Google *Leave It to Beaver* and *Father Knows Best*) is still around, reminding men to make good and be the man! Be *the king of the castle, lord of the debt.*

Fifties and sixties sitcom fathers didn't invent this role, of course. Alan Eisenstock got it right when he said it was a gender thing, not a generational thing. Men and money have been joined at the hip since time began, and basically for the right reasons. Yes, money gets the best of men sometimes. Yes, the love of it is the root of all evil. And yes, contrary to *Wall Street*'s Gordon Gekko, greed is not good.

But what exactly does money mean to men? Simply put, money is a tool in the hands of reasonable men. With it, they can fix things in their domain. They can provide for themselves and their family, which is part of the male thing.

If you live in the kind of subdivision or neighborhood that makes up much of America today—houses on postage-stamp lots with garages that face the street—try this experiment: next time you take a walk after supper, see how many garages you can peer into and spot a large, red, five- to six-foot tall metal cabinet. That is the classic auto mechanic's tool chest, now appearing in countless garages near you. Is your neighborhood filled with mechanics? Of course not—but it is filled with men. And men love tools. Even though they don't work on their own cars, they collect tools like women collect shoes.

And money is a tool. When a man doesn't have money, or is afraid he may not have enough for retirement or to cover exigencies such as a long-term illness, he gets insecure. Okay, he panics. So much so that sometimes he does really foolish things to get the money he thinks he needs.

The whole nation was amazed by the December 2005 story about Al Ginglen, the sixty-four-year-old grandfather of seven who robbed a series of small banks in Illinois to cover the ever-deeper financial hole he had gotten himself into. The amazing part, of course, was that it was his three grown sons who turned him in after one of the sons recognized his father's picture, taken from a bank surveillance video, on an Internet law enforcement Web site. The sad part was that a grown man lost the primary tool by which men define themselves—money—and turned to crime to get it.

Al Ginglen's sons turned their father in because he had raised them to do what was right. Yet such is the power of money that he failed to do what was right himself. I can't help but think that his amateur burglaries were just an open invitation for officials to catch him and put an end to his out-of-money pain. At least in jail he'd have no bills to pay.

No issue strikes the male heart with such a discordant note as the thought of running out of money either now or in the future. It's not running out of money, of course—it's not being able to secure that for which we exchange money: food, shelter, and the rest of life's needs for ourselves and our families, not to mention the "wants" that our creative minds dream about.

For good or for ill, money is almost a synonym of masculinity. That's good in the sense that a man is motivated to earn money in order to fulfill his responsibilities. But it's ill when money becomes an object in itself, an end instead of a means to an end. Walking the fine line between the two is every man's calling.

NEW DIRECTIONS

If men feel secure when they have the tool of money in their hands, then it's not surprising that a majority of men feel insecure today. For only the third time since records have been kept, Americans recorded a negative savings rate in 2005 of .05 percent. The previous two times this happened were in 1932 (-0.9 percent) and 1933 (-1.5 percent) in the midst of the Great Depression. A negative savings rate means that not only did people not save money overall in 2005, they dipped into their savings to pay for increased spending. (The Commerce Department announced in January 2006 that in December 2005 consumer spending rose 0.9 percent while incomes rose only 0.4 percent.)[3]

With those facts in hand, men who are worried about the present and future state of their finances need to assume they have been issued a wake-up call. It's impossible for men to take advantage of their built-in congratulatory mechanism when they are not being responsible with money. And being responsible means spending less than is earned and laying the balance aside.

Saved money for a man is like that tall, red, metal mechanic's tool chest in the garage. It means being able to go to the cabinet and take out the tool that's needed to solve a problem. For a man to go to the cabinet and not find the tool he needs is an affront to his masculinity. Unfortunately, money that wasn't saved when it was available can't be replaced as easily as going to the hardware store to get a new wrench.

So a new practical direction is needed. Fortunately, there is no shortage of information available to help men gain the upper hand in financial planning. And the very fact that information is so readily available suggests that a lack of know-how is not the problem. Indeed, it suggests that something else is needed: conviction. And for men of faith: faith.

It takes tremendous courage to stand against the financial trends of the day. The over-the-top housing boom of 2004 and 2005 gave most people an excuse to pull the windfall equity out of their houses and spend the money on unnecessary purchases. Or they sold their newly appreciated (and previously adequate) home and moved on up, garnering for themselves a larger piece of the pie—and a more oppressive mortgage to boot. There's certainly nothing wrong with selling at the top of the market. But the trend in society is not to save windfalls, or even hard-earned excesses, but to spend them.

It's true that Jesus said we are to take no thought for tomorrow (Matthew 6:25–34). But that teaching was given in this context: "But seek first [God's] kingdom and his righteousness, and all these things will be given to you as well" (v. 33). Therefore, the question is, What does it mean to seek God's kingdom *first* in order to receive His provision for today and tomorrow *second*?

With regard to money, it means to live by the teaching of Scripture: Live modest, frugal, generous lives; work and save diligently as an expression of faithful trust; acknowledge that everything comes from and therefore belongs to God; adopt the attitude of a steward—a manager of that which God has entrusted to you—and seek His approval for what you do with that which is His.

NEW CONNECTIONS

Regardless of whose survey you look at, money always lands near the top of the hot-button issues in marriages. And that shouldn't surprise anyone. Whatever is a critical issue in one partner's life is going to become an issue in the marriage. If 68 percent of the men in America are fearful about financial security now and in retirement, I can assure you that 68 percent of the marriages in America have a measure of tension in them as a result.

In 1985, Richard Foster wrote a book titled *Money, Sex, and Power: The Challenge of a Disciplined Life*. Think of those three subjects in terms of marriage and you'll identify three prime places for couples to either stand their ground or seek common ground. Far too often they stand their ground, holding tenaciously to practices and points of view they either learned from their parents or picked up along the way in life. Most couples enter marriage thinking about money the way their parents did—detailed record keeping or constantly overdrawn; poor credit ratings or great credit ratings; disciplined savers or dedicated shoppers; planning for the future or living for today; hording every penny or enjoying every penny.

Money is a great topic around which to build consensus in your marriage, but it requires making a commitment and connecting with your spouse. The future is coming, like it or not. It's up to you and your husband or wife to decide how you want to spend it.

Ipsos Public Affairs conducted a telephone survey in which they interviewed 1,016 adults ages forty-five to seventy-five. Indications are that there is not a lot of planning for the future going on among pre-retirees. Forty-nine percent of those surveyed had spent five hours or less during the previous twelve months planning for retirement; 18 percent had spent no time. Thirty-one percent of pre-retirees said they would rather clean their bathroom or pay bills than plan for retirement. Thirty-four percent said the most challenging part of planning for retirement is not knowing how much money they would need.[4]

I could cite statistics all day, but they would all reveal the same thing: people don't like to think about the future because it represents a giant unknown. It's easier to live in denial than to make a commitment to gathering the information, creating a plan, and then making the necessary adjustments today to make the plan work in the future. If it's true that two heads are usually better than one (and it is), couples can begin creating their future today by making a commitment to each other to shape the future rather than letting the future shape them.

Merrill Lynch produced "The New Retirement Survey" in February 2005, which charted the changing landscape of retirement in America, especially among the massive generation of about-to-retire baby boomers. Consider some facts cited:

- Seventy-six percent of boomers intend to retire around age sixty-four and then launch into an entirely new job or career.
- Most boomers reject either full-time work or full-time leisure in retirement, preferring a blend of work (part-time or full-time) and leisure. Only 17 percent hope never to work for pay again after retirement.
- Sixty-seven percent want to work in some form during retirement for the challenge and mental stimulation it provides.
- A set age for retirement has now taken a back seat to retiring only when sufficient resources have been accumulated. The uncertainty of government entitlements is motivating boomers to plan "creative" retirements and assume more of their own responsibility.
- One size doesn't fit all. Retiring with a gold watch at age sixty-five is ancient history. Couples are planning their futures with the assistance of advisors who are creating new models for living successfully, creatively, and healthfully in their latter years.[5]

Translation? It's not too late to begin planning. Even if you don't have the traditional pension to depend on, aren't maxing out your 401(k), or have skipped years funding your IRA, you aren't alone. And because there are a lot of people like you, the financial marketplace is creating plans and products to help you gain the security you seek.

Having said all that, here is the bottom line: men, or their spouses, aren't supposed to live in fear of their financial future. I'm reminded of how Dr. Bill Bright, founder of Campus Crusade for Christ, lived his life. Though he was head of an organization with income of hundreds of millions of dollars annually, he and his wife raised their personal support each year just like all Campus Crusade staff—a modest income by any measurement. They did not own a car or any real estate, and when Dr. Bright won the million-dollar Templeton Award for Progress in Religion in 1996, he put the money toward developing a new ministry initiative. Like all CCC staff, he and Vonette had paid into a modest retirement fund, but he even liquidated most of that fund to start a new training center in Moscow. He had no savings account and accepted no speaking fees. When he died in 2003, he left behind few worldly goods, yet God had provided for him abundantly throughout his life.

All followers of Christ are called to a life of faith, not fear. That life of faith may look differently from one person to the next, but the lack of fear will look the same. It will be a combination of wisdom, diligence, and trust that does everything it can to live a responsible financial life while putting ultimate hope in Him for the present and the future.

Chapter 2

IT'S A WORKER'S WORLD

My wife and I hosted twenty-four family members for an old-fashioned family reunion. It was such a wonderfully varied group that my mother said it must be what heaven will be like. Everyone I hoped to be able to see was there, except for one person: my dad. He died more than a decade ago, but I found myself acutely aware of his absence at the reunion.

My father was one of the hardest-working men I've ever known. He died with his boots on, as they say—a massive heart attack while filling out a real-estate contract for a couple. He worked for twenty years at a large university in Texas while also running drive-in restaurants and selling real estate. I think in some ways he must have worked himself to death. But he was a great provider and left my mom with ample provision for the remaining years of her life.

Dad worked so hard because he got a late start in building a career for himself. He was one of five brothers whose father owned a successful machine shop that prospered during the days of the oil boom in Texas. Somehow my dad was chosen to help his father manage that business while the other four sons went to college. Then, when the oil boom ended and the machining business suffered, my dad was left without a career or a college education.

Men's careers often take turns they never planned on. It's easy for men to incur expenses and responsibilities when they marry and feel "stuck" in their jobs. I imagine more men today feel like they have jobs rather than careers, which can be a debilitating feeling for a man who has that "change the world" gene in his system. My dad sacrificed in order to serve his father and played catch-up the rest of his life. But he succeeded at honorably providing for his family despite his late start. And for that I hold him in the highest esteem.

WHAT WE KNOW ABOUT MEN AND THEIR CAREERS

Management guru Peter Drucker wrote with the insight that made him famous about the uniqueness of our modern era:

"In a few hundred years, when the history of our time is written from a long-term perspective, I think it very probable that the most important event those historians will remember is not technology, not the Internet, not e-commerce—but the unprecedented change in the human condition. For the first time—and I mean that literally—substantial and rapidly growing numbers of people have choices. For the first time, people have had to *manage themselves*. And we are totally unprepared for it."[1]

His point was based on the fact that, in pre-industrial times, men simply followed their fathers into a trade (and often gained a surname in the process: Smith, Baker, Joiner, Butcher, Mason). There wasn't a whole lot of personal choosing or managing to be done; life was a predictable path from which one varied little.

But how different things are today! The average American man has choices galore—education, work, career, family, children or not. And as marketing experts tell us, too many choices is not always a good thing. Increased choice leads to increased confusion, passivity, and inaction.

Drucker might link his own observation with those of a trio of career experts who have coined a new term to describe a phenomenon among mid-career-level workers: middlescence. Everyone is familiar with the confusion that arises in adolescence. Middlescence is a second round that is affecting mid-career employees, ages thirty-five to fifty-four years old. Specifically, it is the seeming mental and emotional confusion that comes from balancing the results of all the choices life has so generously extended: job responsibilities, family, leisure, and most especially the attempt to find new meaning in work. At mid-career, most workers are too heavily invested to make changes and are stuck with an "I thought it would be better than this" response to their career.

In a March 2006 *Harvard Business Review* article, researchers reported their findings from surveying 7,700 mid-career U.S. workers. Only 43 percent said they are passionate about their jobs, only 33 percent feel energized by their work, 36 percent say they are in dead-end jobs, and more than 40 percent are experiencing career burnout. A large percentage are trying to figure out a way to make a career change. The authors of the study identified seven sources of frustration for this demographic group. See how many you identify with:

- Career bottleneck: Too many baby boomers chasing too few upper-level jobs.
- Work/life tension: Caring for children and parents at the same time.
- Lengthening horizon: Prospect of working longer to fund retirement.
- Skills obsolescence: Catching up with the information age.
- Disillusionment with employer: Insecurity about downsizing; frustrations over the gap between executive and worker compensation.
- Burnout: Twenty years down and twenty to thirty to go.
- *Career disappointment: Career fulfillment a far cry from what they had imagined* (emphasis mine).[2]

Middlescence affects morale, which affects productivity (which is the corporation's primary concern). But middlescence also affects the individuals who experience it, not only at work but in their personal and family lives as well.

While our survey did not test for middlescence, we did ask about one of its defining characteristics: career disappointment. We presented this statement: "Men are disappointed about what they have achieved in their careers." One percent responded "always," 26 percent said "often," and 66 percent said "sometimes." That's almost all (93 percent) of the 3,600 men we surveyed. As usual, we can discount the high numbers in the "sometimes" category—who doesn't sometimes experience some disappointment over how his career has turned out? But the numbers still suggest that there is a low-grade burn going on out there among men who are disillusioned and disappointed about what they have accomplished in their careers.

WHAT CAREERS MEAN TO MEN

Without doubt, men define themselves by what they do. It won't be more than thirty seconds after two men meet for the first time that one will ask the other, "So, Bob, what do you do?" Usually, it's the one who is the most confident in what he "does" that asks the question—the one who is most proud of his career accomplishments. He doesn't fear the question; he loves to tell what he does. So to get that opportunity (he knows the return will be, "And what about you, John—what kind of work do you do?"), he initiates the exchange.

The older a man gets, the more threatening the question, What do you do? For in those four words is concealed an invitation to self-disclosure, an opportunity to disclose what a man has made of himself in his career. Obviously, the more years that have gone by since a man entered the work force, the higher he should have risen in his chosen field. He might have started as an electrician, but twenty years later he ought to have his own electrical contracting business. If he started as an accountant, twenty years later he ought to be a partner in a CPA firm. If he started as an account manager at a Fortune 500 company, twenty years later he ought to be a regional VP. *Or so the theory goes.*

It's bad enough meeting a stranger for the first time and going through the dance. Fortunately, you may never see the guy again, so if you're a little embarrassed at the path your career has taken, at least it will only be momentary. What's worse is when you return to your high school or college for a twenty- or thirty-year class reunion. There you see men and women who you formed deep emotional bonds with—people who knew you well, people with whom you competed in all things adolescent, especially the guys. And when you've been away two or three decades and show up at the reunion where every guy is supposed to pull out his career report card, it's like show-and-tell all over again. But if you're a man who is disappointed with what he has achieved in his career, it's not a pleasant experience.

A woman or wife in this situation has a hard time understanding a man's embarrassment at saying "what he does" if he feels he should have, or at least could have, done better. Sure, there may have been exigencies along the way—things that were beyond your control—that significantly impacted your career. But there's no time to go into all those details at a cocktail party or a noisy reunion barbeque. You only have a couple of moments and words to describe what you do, to say who you are. And men who are disappointed in themselves grit their teeth at the thought of revealing themselves in a less-than-flattering light.

The words of Henry David Thoreau come to mind when men do a self-assessment of their station in life. "The mass of men lead lives of quiet desperation." Sometimes it's a desperation born out of a sense of entrapment—the middlescence mentioned earlier. Other times, it may be a sense of desperation that stems from a man realizing he has invested everything in the wrong thing and is sorely in need of a course correction.

That was the kind of desperation Bob Buford came to grips with at the height of his success as president of his family's cable television company. In the twelve years Buford had been the president of Buford Television, Inc., the company had grown at a 28 percent compound annual rate. Those were heady days for the young entrepreneur and he was feeling flush with the pride of accomplishment. He was shocked into reality, though, by two words from Peter Drucker. At the end of what Buford calls a "long and profitable day," he and Drucker were talking. "I think most people would give their left arm to be where I am," Buford said. Drucker replied, "I wouldn't." Buford never forgot those two words. That conversation was part of a slow chain of events that led Buford to divest himself of the company and begin a transition from "success to significance."[3]

But Bob Buford is an exception. He had financial resources that allowed him to stop what he was doing and begin doing something different. The vast majority of men are not in that situation. They have to live with the "quiet desperation" they feel and work on understanding it, or changing it, over time.

In the previous chapter, we heard part of the story of Alan Eisenstock, a successful Hollywood screenwriter. Eisenstock had stopped in mid-career to consider doing something else, something that would represent more of his personal values than writing scripts for sitcoms. So he stopped. But to keep paying the bills he agreed to co-write a movie script. You can see in his words the paralysis, the fear, the self-doubt that assails a man who realizes he has not accomplished what he believes he should have:

> Every morning at the crack of ten-thirty, my writing partner scales the stairs to my office, balancing his briefcase with a cardboard carrying tray stuffed with two Grande Lattes, which poke up like stubby Styrofoam goalposts, flanking a bagel or a muffin, or on certain decadent mornings, a chunk of coffee cake. We settle in and [talk] about sports and show business while we snack. Time flies. We break for lunch. We read the trades. We take a walk.
>
> What we don't do is work.
>
> I can't somehow, can't find the words or the motivation. Despite my desperate need to make a living, I am paralyzed.
>
> This is no midlife crisis. This is a whole life crisis, based on the deep, throbbing possibility that everything I have done in my work life for the last twenty years will be revealed to have been a brutal mistake. I am stunned that I am now stuck, in this place, struck impotent and mute. What happened? How did I get here? I wanted to simplify my life. Instead I have overextended myself, committed to doing work I clearly don't want to do. Hell, can't get myself to do. Instead I stand frozen, watching chunks of my savings peel off and tumble into space like shingles falling off a decaying roof. . . . [W]e deliver the screenplay in ten days and retire to my office where we wait for Martin's reaction, wait for the second-draft notes, wait for our agent to get us another movie to write, *and I wait wordlessly for the screaming to stop in my head* [italics mine].[4]

Every man who is disappointed with what he has achieved in his career has his own reasons. He has his own target that he missed, something that he alone understands. He might not even be able to explain it to another person, but he knows it has been missed—and by how much—by the way he feels about his life. He knows if he's moving away from or toward the target, like the game he played as a kid: "You're getting warmer . . . warmer . . . now colder, colder . . . okay, warmer again." These temperature changes happen slowly, but they happen. And one day he wakes up and realizes he is not where he thought he would be after working for decades in his field.

Every man who feels that way should try to think, as best he can, about what he thought he was going to accomplish. Here are a half dozen things to consider as a place to begin:

1. Enjoyment

Very few repetitive motions in life (like going to work every day) remain absolutely thrilling. Some things we do in life because they're the right thing to do, not necessarily because they're a blast. There are elements of repetition in every man's career.

2. Fame

In whose eyes is it most important to be "famous"? A man who is a faithful husband and father has the most important kind of fame. Public fame may have a certain appeal, and there's nothing wrong with achieving it, but it is certainly not the most important level.

3. Accomplishment

Professional status, income level, technical achievement—all are legitimate goals. Disappointment may simply be a messenger reminding a man that perseverance and tenacity are needed. If the accomplishment is not worth pursuing for a lifetime, it might not have been as important as originally thought.

4. Money

Net worth, material accumulation, prospects for retirement, funding for college educations—all these strike hard at a man's sense of worth (rightly or wrongly). Every man has to figure out where money fits in his own personal value system.

5. Legacy

Some men may have wanted to create a life that would impact generations to come. But fame after life is the same as fame in life—it is fleeting at best. One's legacy should be measured in terms of depth, not breadth.

6. Contribution

Some men may be visionaries and dreamers to whom no one listens. Others may read books and make notes in off hours on subjects wholly unrelated to their profession. They would love the opportunity to make a contribution they really care about.

NEW DIRECTIONS

The man who feels disappointed with what he has accomplished in his career should think prayerfully and carefully about the reasons. I don't believe God's image is best reflected in any man whose life is tarnished by frustration and discontent. Some of the reasons for disappointment could be carnal—for example, the desire to be rich in order to boost one's own ego or status among peers. If that's the case, such reasons ought to be reconsidered; a more spiritual value system might relieve some of that disappointment.

On the other hand, other disappointments could be entirely legitimate, and some may be addressable. There are many men who are in careers for the wrong reasons. Their parents may have influenced them. They may have begun a career fresh out of college because they didn't know what else to pursue. They may not have had financial opportunity to get the training needed for the career they really desired. Or they may simply have had a "eureka!" experience at mid-life and discovered a calling that was heretofore unknown to them. In such cases, a career change, if possible, could be a completely legitimate pursuit.

Some disappointments can be resolved by adjusting expectations, especially if the expectation was unreasonable or illegitimate to begin with. But lowering the bar on a legitimate expectation is not a path to fulfillment. Far better to put steps in motion to achieve that which will bring fulfillment than to work another two or three decades in a state of disappointment.

The challenge is making changes at mid-life. If you are financially able to switch careers or make mid-course adjustments, all the better. But if you are so rigidly constrained by financial obligations that you can't move, then the process will be longer. It will require patience and creativity. But for the sake of escaping disappointment, it is worth it.

NEW CONNECTIONS

No one has more power over a man's freedom to escape disappointment in his career than his wife. When a man thinks about making changes, his first thought is, "What will (my wife) say?" If a man senses or knows that his wife is going to resist suggestions of change, he likely will never bring up the subject. He would rather live with disappointment than create a confrontation that could have lasting negative effects.

Because of this, a wife's willingness to explore changes leading to her husband's fulfillment in his career is a godsend for a man. It lets him know that she is willing to consider options, alternatives, even changes. At least she's willing to discuss it.

In the 2000 film *The Family Man*, the husband, Jack (played by Nicholas Cage), is considering leaving his father-in-law's tire business and pursuing his dream of a Wall Street career. His wife (Téa Leoni) has opposed the idea, but then comes to him with these words:

> Maybe I was being naïve, but I believed that we would grow old together in this house. That we'd spend holidays here and have our grandchildren come visit us here. I had this image of us, all gray and wrinkly, and me working in the garden and you repainting the deck. But things change. If you need this, Jack, if you really need this, I will take these kids from a life they love and I'll take myself from the only home we've ever shared together and I'll move wherever you need to go. I'll do that because I love you. I love you, and that's more important to me than our address. I choose us.[5]

"I choose us." Powerful words from a wife to a husband. Interestingly, when Jack saw his wife's love, he realized his disappointment in his career had been unfounded. In his wife's love and his family, he had more fulfillment than anyone he knew. He lost his disappointment and gained new happiness when his wife gave him the freedom to choose.

Chapter 3

PARENTS' EXPECTATIONS: A HEAVY WEIGHT EVEN FOR MEN

I am one of the fortunate men who had a great father. The older I got the more I realized how blessed I was to have him in my life. Like every adolescent I swore I wouldn't become like my father, but of course I did. But he was not a bad man to copy. He led me to faith in Christ and taught me the difference between male and man.

A priceless gift my dad gave me was confidence. He somehow convinced me that I could do whatever I wanted to do and be whatever I chose to be. I had no family business to inherit from him, so he encouraged me to make my own path and follow it. When I would occasionally fail in my efforts to do just that as a young man, he was there to encourage me to pick up the pieces and keep moving ahead.

The refrain of his that plays like a tape in my mind is this: "Steve, I am proud of you." Whenever we parted on the phone or in person those were among the last words he said to me. In fact, I can't remember ever leaving him when he didn't tell me how proud of me he was. Looking back, I hadn't done a whole lot to take pride in, but he kept piling on the pride anyway. Having finally accomplished a few things that I believe he would have enjoyed seeing, it saddens me that he's not here to enjoy them with me. But that doesn't matter because I already know he would have been proud.

As much as I planned not to be like my dad when I was growing up, I know there is one way I plan on imitating him to a T: saying to my own infant son, "Solomon, I am proud of you."

WHAT WE KNOW ABOUT MEN AND THEIR PARENTS' EXPECTATIONS

Everyone has heard the saying, "As the twig is bent, so grows the branch." That's not just true with twigs—it's also true of human beings.

When a young man grows up in our modern culture, when does the influence of his parents stop? America is one of the few cultures in the world where young men do not experience a rite of passage from the world of adolescence to the world of adulthood. But even if every young man in America experienced a rite of passage, that does not wipe the developmental slate clean; it does not mean that the influence of one's parents automatically ceases. Even though a young man leaves his home and begins his own life with a family and a job, it is impossible to erase the tapes that still play in his mind. A parent's influence can be positive in that sense, or it can be negative.

Late in 2005, a political lobbyist in Washington, D.C., named Jack Abramoff came under suspicion of fraudulent dealings involving millions of dollars. And in January 2006, he was convicted on several felony counts. Before his dealings were exposed, he and his "family" of young staff and associates, mostly recruited from other high-profile Capitol Hill offices, were flying high and the money was flowing. His young associates were being paid $200,000 to $300,000 a year, according to a *Washington Post* story. One of the lobbyists told the *Post* that "[Abramoff] hired a bunch of white, middle-class Irish Catholic guys who wanted to exceed their parents' expectations. He was always pushing, demanding."[1] Obviously, "middle-class Irish" boys don't normally make $200,000 to $300,000 per year. So "exceeding their parents' expectations" would have been an opportunity too good to pass up, even if it meant skirting, or breaking, the law.

Apparently, a lot of men have not been able to brush that small parent off their shoulder—the one who sits there whispering, "Make me proud!"

long after the man has left home and has supposedly become his own person. Lots of men live with guilt for not making Mom or Dad proud. Lots of men live with frustration because they are doing what their parents wanted them to do with their lives instead of doing what they themselves wanted to do. Lots of men live in fear of hearing the same criticisms as adults that they heard as children. If an A- should have been an A+ as a child, as an adult a promotion to vice president should have been a promotion to executive vice president. A lot of men would like to someday live in freedom, free of their parents' expectations.

This was born out by the responses of 3,600 men to this statement on our survey: "Men have a deep-seated fear of not living up to their parents' expectations." Fully one-fourth of the men said "always" (4 percent) or "often" (21 percent). Another 51 percent indicated that they "sometimes" experience that fear.

WHAT PARENTS' EXPECTATIONS MEAN TO MEN

In this chapter I am going to boil the issue of parental expectations down to one word: acceptance. If a young adult man does not sense, or hopefully know, that he has been fully accepted by his parents—and most importantly, his father—the cloud of parental expectation will potentially hang over his head the rest of his life. If a young adult man does not know that his parents accept him—and again, most importantly his father—he has little hope of achieving the goal of self-acceptance. A man listens for his father's words: "You are good . . . you are a wonderful son . . . I'm proud of you . . . I love you for who you are . . . I have every confidence in your abilities to succeed in life." If he doesn't hear those words as an adolescent, he may physically leave home to begin his own life, but he leaves without closure and without confidence that he is ready and capable to lead his own life.

What does it mean if a young man doesn't hear those affirming words? The logic of the human mind says, "There must be something I haven't done right, so I'll keep trying; I'll keep working at it to prove that I can get it right. I'll keep at it until I hear that I'm okay . . . that I'm a man." And that's how the majority of men in our culture leave home, with the fear that they still haven't met their parents' expectations. It's tragic when you consider how this repeats itself from generation to generation. Only a man who heard from his father that he is a man is free to tell his own sons at the appropriate time that they are men. Acceptance cannot be conferred by someone who has never known acceptance himself.

Gordon MacDonald shares some personal insight on this:

I have a friend who always seems to be telling Dad-stories. "My dad once said . . . ," he will recall, or "I remember the time my dad asked me to . . . ," or "You know, my dad always had a way of . . . ." I love my friend's Dad-stories. They always convey some nugget of wisdom. But even more, they remind me of the connection that is supposed to exist between the generations, a connection marked with affection, understanding, stability, and direction. I guess there is hardly a man who wouldn't crave a bevy of positive Dad-stories as part of his heritage.

It's my observation that the men with positive Dad-stories tend to be in the minority. Frankly, the majority of Dad-stories I hear are mostly stories of regret and anger: "I never really knew my dad," or "My dad never seemed to be there at the right moment," or "My dad wasn't able to give me the slightest impression that he was glad to be my father, that he approved of anything I did."[2]

It seems MacDonald's observation parallels our own survey results. There are a lot of men who don't have as many "positive Dad-stories" as they need to have. If they did, they wouldn't have this lingering fear that somewhere their parents are lying in bed at night wishing their son was doing something better with his life.

There must be a connection between the fact that Jesus of Nazareth appears to have been the most assured person ever to walk the face of the earth and what His Father said to Him when He was beginning His public life: "This is my Son, whom I love; with him I am well pleased" (Matthew 3:17). In that simple statement are the two things every man needs to know from his father: that he is loved and that he is pleasing. To pronounce such a blessing upon a young man—or a man of any age—releases that pent-up anxiety that constantly wants to know, "How am I doing, Dad?"

Patrick Means says this about what Jesus' Father said to Him:

"The model for the Father Blessing given in Matthew 3 is all the more striking in that the Father gave his blessing before Jesus had even begun his ministry, before he 'proved' himself or 'accomplished' anything. When given in this kind of healthy, unconditional spirit, the Father Blessing affirms the son's unique personhood, rather than requiring him to be made over in his father's image before the blessing can be given."[3]

Young men grow up hearing mostly conditional acceptance from their parents. If acceptance or affirmation is expressed at all, it is usually in connection with some accomplishment: academics, athletics, Scouting, civic work. Achievements in those areas are definitely commendable. But if a young man only hears affirmation when he performs, he leaves home "trained" to perform in order to continue hearing the words of acceptance he so desperately needs to conclude that he is "okay."

When a young man is blessed by his father, he is released to become his own man. The father says, "My days of training and influence are complete. I am always here to help you should you need something I can provide. But I am now stepping down from my position *over* you to assume a position *beside* you. Instead of your teacher and corrector, I am now counselor and friend. I believe you are well prepared to achieve everything that is your heart's desire. You have my blessing not because of what I believe you will accomplish but because of who I know you are. My only dream and expectation for you is that you will fulfill all your own dreams, in your own way, according to your own timetable."

MacDonald has outlined five things that a young man needs from his father:

1. Identity

The most basic sense of identity in life is genetic. When Alex Haley published his novel *Roots*, it touched off an interest in genealogy in America that remains unabated to this day. Everyone wants to know who they are and whose they are. In other cultures in times past, this family tradition and legacy was taught at a father's knee or around a village fire, as portrayed in *Roots*. We see the listing of genealogies in the Bible that established a sense of time and place, a sense of belonging. Even in today's world, a young man looks to his father to tell him who his "people" are and what they believe.

2. Three Assurances: Belonging, Value, and Competence

All three of these declaratory parts were in the statement made to Peter, James, and John when they witnessed the transfiguration of Jesus: "This is my Son, whom I love; with him I am well pleased. Listen to him!" (Matthew 17:5). The words "my son" tell a son he belongs; "I am pleased" conveys value; and "Listen to him" expresses competence. The son who hears these messages regularly from his father will believe he is wanted, that he has value, and that he has something to offer the world.

3. Modeling
A young man needs to be able to watch his father for years to learn how to manage feelings, how to control his emotions, and how to respond to the vicissitudes of life. Does a young man know how to do these things innately? Of course not. All that is needed is a look around our culture at the multitudes of angry young men, especially those who have landed in our bulging prisons, to see that many are growing up without a model.

4. Introduction
A young man needs his father to introduce him to the "men of the village"—the father's friends who reinforce what the father has been teaching. When a young man is accepted by these men, figuratively if not literally, he develops an additional sense of belonging that is beyond what his father alone can provide. This is accomplished literally in rite-of-passage ceremonies in African cultures, but can be carried out informally in our own with a positive effect. The inclusion of a son in the life of the father and his friends—in their vocational, religious, political, social, and recreational events—conveys acceptance by the very group of which a boy stands in awe.

5. Release
How and when release is accomplished will vary. But there are many opportunities, ranging from a son's going away for a two-week summer camp to his departure for military service or college to his wedding day. These and other transitional events ought to be marked by the blessing of the father; a way for the father to convey higher and higher levels of trust and affirmation to a young man.[4]

A father's conveyance of these blessings to a son is a not a black-and-white issue; no father conveys perfectly everything he should at all times. But over the long term of a young man's life, the more of this kind of affirmation that is conveyed the less likely a man as an adult will live in fear of not meeting his parents' expectations.

NEW DIRECTIONS

The obvious question in this discussion is, What should a grown man do who did not receive these gifts from his father and sees little likelihood that he ever will? What if, despite his chronological growth, he still thinks of himself as a child who strives to meet his parents' expectations?

Of course, the most important thing is not to give up on the possibility of reconciliation. Many men, well into their adult lives, have experienced a healing reunion with a father who never affirmed his son as he should have. Perhaps he didn't know how or was not well enough himself to bestow blessing on his son. But people and circumstances change. There is a wisdom that comes with age, and many fathers in the sunset years of their life have found ways to convey blessings, love, acceptance, and affirmation on sons who grew up lacking those elements.

Still, for some that may never happen. For a variety of reasons, a man may be left without an opportunity to gain the emotional and personal closure from his own father that he needs. In that case, the ever-available affirmation and blessing of his Father-God becomes even more crucial. A child learns acceptance and affirmation subconsciously; an adult man must choose to believe he has already been accepted by God in Christ. Leanne Payne puts it like this in her book *Crisis in Masculinity*:

> Without a doubt, masculinity and the true self have a special tie-in to the will of man. Oswald Chambers has written: "The profound thing in man is his will. . . . Will is the essential element in God's creation of man." The will is that in man which chooses whether to be or not to be. It is with the will that we choose the heaven of becoming or the hell of failure to become.[5]

When a man chooses to believe that, despite how he feels, he has been fully accepted by God, he is free to accept himself. In another of her books, Payne quotes Roman Catholic philosopher-theologian Romano Guardini, who has written, "The act of self-acceptance is the root of all things. I must agree to be the person who I am. Agree to have the qualifications which I have. Agree to live within the limitations set for me. . . . The clarity and the courageousness of this acceptance is the foundation of all existence."[6]

Patrick Means suggests three questions by which a man can identify whether or not he has moved beyond his parents' expectations:

1. Did my father communicate to me that I was "beloved"?
2. Did he let me know that he was "well pleased" with who I am?
3. Was the blessing unconditional?[7]

In terms of parental expectations, to me the last is the most important. When parents, or a father, tell a young man (in any of a thousand different ways), "I will love you if/when . . . ," then conditions are put in place that will haunt him the rest of his life. Means tells of a pastor friend who was discontent in his ministry, unsure if he was doing what he was supposed to do. The pastor's own father had been a successful pastor and church planter, and had always verbally told his son, "I want whatever's best for you, son, whatever God wants for you." But when the father would speak to groups of young people, he would say, "Young people, if God calls you to be a preacher, don't stoop to be a king!"[8]

There it is! A subtle message that only by becoming a pastor or preacher could the son fulfill what his father thought was the highest calling. What if the son wanted to be a king instead?

The marvelous thing about the grace of God in Christ is that we are accepted by God with no strings attached. Christ met every expectation God had for the human race, which allows us to be freed from our own failure to measure up (i.e., our sins). We are free to explore our God-directed destiny, to fulfill our God-given dreams and ambitions, knowing that we have a loving Father who encourages us along the way. Every man was created by God to stand straight and tall and look into His face to find true identity. When we look into the imperfect face of human fathers we can only receive an imperfect reflection. Even men raised by the most loving of earthly fathers still need to experience ultimate acceptance and affirmation in Christ. If we hope to live free from the shackles of others' expectations on our lives, it's essential that we move beyond the authority of our earthly fathers to our one true heavenly Father.

NEW CONNECTIONS

Husbands and wives who are not free from their own parents' expectations live in danger of trying to parent each other. Wives treat their husbands like boys that track mud in the house, and husbands use "I'm the head of this house" as an excuse to force wives to conform. The imposition of such expectations only creates an environment ripe for failure that's seen all too often in our current culture.

You and your spouse can help each other break free from lingering parental expectations by not heaping on more of your own. We all live with expectations—to keep the law, to be morally upright, to be financially responsible, and so on. Those are givens, and living "free of expectations" should not be taken as a license to live in a perpetual state of midlife crisis in which you go out and spend your family's savings on a sports car.

What I'm talking about is being free of the kind of expectations parents put on children: "Stand up straight, eat your vegetables, tuck in your shirttail" when they're little, and "Become a doctor, be a leader, make us proud, be a pillar in the community, live in our hometown and join our clubs" when they grow older. President George H. W. Bush had it right when he finally put his foot down about broccoli, food lobbyists notwithstanding: "I do not like broccoli. And I haven't liked it since I was a little kid and my mother made me eat it. And I'm president of the United States and I'm not going to eat any more broccoli." He even banned it from the White House kitchen and from Air Force One, and replaced President Reagan's famed jelly beans with Texas pork rinds and dipping sauce. President Bush decided, as president of the United States and a man in his mid-sixties, that it was time to break free and become his own man—at least as far as veggies and snacks were concerned.

When you and your spouse can identify and laugh about the repetitive motions you go through that are holdovers from your upbringings, you will learn to relax in each other's acceptance and affirmation—and pursue the life *you* want to live.

Chapter 4

WHO'S BRINGING HOME THE BACON?

Bob Mecca is a certified financial adviser in Mt. Prospect, Illinois, outside Chicago. "When I started as a financial adviser twenty years ago, there were almost no couples in this situation," he says. "Now 40 percent of the couples who come through my door have a wife who earns more than her husband."[1]

Implications? Stephanie Coontz of the Council on Contemporary Families says, "Women have earning power, so they're less intent on finding a husband who is a high earner and more interested in finding someone who is an all-around good partner. And men are letting go of the idea of, 'I should make more or have the more prestigious job because I'm the man.' Instead they're both saying, 'Let's do what's best for all of us.'"[2]

Don't look now, dear reader, but four decades after Bob Dylan first said it, the times they are still a-changin'. In fact, some of the changes still evolving in our culture began when Dylan started his career as a cultural commentator in song.

WHAT WE KNOW ABOUT MEN AND THEIR WIVES' EARNINGS

In 1963, President John Kennedy signed the Equal Pay Act that made it illegal for employers to pay people differently for the same work. The Act was focused primarily on women who had entered the labor force *en masse* during World War II when men left to fight overseas. During the war (in 1942), the National War Labor Board had urged employers to voluntarily equalize the pay of men and women. When that suggestion was ignored, the Equal Pay Act was eventually enacted.

But for all its legality, the EPA has almost been treated as a suggestion itself. The wage gap has narrowed between men and women since 1963, but it is still there. Back then, women earned 58.9 percent of the wages paid to a man doing the same job, and in 2004, they earned 76.5 percent—an increase of less than a half-cent per year.[3] And the gap is not just among low-wage or hourly workers. In 1999, female physicians earned only 62.5 percent of the median weekly wage of male physicians.[4]

By one estimate, a twenty-five-year-old woman who works full time and retires at sixty-five will earn $523,000 less than a man following the same career path. At the current rate of change in the wage gap between men and women, working women will achieve equal pay with men sometime after the year 2050.[5]

Despite the fact that women's overall pay still does not equal men's, significant changes involving women, money, and family structures have taken place in recent decades. For instance, *Money* magazine surveyed one thousand spouses (five hundred men, five hundred women—not couples) and discovered that working wives now contribute more than a third of the typical family's income. And, more significantly to the purposes of this chapter, in a third of married households, *wives brought home more money than husbands.* Contrasted with that new trend is the fact that the vast majority of married couples still divide financial labors along traditional lines: women handle everyday spending and budgeting while men plan and invest for the long-term.[6]

When traditional values meet new trends it's like a high-pressure system and a low-pressure system, a cold front and a warm front, colliding over the heartland. Disturbances in the weather patterns become highly likely. And that's what's happened in some marriages.

The idea of women moving out of traditional roles—working outside the home and bringing home the larger of the two salaries—is threatening to some men. How many men are we talking about? In our survey of 3,600 men we found a fourth of the men (24.3 percent) being either "always" (3 percent) or "often" (21 percent) threatened by their wives making more money than they do. Throw in the 50 percent who are sometimes threatened by this situation and we're looking at three-fourths of the male population. (I don't interpret these numbers as meaning three-fourths of our respondents are married men making less than their wives. That would be out of sync with the one-third of marriages where the wife does make more than the husband. Rather, I interpret our survey's respondents to be saying, "I am threatened by the idea [sometimes, often, always] that my wife either does or might bring home a salary larger than mine.")

In this chapter we're going to talk about the gray area of money and marriage, and why so many men harbor a secret that they're threatened by their wives' financial success.

WHAT WIVES' EARNINGS MEAN TO MEN

Why are men threatened by their wives' rising salaries? Based on the "wage gap" statistics, every man alive in America today (and virtually all the world) has grown up in an era in which men, using wages as a measure, have been valued more than women in the workplace. And with higher wages came power, including power over the women who earned less and who filled out the bottom rungs of the organizational chart. Basically, all a man had to do to feel more valuable in his vocational life was show up. His job wasn't guaranteed, of course. But if he lost his job due to incompetence, it was likely he would be replaced by another man, not a woman.

I don't think most men realize how pervasive this cultural paradigm has been or how ingrained it is in our psyches. Women expect to be paid less and men expect to be paid more. When a man finds himself in a situation where this reality field is reversed, it strikes him that something is out of order. If the culture normally values men more than women and suddenly a man finds himself valued less than a woman, the implication is that he must be seriously substandard. And if that's how a man might think in the general workplace, think what it might mean if his wife, based on her greater salary, is the one who is now more valuable (more powerful, more important) than him.

It's possible that a man could be the cause of his own failure to keep up with women in terms of promotion and pay. But it's also true that many other variables are part of the decision matrixes that result in women earning higher salaries: skills, experience, government quotas, corporate culture, gender mix, and so on. When a man responds emotionally to being "demoted" in his marriage from breadwinner to assistant breadwinner, he is not analyzing facts. He sees himself as an exception to a well-established cultural rule: men are supposed to be paid more than women.

Let me make it clear at this point that what I've already said, and will say, in this chapter is not based on a position or point of view on the legitimacy of a woman earning more than a man. My goal is to hold a double-sided mirror up to our culture, one side reflecting tradition (the past) and the other the present (and the future), and talk about what we see. What to do with money is one of the main points of contention in any marriage. Throw in the additional elements of deciding on the basis of who earns how much and you have a recipe for even greater conflict.

The following story of one couple illustrates how confusing things can get when new realities impact a traditional setting and there is no game plan in place to accommodate them:

Jenny is now forty-five and runs her own management consulting firm in New Jersey. She and Bob began their careers as co-workers, but after they planned to marry she decided to switch to another part of the company. "Every job available was a higher-grade, officer-level position. Then I learned that my career was moving along fine while Bob's wasn't. I didn't want to bruise his ego, so I reasoned, 'If I can do it here, I can go anywhere,' and said to Bob, 'Let's shop around for another location to start our family.'"

Then she was the first to get hired for a new job, which left Bob to assume "the wife's role" of selling the house and arranging the move. It took Bob, an aggressive M.B.A. graduate of Wharton, six months to land a position.

"It got to the point where I wasn't telling him about raises or any of the perks associated with my new job because I didn't want to make him feel bad," Jenny recalls. "But it got harder to hide; we had a joint bank account. When he noticed an increase on my pay stub, I'd act like it was no big deal, but each deposit was a reminder that I was doing better than he was. He never mentioned my promotions to his family or celebrated my raises. Now I see that was because he saw my success as a poor reflection on him, rather than a triumph for us as a couple."

Jenny was relieved when Bob was finally offered a post as a vice president at a major bank. "In his mind, he had reached some level of status. He played the VP role to the hilt—including having an affair." Unfortunately, Jenny says, "Image became more important to him than his marriage or his new baby on the way."

They separated. Then Bob sued for—and won—half of Jenny's pension and savings. He later remarried a lower-level professional with whom, Jenny says, he doesn't have to compete.

Looking back, Jenny sees that, "A lot of the problems in my marriage had to do with what I had accomplished versus what Bob had. It finally dawned on me that he was in competition and that he wasn't winning."[7]

This is not an isolated case. The number of married women in the workforce increased from 35 percent in 1966 to 61 percent in 1994. Women with children under three years of age increased at an even higher rate during the same period, from 21 percent to 60 percent.

Also, the traditional model of "breadwinner husband" and "homemaker wife" is being replaced by the dual-income couple—an increase from 39 percent to 61 percent of all married couples from 1970 to 1993. (Interestingly, the dual-income marriages peaked at just over 60 percent in 1999 and have begun to decline, offset by an increase in the husband-only wage earner marriages.) With these changes, the proportion of dual-income marriages in which the wife earns more than the husband increased from 16 percent in 1981 to 23 percent in 1996.[8]

These changes are a problem for some and not a problem for others. In an online poll conducted by *Redbook* magazine, "breadwinner wives" contributed the following information:

- Forty-six percent said that both partners in their marriage are equally happy with the arrangement. But 30 percent of women admitted they're happier with it than their husbands are.
- Twenty-six percent of high-earning women report that their friends or family members have hinted or said outright that their situation is weird.
- The majority of couples with a breadwinner wife share big-purchase decisions.
- Forty-one percent of big-paycheck wives said they still do more than half of the household and parenting duties.
- Thirty-five percent of breadwinner wives admit wishing their husbands would step up and earn more.
- The majority of female breadwinners would not trade salaries with their husbands.[9]

A *Psychology Today* study quotes a number of therapists and psychologists on the impact a wife becoming the breadwinner has on a husband:

- Dr. Ronald Levant, therapist and Harvard professor: "Men have been slower to respond to the change in women's roles, in part because it challenges the notions of male privilege and entitlement. Males aren't ready to give up their advantage in terms of earnings and social power. The idea of women having the upper hand in any way threatens traditional male identity."
- Dr. Barry Dym, family psychologist: "[A wife earning more] violates the imagery we have of ourselves as providers. Money is so charged in American culture. It's our only reckoning of status. People are more willing to talk to me about their sex life than they are about their income."
- Dr. Lori Gordon, marriage and family therapist: "[When a wife earns more, the husband] sees his partner as 'the opponent.' He finds fault with her to feel better about himself."
- Dr. Dorothy Cantor, psychologist: "The societal norm still says there is something wrong with a man if a woman is making more money. But as more couples earn equal pay, the gap will begin to close, and such notions will begin to fall off."[10]

Maybe they will and maybe they won't. Having looked at our societal standards, it's time to ask questions about matters that a cultural mirror won't reveal. Specifically, why should it matter to a man at all what his wife makes? If the money is made honorably and no one, including children, is harmed in the process, why would a husband feel anything but appreciative of his wife's efforts and rewards?

NEW DIRECTIONS

Indeed, for many men it is not a problem. But for many more, it is sometimes, often, or always a problem. For a husband who adheres to the Christian faith, there is another mirror that can probe deeper than the mirror of cultural trends in government and academic research posted on the Internet: the Bible. The apostle James likened the "perfect law of liberty" to a mirror that allows us to measure ourselves against God's ideals (James 1:22–25 KJV). The apostle Paul said the Bible is "living and active. Sharper than any double-edged sword, it penetrates even to dividing soul and spirit, joints and marrow; it judges the thoughts and attitudes of the heart" (Hebrews 4:12).

Unfortunately, the Bible doesn't say explicitly whether a wife should or shouldn't work outside the home; neither does it mention the dynamics that can arise if she does and if her income is greater than her husband's. Ideally, husbands and wives should prayerfully and carefully plan for the "what ifs" in life and make decisions based on the values they agree on. But "what if" a wife goes to work when the couple has no children, experiences rapid promotions that no one could foresee, resulting in an income greater than her husband's, then unexpectedly gets pregnant . . . and so on? Things happen, and husbands must ensure that their responses are based on love and honor instead of jealousy, envy, resentment, or anger.

For us men, that often requires us reaching to the core of how we value ourselves (be that right or wrong). Most of us instinctively know we are to support our wives in every endeavor that allows them to flourish with their God-given talents and abilities. Yet when that results in a reward greater than our own, it's a case of the rubber meeting the road. On a level playing field, a woman being compensated generously for the excellence of her work is to be celebrated. Scripture exhorts us to "rejoice with those who rejoice" (Romans 12:15).

Obviously, I can't prescribe to you and your wife exactly how you are to work out the particulars of your own marriage and the money you both earn. But there are some principles you can consider as you face the challenges that may arise:

1. Think long-term, not short-term. If your wife's income begins to exceed your own, don't panic. Sit down and talk with her about what it might mean to your future as a couple.

2. Don't assume anything. The way things are today is not likely to be the way they will be forever. It's possible that you're completely content with being the only or primary breadwinner now, yet your wife may feel held back. The only way to clear the table of assumptions is to . . .

3. Communicate about everything. Remember the high point of Frank Costanza's Festivus celebration on *Seinfeld*, the "airing of grievances"? Money certainly qualifies as an issue you or your spouse may need to finally open up about in complete honesty. Just make sure you air your grievances in an honorable way.

4. Don't base worth on money. For a man, this is easier said than done, given the cultural expectations we've already discussed in this chapter. Yet it's vital that you remind yourself of this fundamental truth: The person who makes the most money in a marriage is not the most important, talented, valuable, or powerful. Think your stay-at-home wife has it easy meeting your three kids' every need twenty-four-seven? Go ahead, try walking in her shoes for a day, a week, a month. See how "valuable" she is then. The bottom line? Don't get caught in the trap of basing how much you or your wife is "worth" on the monetary amount earned. It's a foolish game. Likewise . . .

5. Don't compete. All it takes to ruin a great relationship is for two friends to start competing. It's easy to laugh about it at first, but the moment you stop laughing is the point at which you know you've crossed the line.

6. Strive for unity. If it truly doesn't matter whether you or your wife gets the credit for something, you'll go far together. You are partners, and partners have different roles and responsibilities yet come

together to form a cohesive unit that's stronger than either individual. Many couples have solved the "who makes more" issue by having only one checking account into which all the income is dumped every month. I advise you to do the same. "His" and "hers" accounts don't paint the clearest picture of unity.

7. Plan ahead. If you're a single guy reading this, think about the issue of unequal salaries. Will you be comfortable only with a more traditional view of wage earning? Or are you flexible, willing to accept and make changes as they come? If this subject is important to you, make it a topic of conversation before you get to the altar.

NEW CONNECTIONS

Anybody who's married knows that a spouse is a different person five, ten, fifteen years after the wedding date. Change is a normal, healthy progression of both an individual and a married couple. But one of the most volatile subjects that can drive couples apart during these changes can be who makes the money—and how much. It can be a source of delight in the ever-changing kaleidoscope of life as viewed through the lens of marriage, or it can be a constant thorn in the collective relational side. If couples will commit that the sacredness of their union is more important than any single dimension of it, they can work through financial changes.

Money is like any other issue. It is not the disease; it is a symptom. If money matters reveal tension and discord in your relationship, money is not the problem. If you're not sure what the real problem is, seek help in finding it. You can't agree to disagree about money—that much is true. As earth, wind, and fire are powerful forces of nature, so money, sex, and power must be handled delicately in marriage. It's essential that you resolve and agree on issues this important. If you don't, an agreement to disagree could easily become an agreement to dissolve.

Chapter 5

"ME TIME" FOR MEN

When I first began to read the four Gospels in the New Testament I was struck by several things: Jesus didn't heal everybody; He was willing to say "No" in a way that would be considered rude today; and He often left the public scene to rest—sometimes alone and sometimes with His disciples. The popular image of Jesus as a passive guy who couldn't say "No" and who served at everyone's beck and call is wrong. For someone who was the Son of God, it's amazing just how human Jesus was. He argued, used strong language, said "No," and walked away. In fact, when it came to taking time for Himself, He was far more balanced than we are.

Or take someone more on the human scale like Mother Teresa. This tiny dynamo spent most of her life taking care of the poor and indigent in India, never seeming to stop. Yet she did—she had to eat and sleep and rest. If she hadn't, she would have died long before she did. Everyone, including men who are husbands and fathers, has to take time off for "R&R" in order to get new strength and a fresh perspective on the tasks at hand.

Men have responded pretty well to the current mindset in our culture that suggests men need to "be involved" at home. They do housework, change diapers, shop for groceries, play with the kids, date their wives, and help with homework. Adopting that mindset, a lot of men feel guilty about taking time off for themselves. I don't mean a ski trip to Colorado. I'm talking more about just taking a few hours here and there to regroup. Often, husbands will stay with the kids while their wives get together with "the girls," but they don't plan similar events for themselves. Most men think their wives need the break and they don't, which is a big mistake.

If "all work and no play makes Jack a dull boy," it also makes him a gradually more dull husband and father.

WHAT WE KNOW ABOUT MEN AND THEIR PRIVATE TIME

In both of the major commercial revolutions in our country's history—the Industrial Revolution and the Digital Revolution—something that was expected did not happen. In the Industrial Revolution machines were supposed to increase human productivity so measurably that America's workforce could live a more balanced and leisurely life. And in the Digital Revolution the "paperless office" and a panoply of digital tools and devices were supposed to save us massive amounts of time.

Never happened. When machines were introduced, instead of workers producing the same thousand widgets in less time and going home early, everybody stayed on the job and produced 1,500 widgets instead. Same deal with the digerati that now inhabit America's offices. After subtracting the number of hours wasted every day fooling with computers and other marvels of technology, any time saved by their use is spent creating more work. A version of Parkinson's Law—"Work expands to fill the time available for its completion"—is always at work. Despite two revolutions destined to change our lives, Americans still work more hours per week than workers in any other developed nation.[1]

You'd think with all that work we'd be floating in cash, right? We all know that's not the case. In 1974, consumer debt (including mortgages) in America was $627 billion. In 1994, it was $4.2 trillion, and in 2004, it was $9.7 trillion. The Federal government announced in the second quarter of 2005 that the nation's debt-service ratio (personal debt payments as a percent of net personal income) was 13.6 percent, the highest since the Fed began tracking the ratio in 1980. In October 2004, USA Today reported that the average personal debt per household in America was $84,454 (including mortgage). Each household's share of the national debt was $473,456.

Okay, we're working more than ever and getting further and further in debt. Stress must be increasing as a result. The National Consumers League's 2003 survey of 1,074 adults found that 80 percent of respondents have problems with stress, including 76 percent of men. Fifty-seven percent of those surveyed said their stress level is higher than they would like it to be. Here are the chief sources of stress they found among those queried:

- Seventy-four percent worry about their own health and that of their family.
- Seventy percent worry about family finances.
- Sixty-eight percent worry about safety.
- Fifty-eight percent say they don't get enough sleep.
- Forty-one percent are burned out and overloaded with work.
- Twenty-five percent are overextended with too many involvements and commitments.[2]

Here's how bad the stress has become for men: the International Spa Association reports that men now make up 29 percent of spa-goers nationally.[3] Men are finding that the quiet, calming, downtime of a spa is helping them decompress from the overamped lifestyle they're living. Which leads me to the point of this chapter.

We all know that life in America is busier than ever, but it's translating into something new that men are looking for: private time. Private time basically means time away from family, and here's why. Most men see work as an obligatory forty- to fifty-hour weekly commitment. It's something they have to do whether they want to or not. But it's the rest of the day that's getting to be a frustration for men.

Let's divide the day into the three traditional thirds: eight hours of work, eight hours of sleep, and eight hours for "everything else." It's that last category in which a lot of men feel they're getting shortchanged. Most of that time (what's left after commuting) is spent on the home front—cutting the grass, paying the bills, eating meals, washing the car, repairing the house, and spending time with wife and children. Some men who have children in their home see their discretionary time being completely consumed by domestic activities. And they need time to get away.

Obviously, many women who are wives and mothers feel the same way. But for some reason, we've always known that women need a "night out for coffee with the girls." This is a carryover from when more women were stay-at-home moms and spent their day conversing in kidspeak and needing to interface with adults. Because men had adult interaction at the office, it was assumed they were okay and good to go when they arrived home from work.

But times and people change. In the survey we conducted, 22 percent of the men said they "always" (3 percent) or "often" (19 percent) "wish they had more private time away from their families." Throw in the "sometimes" (60 percent) and we're (again) talking about well over three-fourths of the men who agreed with this statement.

WHAT PRIVATE TIME MEANS TO MEN

Women looking at these numbers might ask, "What do men need the time to do? It's not like they're going to go out and talk about their feelings with their pals." True, that may not be the first thing on men's minds. But what we're talking about is getting *away* from something (domesticity), not going *to* something. What men are going to—sports, the outdoors, a concert, the gym, car races, the tool section at Home Depot—is definitely important, but not as important as what they are taking a break from.

For men and women today, there is little downtime. Because of the digital and communications revolutions, all of life happens in real time. At one point in our nation's history it took weeks for mail and news to travel from one coast to the other. People didn't sit around twiddling their thumbs during those weeks, but those delays were indicative of how life worked then. There was more time to think; decisions weren't made instantly. Gradually, the time was reduced to a week as trucks and trains replaced ships and stage-coaches, then a few days as airplanes started hauling the mail. Then FedEx gave us overnight delivery. Somewhere in there telegrams and telephones made on-the-spot decisions commonplace ("Buy! Sell!"), and the idea of work being a leisurely pursuit disappeared.

Now, with faxes (minutes) and email (seconds) we're living at a whole different pace. We don't even have to wait the fifteen seconds necessary to dial up and log on to the Internet. Now our connections to the world are always on. Broadband Internet connections have made the world one giant network with every computer being a node. There is no delay, and with the absence of delay we lose the time to think and to reflect. As much as we hate our drive-time commutes, those hours have become a weekly sanctuary for the modern worker. Not a great sanctuary, what with road rage and all, but a sanctuary nonetheless.

Think about the time when a man mounted a horse or climbed in a wagon to go into town for supplies. If the trip was two miles, and he plodded along at a top speed of two miles per hour, that gave him an hour of private time—no radio or CD player, no cell phone, no horns, no road rage. Just the simple delight of the purest sanctuary of all, nature, where he could think and reflect and gather his thoughts. Today, two miles takes us two minutes on the freeway, during which time we've already talked to a couple of friends via cell phone while listening to music or talk radio. That's not enough time to gather our thoughts, much less do anything with them.

I'm using absurd examples to make a point. I'm not suggesting we should return to the horse-and-buggy days. But I am noting that our lives today have far fewer empty spaces in them, spaces that have been a natural part of life in other eras. And because the need for those spaces (those "private times") doesn't go away (witness our survey), if the space is not created naturally in the ebb and flow of life, we have to create it. We have to schedule a space for diversion and downtime.

Again, most of this is not a secret where women have been concerned in the recent past of our modern era. What's new is that men are feeling the need for this space as well.

In his book about men written for wives, Patrick Morley lists five "thorns" that put increasing pressure on men today, resulting in the need for private time away from families to decompress:

1. Time

Morley quotes medical doctor Richard Swenson from his book *Margin*:

> Something is wrong. People are tired and frazzled. People are anxious and depressed. People don't have the time to heal any-more. There is a psychic instability in our day that prevents peace from implanting itself very firmly in the human spirit. And despite the skeptics, this instability is not the same old nemesis recast in

modern life. What we have here is a brand-new disease. . . . It is the disease of marginless living.

Margin is the amount allowed beyond that which is needed. It is something held in reserve for contingencies or unanticipated situations. Margin is the gap between rest and exhaustion, the space between breathing freely and suffocating. It is the leeway we once had between ourselves and our limits. Margin is the opposite of overload.

Margin is the space men are looking for in their lives.

2. Money

The personal debt statistics I cited earlier have created another category of expense that men (and women) struggle with: insurance. We have accumulated so much stuff, and owe so much money on it, that it all has to be insured to protect our debt, not to mention protect us. There's life insurance, health insurance, major medical insurance, car insurance, house insurance, disability insurance, liability insurance, boat insurance, business insurance, and others. That list alone indicates just how complicated the financial life of men has become.

3. Work

The pressure of money increases the pressure to work. Even if men work at salaried jobs where putting in more hours doesn't result in more immediate income, there's always the pressure to perform. Not only do most men *want* to perform well (an internal pressure that most women don't understand), there is the pressure to perform in order to survive. And for those men who are self-employed or paid on commissions, the temptation of "one more sale" is often too strong to resist.

4. People

Men are different about this one, but far too many men say "Yes" to more people than they should. Unfortunately, most men are so committed with work and family that they have little time to commit to others. But it's better to face that reality and stay balanced than to commit the last bit of margin in our lives to something we can ill afford. If we want to be involved with people, something else will have to be eliminated to make room.

5. Religion

If there is one part of the week where many men feel the option not to show up, it's Sunday morning. It's the last day of the week, and a normal week has left men exhausted and in need of time to catch their breath. Quite frankly, many man don't see church as a good place to be refreshed (see Chapter 12). Sunday morning is their last chance to grab a minute for themselves before the crunch begins again on Monday. Criticism from wives and pastors notwithstanding, men are features-and-benefits oriented. They are going to trust that God will give them a break if they stay home, even if others don't.[4]

NEW DIRECTIONS

Despite the pressures on his life, it is not easy for a man to justify time for himself. A man has an image of driving away from his house leaving a tired wife and daddy-deficient children standing in the doorway. That's a bit melodramatic, of course, but most men carry a load of guilt about "requesting" time off from the family to get a few hours alone or with other men. Psychiatrist Scott Haltzman proposes men take the following short quiz, seeing how many of the following they can answer "No" to:

1. I spend more time per week doing my own thing than my wife spends doing her own thing.   Yes   No
2. Commonly, when I tell my wife that I got home late because I was working, I was actually hanging around the office shooting the breeze with co-workers.   Yes   No
3. I've lied to my wife about working late, when the truth is I stopped at a bar for a quick drink with pals on the way home—or worse.   Yes   No
4. I erase e-mail or phone messages because I don't want my wife knowing about my interests outside the home.   Yes   No
5. In the past three months, I've complained when my wife announced plans of her own that I felt conflicted with my personal plans.   Yes   No
6. In the past three months, my wife and I have exchanged harsh words over how I am spending my leisure time.   Yes   No

7. My wife agrees with the following sentence: my husband gets to do more cool things with his friends than I get to do with mine.
   Yes   No
8. When I am at home, more than 50 percent of my time is spent on a solo activity (such as watching TV or sitting at the computer).
   Yes   No
9. Even when I'm home from work, the housework and child-care load still fall primarily on my wife.   Yes   No

Dr. Haltzman suggests that the more "No" answers you recorded, the better relationship you have with your wife in terms of maintaining a balance between your need for private time and her needs. The more "Yes" answers you gave, the more careful you need to be about demanding personal time at the expense of your family.[5]

I like the ideas of Dr. Sam Keen on how a man can cultivate private time by cultivating solitude. That is, it's not always necessary to leave home and spend money you don't have in order to take a break from the routine. Too often, such activities only constitute one more form of busyness and distraction, taking away from the real goal of spiritual and emotional reflection and refreshment.

Here are his thoughts on creative ways, at home and away from home, to achieve the rest you need (I've added some of my thoughts to his points):

- Take separate vacations—not in place of family vacations, but as an occasional, inexpensive source of R&R. Many close-by resources exist for you and your wife to take separate, individual breaks from the pressures of life—a rental cabin in a state park, a monastery, a bed and breakfast. Find a cheap way to power down in order to power up.
- Design a sanctuary of solitude—a corner of the basement, a back corner in the yard, a carrel in the local library, a favorite easy chair at a local bookstore—where you can grab an hour on occasion to read, nap, write in a journal, or pray.
- Keep a journal. A journal is a record of a journey—your life journey. It's a significant way to "talk" to someone even when you're alone.

.• Pay attention to your dreams. This is, unfortunately, an unknown to many modern men. But the work our minds do during our sleeping hours can often speak to us after waking about what's going on internally. That's six or eight hours of lost data if we ignore the content of our dreams.

• Walk. "The philosopher Friedrich Nietzsche once said that the only ideas that were worthwhile were those that came when he was walking under an open sky," writes Keen. Besides being an excellent form of exercise, walking alone is a perfect, free way to take advantage of the aerobic stimulation of the brain. Creativity seems to get a jump start when we walk.[6]

NEW CONNECTIONS

Wives who have read this chapter need to guard against any resentment that may surface at the thought that their husbands need "private time." That is not to say wives don't either. The new idea here is that men need this as much as women. Discussing this thought together is an excellent opportunity for a couple to assess their schedules and their needs, and purposefully create the individual space that's required for each to be as healthy as possible.

Life in our culture, especially during the child-rearing and midcareer years in any man's life, is not going to get slower and calmer. If anything, it's only going to get more demanding in the future. That reality makes creating private time an imperative for both men and women. It's a way for individuals to make themselves stronger as an end in itself, not just as a means to the end of a stronger marriage (though that probably will happen). This chapter is a call for individuals to renew their uniqueness by breaking out of the conforming ways of our culture and to go deeper within themselves. Whether it's done alone as a quest for solitude, or in a collegial setting with close friends, private time is a necessity for good mental, spiritual, and emotional health.

Nothing hides us from who we really are, and who we are becoming, like the clamor of busyness.

Chapter 6

DADDY DEAREST

In 1990, I became a father, something I had looked forward to for a very long time. I didn't just want to be a father; I wanted to be a good father. I knew being a good father would make me a better man. While not perfect in either category, I have seen the truth of that correlation over the years. Parenthood forces a man to get out of himself and into the life of another human being.

I've heard many dads express regrets over missing so much of the fatherhood experience because they were busy making their mark on the world. The irony in that reality is that there is no stronger or more permanent way a man can make his mark on the world than by investing himself in his children.

My daughter and I made a trip to Africa along with another father-daughter pair in conjunction with a mission organization. One night over dinner the other father asked my daughter to tell him what she appreciated most about me, her father. Gulp! One never knows what a fifteen-year-old might say—or want to say—about her parents, given the opportunity. But here's what Madeline said: "First, I know he loves me. Second, he's always been there for me. Three is yet to be determined and four is unknown."

We all laughed together over numbers three and four, but I was holding back the tears over numbers one and two. She couldn't have said anything to bless or humble me more as her father, because that's what I've wanted to do for her: love her and be there for her.

I've made plenty of mistakes as Madeline's father. Saying the wrong things and not saying the right things. Being insensitive. Forcing my adult male grid onto her adolescent female personality. But even the mistakes pay off when I'm there to acknowledge them, apologize, and ask her forgiveness. That's what I mean about fatherhood making me a better man. Where else can you be humbled like you are when asking the forgiveness of a seven-year-old?

In 2005, I made a new journey into fatherhood as two little boys became my step sons. James and Carter have added so much to my life. They are so smart and so very loving. It is such a privilege to be what we call their "bonus Dad." It is a different experience because my role is more about just icing a cake that was prepared by two very good parents before me. I had heard that being a stepdad could be a very difficult role, but so far it has been nothing but a blessing.

Being an adoptive father (Madeline) and a stepfather have been sources of joy and fulfillment for me. Now with the birth of Solomon, I am becoming a biological father, making me a thrice-blessed man—and I believe no less than three times a better man as well.

WHAT WE KNOW ABOUT MEN AND FATHERHOOD

Some of what we know about fatherhood today is good, and some not so good. Let's start with the good, which is linked to a piece of good news from the survey of men we conducted. Of the twenty-five statements to which we asked 3,600 men to respond, the two lowest numbers of agreement were on these two statements:

No. 24: "Men wish they had married someone other than their wife."

No. 25: "Men are bored or impatient with their role as a parent."

If I had been asked to choose the two statements that I hope men in America would respond most negatively to (which is a positive thing in terms of the survey), it would be these two having to do with marriage and fatherhood. This is indeed cause for celebration in terms of how men are feeling about their wives and their children.

I discussed question number 24 in Chapter 20, and in this chapter we'll look at question 25 concerning men and fatherhood. In our survey, only 1 percent of the men said they are "always" bored or impatient with being a father, and 10 percent said "often." If I were going to ignore the "sometimes" category on any question it would be this one (56 percent). What father doesn't get bored sometimes after reading *Curious George Visits the Zoo* for the fiftieth time? And what father doesn't have to pray for patience as he watches and waits while his four-year-old s-l-o-w-l-y and c-a-r-e-f-u-l-l-y ties her sneakers—while he's late for work. So we'll give the "sometimers" a break on this one—it comes with the fatherhood territory.

While it appears the vast majority of fathers in our survey are pretty committed to being there for their children, the fatherhood landscape is not so positive overall. The *Father Facts* book, published by the National Fatherhood Initiative, is filled with 182 pages of information about the state of the fathering art in America. On their Web site, they list the top ten father facts from the book:

1. Twenty-four million children (34 percent) live absent from their biological father.
2. Nearly twenty million children (27 percent) live in single-parent homes.
3. In 2000, 1.35 million births (33 percent of all births) occurred out of wedlock.
4. Forty-three percent of first marriages dissolve within fifteen years; about 60 percent of divorcing couples have children; and approximately one million children each year experience the divorce of their parents.
5. More than 3.3 million children live with an unmarried parent and the parent's cohabiting partner. The number of cohabiting couples with children has nearly doubled since 1990, from 891,000 to 1.7 million today.
6. Fathers who live with their children are more likely to have a close, enduring relationship with their children than those who do not. The best predictor of father presence is marital status. Compared to

children born within marriage, children born to cohabiting parents are three times as likely to experience father absence, and children born to unmarried, noncohabiting parents are four times as likely to live in a father-absent home.

7. About 40 percent of children in father-absent homes have not seen their father at all during the past year; 26 percent of absent fathers live in a different state than their children; and 50 percent of children living absent their father have never set foot in their father's home.

8. Children who live absent from their biological fathers are, on average, at least two to three times more likely to be poor; to use drugs; to experience educational, health, emotional, and behavioral problems; to be victims of child abuse; and to engage in criminal behavior than their peers who live with their married, biological (or adoptive) parents.

9. From 1960 to 1995, the proportion of children living in single-parent homes tripled, from 9 percent to 27 percent, and the proportion of children living with married parents declined. However, from 1995 to 2000, the proportion of children living in single-parent homes slightly declined, while the proportion of children living with two married parents remained stable.

10. Children with involved, loving fathers are significantly more likely to do well in school, have healthy self-esteem, exhibit empathy and pro-social behavior, and avoid high-risk behaviors such as drug use, truancy, and criminal activity compared to children who have uninvolved fathers.[1]

It's a little hard to read those top-ten facts and not grieve for the state of the family, and fatherhood, in America today. It would be hard to find a father who set out to be a bad one. But things don't always turn out the way we plan. Fortunately, God is committed to turning the hearts of fathers to their children and the hearts of children back to their fathers (see Malachi 4:6).

WHAT BEING A FATHER MEANS TO MEN

Trained botanists and weekend gardeners alike know something that applies to fatherhood, and that is concerning the purpose of plants. There is something in the dirt that covers our planet that is fundamental to human health, and that is minerals (calcium, iron, magnesium, potassium, zinc, and the like). Scientists have identified one hundred-plus elements of which our planet is built (the dreaded periodic table of elements you had to memorize in high school science or physics class), and which all animal life must consume in order to survive. (Recall that Adam was created from the dust of the ground—Genesis 2:7.) The challenge is getting the minerals out of the ground and into the human body. To that end, some mountain folk have made a practice of eating a spoonful of rich, natural dirt every day. Unfortunately for them, that folk remedy doesn't work since the human body can't absorb chemicals in their mineral state.

Enter the plant. When a plant sends its roots deep into the soil, it has the ability to absorb molecules of the earth's chemical elements. Those molecular elements make their way through the roots, up the stem, out through the branches, and into that juicy apple or tomato that you love to eat. Therefore, at the risk of overstatement, we can say that the plant kingdom is God's vehicle for delivering life-sustaining chemicals (minerals) from the earth to the animal kingdom. Plants, whether grass or fruits and vegetables, are a temporary intermediary, a transmission device to get chemical elements from one place to another. A brilliant plan from the creative hand of the Creator.

In that same vein, God has devised another temporary transmission device, a way to transmit truth from His heart to the hearts of developing young adults. And that transmission device is the subject of this chapter: fatherhood. I use that term in a biblical way, not to the exclusion of mothers, to focus on the role the Bible seems to assign fathers (especially in the Old Testament) for raising their children in the nurture and admonition of the Lord.

Think about it: fathers are assigned the task of mentoring and tutoring one or more developing adults for eighteen or so years. During that time a continual process of transmission is going on through many means: teaching, correcting, being an example, answering, challenging, disciplining—all in a context of love. The father's purpose in those two decades of leading is to prepare a child to become an adult, to be a conduit of truth from the heart of God to the heart of the child. By the time a child is a mature teenager he or she ought to be making "the turn"—turning their eyes from their earthly father to their Father-God. That's the whole point: to show children what God is like so they will let loose of their parents' hands, reach out and grasp God's hand, and walk with Him for the rest of their adult lives. There are several critical implications in that process:

1. A father's role is not optional.

Think of the plant example. If the plant is not there, how do the minerals get out of the ground and into the human body? They don't, and the animal kingdom dies. If a father is not present to speak for Father-God to developing children, how will they hear His truth? I'm not going to be melodramatic and say, "They don't, and the children die." There are other ways that children can learn about life and God, especially through thousands and thousands of godly single mothers who labor faithfully to ground their children in a biblical worldview. But even those moms know that their love and efforts are not enough, that their children need the balancing influence of a male presence. And thank God again for godly brothers and uncles and grandfathers and others who stand in the gap for children. But those exceptions prove the rule: a father's role is not an option.

2. A father's role is temporary.

It seems anything but temporary when a father is going through the child-rearing process, but it is. We fathers have fifteen to twenty years to impact our children with God's truth before our role changes from teacher/influencer to counselor/advisor. If that's not scary enough, I recall Dr. Paul Meier's statement in *Christian Child-Rearing and Personality Development* that 90 percent of a child's personality has been set in place by age six. Every day counts. Every day that passes is a day fathers are impacting their child with some idea of what fatherhood is about—ideas that will greatly influence their understanding of what the fatherhood of God is all about. Plants are temporary; the seasonal cycle allows them to bear fruit and then expire. A father's cycle is fifteen to twenty years. What's not transmitted in that season will have been missed.

3. A father's role is to pull, not push; to create a hunger, not force-feed.

A plant has no heart, no pump, to force chemicals to go from its cells and veins into the fruit. In some mysterious, capillary-like fashion, chemicals travel from the ground to the fruit where they are deposited, waiting to be consumed. Fathers have to create a setting in which truth is drawn into a child because he is hungry. In biblical times mothers would dip a finger in the juice of a date and put it in the mouth of a newborn to stimulate its sucking reflex before putting the child to their breast. The Hebrew word for "train" in Proverbs 22:6 ("Train up a child . . .") is a word based on that idea, the notion that training a child involves stimulating his or her desire to know truth, and ultimately to know God.

4. A father's role is to be a clear channel.

Unlike North America, which, for the most part, has lost its precious mineral-rich topsoil through erosion and poor agricultural practices, there is no deficiency of truth with God. Even in the best soil, however, a plant can be diseased and fail in its purpose, as can fathers. We have access to all the truth our children need by connecting with the heart of God ourselves. The question is whether we are pure enough, strong enough, present enough, and full enough of that truth to transmit it in the time we're allotted.

5. A father's role is to be a steward.

This biblical word is used to reflect the idea of managing something for someone else. A steward was a trusted household servant into whose hands a head of household would entrust the managing of his properties, other servants, and even his finances. The steward owned nothing and had no authority that wasn't bestowed by his master. So it is with a father who is a steward of the children given into his care by God. The children are not his to keep; they are his to train in the ways of God. Everything needed for that task is supplied by God, but it is the father-steward's job to choose and introduce the right elements at the right time. Just as a plant knows which chemicals to pull out of the soil and deliver to the fruit, so a father knows how to manage what has been entrusted to him.

6. Finally, a father's role is to be a servant-leader.

A plant is not a utilitarian device. It provides shade, beauty, by-products, refuge for parts of the animal kingdom, and keeps the soil in place with its roots. But every plant ultimately serves only one purpose in life: to reproduce itself. Everything else a plant does is subsidiary to that goal.

Contained in the fruit of an apple or tomato are the precious seeds that ensure the plant's survival and reproduction in the next season. To that same end, while a father accomplishes many other beneficial and noble tasks in his own life, everything in him is geared toward serving the end of spiritual reproduction—of sending out into the world young adults who are not like him, but like God.

NEW DIRECTIONS

This chapter is obviously not a "how to" manual on being a good father. It's an attempt to once again step back from the trees and look afresh at the forest, to remind ourselves of the big picture to which fathers have been called by God. To that end, let me suggest three things that every one of us fathers can focus on today—and every day—that are absolutely mandatory for accomplishing God's purposes in the lives of our children.

First, fathers must love God. As I've already stated, I don't think there are many men who purpose in their hearts to do a bad job as a father. But there are *multitudes* of us who have the idea that somehow our children will get raised without much of our personal involvement. We believe that by taking our children (or in many cases sending them) to church, sending them to school, getting them involved in various activities, that our children will turn out okay. And from the point of view that "all truth is God's truth," our children will indeed pick up a lot of what it takes to survive in this world, even succeed in some sense. But the only way a father can be assured that his child will learn the most important truths in life—truths about living under God's lordship—is knowing those truths himself and assuming the responsibility for transmitting them to his children. A father cannot give away to his children what he himself does not possess.

Second, fathers must love their own fathers. There are millions of walking wounded men in our culture who never received from their fathers the love, truth, and affirmation they needed. They were raised by fathers who were raised by fathers who were raised by fathers . . . who were not equipped to reproduce healthy and whole young adults and release them into the world. There are open wounds and sores that must be healed and closure that must be gained in order for the cycle of dysfunction to be stopped. Men who are not loved by their fathers cannot love their own children. And where a father can't, or won't, provide that love, fathers must get it from God Himself. Fathers must find healing for their own broken hearts to prevent breaking the hearts of their children.

Third, fathers must love their wives. I mention later in this book the principle that the greatest thing a father can do for his children is to love their mother unconditionally. In that love, boys see what it means to provide for and protect the love of the husband's life, and girls see the kind of man with whom they should try to spend the rest of their life. Parenting is a partnership. As both the male and female in the Garden of Eden were created in God's image, so it takes both male and female in a marriage to adequately represent God in His fullness to children who are just coming to know Him. Nothing will embitter children more toward God than living with a mother who has been turned resentful by the callous affections of their father. The contradiction, the disconnect, this sets up in the heart of a child is spiritually and emotionally life-threatening.

If we as fathers will set our hearts on these three loves, the various details of raising children will find their own place in their own time. To try to accomplish the details without the context of these loves is like spinning a wheel bearing without lubrication. In due time it will grind to a stop.

NEW CONNECTIONS

I dislike ending with a negative example, but the following true story is given such a prophetic interpretation by the observer that its meaning for fathers, and their wives, will be immediately apparent. The spokesman is Weldon Hardenbrook, as told in the chapter he wrote for the widely respected volume *Recovering Biblical Manhood and Womanhood: A Response to Evangelical Feminism*. His chapter is titled "Where's Dad? A Call for Fathers with the Spirit of Elijah":

I was with a friend some time ago, driving home from Los Angeles. It was midday, and we were coming down a steep grade. In front of us was a new pickup truck with a family. The mother was driving, and the father was beside her in the cab. In the open bed of the truck were four small children. They had a picnic basket, fishing poles. The children were obviously excited to be going on vacation.

Suddenly, one of the back wheels snapped off. The truck veered sharply to the right and shot off a sixty-foot cliff. My friend and I were the only ones there. We stopped our car and started down the hillside. We ran to the children, doing what we could do. All of them were unconscious.

The mother was seriously injured. It looked as though she had broken her legs and pelvis. But she started crawling on her belly to each child. We couldn't prevent her. The father could not restrain her either, although he tried. He was in the best shape of anyone, but he stayed in the truck, and called out to his wife to stop.

The scene is forever engraved in my mind. It says something to me about the fathers of our country. The children of America are lying wounded, strewn throughout our cities. In too many cases, their fathers are leaving them to their mothers' care. The children need the father to get out of the truck and join the mothers who care for them. The fathers of America need to have such an extraordinary passion for God and be so consumed with the vision of responsible fatherhood that we will allow no obstacle to stand in the way of the healing of the American family.

This is our greatest challenge at the end of the twentieth century: turning the hearts of fathers to their children so that, as the prophet promises, the hearts of the children will turn back toward them.[2]

May God give grace to fathers everywhere to yield to the spirit of Elijah being sent into the world before the coming day of the Lord (Malachi 4:5–6), that the hearts of fathers and children will turn toward one another again.

SECTION 2

SECRETS ABOUT FEELINGS

Chapter 7

SHARING WHAT'S ON THE INSIDE

Dan loved his wife and would never be unfaithful to her, but a woman at work had caught his eye. She was beautiful and showed an interest in him. She would stop by his office to talk—always about safe subjects such as her boyfriend or Dan's wife. But this woman's presence had become a factor in Dan's life. He didn't know what to do, but he managed to narrow his choices down to two: defuse the situation by talking to his wife about it, including her, and seeking her help in resolving his feelings; or keep the situation and his feelings to himself so as not to threaten his wife.

He decided to talk to his wife, to invite her into the situation as an ally. After dinner one night, when the children were in bed and the two of them were alone in the kitchen, he broached the subject as carefully as he knew how. He reaffirmed his love for his wife but told her he wanted her to be aware that there was a woman at work showing interest in him. Trying to be honest, he told his wife she was attractive and that he had been surprised by the fact that he looked forward to their chats.

Up to that point, his wife had been with him. But when he told her how he felt about the woman stopping by his office, she began to cry and ran upstairs to their bedroom. She was inconsolable, and he ended up spending the night on the sofa downstairs. Naturally, he concluded that he had made a gigantic mistake by revealing what was going on at work and, more importantly, his own feelings about the events. Wishing he could take the whole conversation back, he decided he would never risk that kind of honesty again.

He kept to his word, and within a month he had slept with the woman at work. It only happened once. But he decided that "once burned, twice shy" was a good reason not to tell his wife.

WHAT WE KNOW ABOUT MEN'S (UN)WILLINGNESS TO TALK ABOUT THEIR FEELINGS

For many men, the world is not a safe place to share feelings. In his book *When Men Think Private Thoughts*, Gordon MacDonald tells about being invited to speak at a men's retreat. At the beginning of one session he told the group of several hundred men that, when he concluded his talk, he was going to extend an invitation. Any man who felt God was speaking to him about significant life issues could come to the front of the room for prayer. And any friends of those men would be invited to come and pray with and for them.

MacDonald delivered what was, in his estimation, a poor talk—halting and unconvincing—and felt sure there would be little response from the men. But when he issued the invitation, he was shocked to see scores of men coming forward to pray, and many more coming to pray with them. When all had come, he dismissed the rest of the crowd and allowed the auditorium to become a room of prayer. He slipped out a side door to get a breath of fresh air and ask God's forgiveness for his lack of faith.

When he returned to the auditorium he was shocked by what he saw. It seemed not a single man had left. The men were scattered throughout the room in groups of twos, threes, and fours. He was struck by two things: the tears and the intimacy. Men were talking softly, weeping, praying, hugging, holding one another. In MacDonald's own words, "I remember standing there in a state of total surprise. I'd never seen anything quite like it in a spiritual setting. I recall thinking, almost out loud, that there are two things men desperately need from one another that, generally speaking, they are not getting or giving: *permission to express their deepest feelings to one another and the freedom to be affectionate.*" [1]

This experience, and Gordon MacDonald's observations about it, confirms the fallacy in a common stereotype about men—namely, that men don't have deep feelings, period. While some people (okay, some women) buy into that notion, another group of women believes that men don't have deep feelings about anything other than work, sports, guns, cars, and other traditionally male foci. But here's what a third group of women (the majority) holds as truth: men have deep feelings about lots of things—most of the things women have deep feelings about—but they either don't know how to express them or are unwilling to express them.

Men will tell you that this last group of women is correct. Men do have deep feelings. We see soldiers on the battlefield weeping over the loss of a comrade. We see retiring athletes break down emotionally as they say good-bye to their fans. We see fathers shed tears at the births of their first sons or their daughters' first recital. We see men barely able to make it through the giving away of a daughter at the altar. And we see men riled with anger when they encounter injustice in the world.

What is unique about men is that it often takes a precipitating event to trigger the release of their feelings. When no such event has occurred, men are "business as usual." For women, however, life itself is a precipitating event. They are almost always willing and able to reveal how they feel about life—and get frustrated that their men are not that willing and/or able.

Apparently, most men, if not aggravated by the fact, at least agree with the perception that "it is difficult for them to talk about their feelings." In our survey of 3,600 men, a total of 52.7 percent agreed with that statement. Interestingly, a higher percentage of Christian men (53.5 percent) than non-Christian men (50.4 percent) agreed. While the difference may represent nothing more than the margin of error in the survey, it raises the question of why Christian men didn't score "better." That is, why aren't they more comfortable verbalizing their feelings? In a religion that places a high value on honesty, acceptance, and forgiveness, it would seem that openness of expression would be a much higher value among Christian men than among men in general.

WHAT TALKING ABOUT FEELINGS MEANS TO MEN

It is common knowledge among women that there are two things men never do: men never talk and they never listen. If that's true, I'm not sure what we men are doing most of the time. That's like saying to someone who is standing in front of you, "You're never here." "I'm here right now," we counter. "But that's not what I mean," our women will say. Apparently not.

When women tell their men that "they [the men] never talk," and the men respond by saying, "I'm talking right now," that is obviously the wrong answer. A man is referring to the physical act of forcing air past his larynx so that his vocal cords vibrate and produce recognizable sounds. A woman, however, is referring to the act of communicating feelings through the medium of talking.

For men, talking is a means to an end, the shortest path from Point A to Point B. Talking is something we do to accomplish something important. For women, talking is an end in itself—a beautiful, relaxed journey. The journey *is* the destination; it's what is most important. A conversation can be interrupted at any point and still be a success because it was not about getting somewhere beyond the conversation itself. For women, every item that is shared in a conversation represents the destination of intimacy, closeness, and simply sharing life. Men aren't opposed to reaching those goals; they just don't usually achieve them by spontaneously sharing their feelings.

An exception to that rule may be David Bentall, former third-generation owner of a respected construction conglomerate in Vancouver, British Columbia, who's now a consultant and life coach to business executives. At a gathering of fifty successful businessmen, each was asked to describe himself using just three words. After careful thought, Bentall chose *faith*, *integrity*, and *transparency*. Faith and integrity were received well, but he got some strange looks with transparency. He explains:

"It seemed that transparency was such a foreign notion to these men that they thought I must have been mistaken in my thinking. When the session was over several approached me to say, 'You didn't really mean to use that word, did you?' Some of them thought I was referring to myself as invisible! The dictionary defines *transparent* as 'open, frank, or candid' and I certainly want to be like this, so yes, I really meant to use *transparent*."

In a small accountability group of men Bentall meets with, the other members are wont to say they always know what's going on with him. Why? Because he's a man who is obviously unafraid of expressing his feelings.[2]

Such is not the case with all men. Noted counselor and author Dr. H. Norman Wright has taken self-reporting surveys for years in churches and conferences and compiled the results. Following is what a number of men said they are afraid to talk about, in their own words:

- "Deep personal feelings that perhaps we ourselves are afraid of or don't understand."
- "Deep needs or insecurities, inadequacies, and temptations."
- "In short, our own vulnerabilities. In our society men are supposed to be strong, self-sufficient, Clint Eastwood types. Men impose this on themselves. It is difficult for men to show weakness or vulnerability, especially to women."
- "True heartfelt problems. A woman's emotional makeup many times does not enable her to just *listen*. She starts talking and makes it worse."
- "Masculine and feminine role issues. Men fear being accused of being sexist."
- "Getting older, reaching lifetime goals, mortality."
- "Men's feelings of insecurity, incompleteness, inadequacy, loss of control of family and situations, lack of self-confidence, and relating to past mistakes."
- "Personal fears and 'perceived inadequacies.' Any subject that triggers my wife's insecurities, resulting in hours of defensive discussion to alleviate her fears."
- "Risk is a big factor in the man-woman relationship. Men are risk-takers in many areas of life, but only in areas where they can fall back onto other resources. For men, sharing feelings presents a risk with a bottomless abyss waiting for them if they slip."

One of the men responding to Wright's surveys was a family law attorney who had interviewed thousands of men over his decades of practice, specifically asking them about marital legal issues. Here is his summation:

"If there is one category to define all the subjects that men hesitate to talk about, it would be in the area of emotions. Men do not like to discuss their hurts, stress, lack of accomplishment, and questions related to their energy levels. All of these, of course, would fall under the general heading of the inability to express personal feelings."[3]

Whether you're a man or a woman reading the various quotes from Wright's respondents, you're probably nodding your head in agreement. Men are definitely less willing to talk about feelings and emotions than anything else. But there are two factors that seem to give men the permission they need to talk: trust and time. I'll let Bentall state both points clearly before elaborating on them.

Men and trust.

"Most of us don't like to tell our most intimate secrets or experiences to anyone but close friends, with whom there is a preexisting bond of trust."[4] Bentall makes an excellent observation, yet there is a catch-22 for every married man in this type of situation. On one hand, how is he to know he can trust his wife without revealing his thoughts to her? On the other, he refuses to reveal those thoughts to anyone he doesn't know he can trust. For any husband who has revealed a deep, dark secret to his wife—only to find out that she told it to her best friend or a pastor or counselor—that's likely to be the last secret that wife hears for a long time, maybe ever. A man's innermost thoughts are like the secret rites and "mystic goodies" of a Middle Ages secret society. If you haven't earned and received the coat of arms, password, and secret handshake, then you don't get to enter. Once in, to violate the code of secrecy is the kiss of death.

Breaking the catch-22 mold requires someone taking a first step. When a man takes the initiative by revealing some of his feelings and fears to his wife, it's a risky move since he doesn't know what kind of steward she will be. If she passes the information on, makes light of what is shared, doesn't appreciate what her husband has done by opening up, or otherwise rolls her eyes (figuratively or literally), up goes the drawbridge. No more access to the sacred hall where the secrets of the society are stored.

Ideally, if a husband shares something new, difficult, personal, or fearful, his wife will respond with trustworthiness, treating his words with respect. Such receptivity says, "This is going in the vault and you have the only key. I'm receiving this not so I can spread it around to all my friends or pass judgment on it, but so you will know that I care about what you think and feel. I'm not going to comment or offer an opinion or feedback unless you let me know it's okay. My purpose is to be an extension of you, as if you're talking to yourself and mulling things over, only out loud."

Men and time.

"Despite the benefits of transparency," Bentall says, "it is a fact that many men are willing to share difficulties and struggles only when they are past."[5] Allow me to introduce Arterburn's Corollary: "A man's willingness to talk openly about personal issues is inversely correlated to today's date." Put another way, the likelihood of a man being willing to talk about a serious or meaningful issue, experience, fear, or question *increases* with every day since the occurrence of the issue or experience.

Men are unlikely to come home in the afternoon and say to their wives, "You know, babe, our human resources staff did a presentation today about financial planning and retirement, and it made me realize we are way behind the curve in saving. In fact, I figure I'll probably have to work as a greeter at Wal-Mart once I do retire just for us to make ends meet. This really strikes at the roots of my self-esteem regarding intelligence, self-discipline, the ability to plan, and success in my vocation. It makes me want to move to another city so I won't be embarrassed when my comfortably retired friends come into Wal-Mart to buy fishing gear and a boat battery to take to their lake houses, and I'm handing out smiley face stickers to their grandkids and saying, 'Have a nice day.'"

Obviously, it's doubtful you'll ever hear a man be this descriptive with every aspect of how an event made him feel. But the more time a man has to think about difficult issues—once the initial panic, shame, embarrassment, or fear has subsided—the more willing he may be to open up about them. A wife who understands this, then, will give her man time to process his thoughts and not press for a revelation when he comes home in a preoccupied or distant mood. She'll respond with something like this: "Honey, there was a day last week that I remember you coming home from work seeming sort of thoughtful, maybe a bit discouraged. I remember you said there was some sort of seminar at work that day. I just wondered if they were connected, if something happened that day that put you in a thoughtful mood. If not, that's fine. I just wanted to make sure you were okay."

Trust and time. Those two conditions are commonsensical in their simplicity, yet so often overlooked. Even if women don't completely understand this, it's important for them to accept by faith that these two factors represent the hardwired reality of how most men live and think. Living in step with these dynamics, rather than denying them, will lead to debunking the idea that "men never talk."

NEW DIRECTIONS

A man who wrote to counselor and author Dr. Emerson Eggerichs said this about his relationship with his wife: "I did not reveal myself to her. I stuffed many of my thoughts, emotions, and needs that I feared would lead to rejection if I voiced them. . . . This was cutting her off. . . . I believe this was an abdication of my responsibility. *I have known for many, many years that honesty and openness is God's way but had not really come to terms with it until recently*" (italics mine).[6]

As men, we need to agree that not every emotion we feel—for example, fear, inhibition, or intimidation—is good. We often know that honesty and openness is "God's way" but struggle to obey. Following Dr. Larry Crabb's insightful suggestion, I've often wondered if Adam ever said "I'm sorry" to Eve. There he was in the garden, listening to Satan tempt his wife, and he did nothing to interfere, to keep her from giving in and plunging the two of them into chaos. As Crabb says, "He was there and he was silent."[7] I wonder if Adam lived his near-millennium-long life never talking to Eve about his shame. And I wonder if we modern men have inherited his silence.

We do not have to give into the temptation to be silent. We can talk to our wives in complete freedom. And it's important for our wives to receive, with trust and over time, what we need and want to say. Before we can get to that point, however, both husbands and wives must come to terms with the silence that fills our houses like a fog, obscuring us from each other.

NEW CONNECTIONS

The stereotype I noted earlier, that men "never talk and never listen," is not true. Likewise, it is definitely not true that men don't feel. The problem is that we don't talk and listen with our wives as much as we should. We talk to other men on spiritual retreats, even cry and confess with them. And we listen intently in strategy sessions related to success on the job. We talk and listen plenty.

The challenge is for two people who have sinned against one another, betrayed each other's confidences, raised their voices toward each other, and done a thousand other things that could easily put an end to intimacy, to establish new ways of connecting. And truth be told, two such sinners are prime candidates for establishing an open, transparent relationship.

When it comes to open sharing between two people, we're talking about a friendship. In the words of scholar and Oxford professor Dr. James Houston, "Friendship is built on the mutual sharing of weakness."[8] When two people—even two people as radically different as a man and a woman—are willing to admit their fears and weaknesses to one another, they immediately take the elevator together down to the lowest floor of the common human condition, a floor called Fallen-ness. There, pretenses are off, posturing is removed, and presumption is done away with. There, they can look at each other with the kind of realization that says, "What's left to hide? We know each other too well to believe anything except the truth. Let's talk. There's nothing to lose and everything to gain."

Chapter 8

WANTED: MALE BONDING

As I write this I am waiting patiently for the arrival of my son, Solomon Russell Arterburn. I think about him constantly because I can't wait to be the father of a little boy. If it is half as wonderful as being the father of my daughter, it will be a grand experience.

Of course, I want the best for my son. His middle name is Russell in honor of my mother's side of the family. I never met her father, my Grandfather Russell, but I wanted my boy to carry his family name. I've heard stories of my grandfather and how he was loved by so many. But he also had secrets that he never shared. He sank into a deep depression and had to be admitted to an institution that was not such a wonderful place to be. They gave him electric shock therapy that actually helped him for a while. But the depression returned. He had sworn if it ever did he would not go back to that institution. And he was true to his word. The next time he started to sink down into his own sadness, he shot and killed himself.

I always wondered what secrets he carried that were so powerful that he could not bear facing them. I also wondered what would have happened if he'd had some great male friends to share those secrets with. If there were close male friends who cared for him, I believe I would have known my grandfather. No one but men who have experienced it can understand the saving power of two or more men in an authentic and transparent friendship.

WHAT WE KNOW ABOUT MEN AND THEIR RELATIONSHIPS WITH OTHER MEN

Most men who are football fans know Pepper Rodger's name—it is almost a synonym for football, especially at the collegiate level. While head coach at UCLA in 1971, Pepper Rodgers installed the now-famous "Wishbone" offense to less-than-spectacular results. UCLA lost its first four games, won the next two, lost the next three, and tied the last game. Pepper Rodgers was in the doghouse big-time in the football-crazy UCLA community. Alumni and fans were making his life miserable. Even his wife was giving him the cold shoulder.

Years later, as he commented on how even his wife had sided against him during those dark days, Rodgers would say, "My dog was my only true friend. I told my wife that every man needs at least two good friends. So she bought me another dog."[1]

Pepper Rodgers was in a situation with which many men today can identify, though for different reasons. He had a lack of close friends. Indeed, for many men their Labrador retriever or German shepherd becomes their best, and sometimes their only real friend—"someone" with whom they can be real without condemnation.

This chapter is about the secret that "men are afraid of close, self-disclosing relationships with other men." When the men we surveyed responded to that statement, just under 37 percent agreed. (More Christian men [37.3 percent] than non-Christian men [35.6 percent] responded positively.) If the one-third-plus who responded affirmatively to that question were reading carefully, then they are the ones who are afraid of self-disclosing, close friendships with other men. If we had asked this question—"I have no friends that I would describe as close, friends with whom I bare my soul and to whom I tell my secrets"—the affirmative responses would probably have been higher than one-third. After being in touch with thousands of men in conferences and personal counseling in recent years, it's my feeling that men in America are essentially friendless if we define "friend" as a covenant-type partner, a soul mate, and a brother.

Christian counselor Dr. Larry Crabb reported on a survey of four thousand men in which only 10 percent said there was someone in their life they looked to as a father, meaning a mentor, advisor, or role model to follow. In the same survey, only 25 percent said they had a friend, a peer, or a brother with whom they felt no shame. "If that survey is accurate," Crabb concluded, "then ninety men out of every one hundred are unfathered, men without a mentor. Seventy-five of that same one hundred have no brother. They are men who live with secrets."[2]

Patrick Morley, doing research for his own book on men, asked a large number of men to complete this sentence: "My greatest need in marriage is _____." After analyzing the plethora of answers that were submitted, he summarized them into two major themes: companionship and support. "By degrees," he wrote, "most men are loners." One man he knows told his wife, "I don't have any *real* friends besides you."[3]

Shouldn't a man seek companionship from his wife? Doesn't Genesis 2 say that man was given a wife, not another man? Aren't the two supposed to become "one flesh," which essentially means they fill the roles of soul mates? Yes, yes, and yes. But it's the words of Morley's friend to his wife that explain why most men are so hungry for companionship from their wives. If it weren't for their wives, they might not have any friends at all!

I believe there are two secrets at work here. First, many men are afraid of intimate, personal friendships with other men. And second, many men are pretending that it doesn't matter to them that they don't have those kinds of friendships. I believe every man would like to have a few really close friends with whom he could be transparent, vulnerable, confessional, and real. Being made in the image of God, it would be unnatural for men not to want that in the deepest part of their souls.

WHAT RELATIONSHIPS WITH OTHER MEN MEAN TO MEN

Dr. Warren Farrell, best-selling author of several books about men, tells the story of a man he calls Ralph. This man had spent his career working his way up the ladder to become a senior partner at his law firm. His newly empowered and liberated wife, Ginny, (vis-à-vis the women's movement) was excited about her involvement in various women's groups and the "growth" she was experiencing. In fact, she told Ralph that if he didn't get involved in a men's group and begin to grow along with her, she would leave him.

Under such orders, Ralph joined a men's group he had heard about for the sake of his marriage. For weeks he attended without contributing. Then one week he told the group he'd like to share some thoughts, resulting in a lengthy monologue about the state of his life, career, marriage, and family. He summarized by saying, "I feel like I've spent forty years of my life working as hard as I can to become somebody I don't even like."

He then added, "I was mentioning some of my doubts to a few of my associates at work. They listened attentively for a couple of minutes, then one made a joke, and another excused himself. Finally I mentioned this men's group—which I never should have done—and they just laughed me out of the office. I've been the butt of jokes ever since: 'How are the U.S. Navel Gazers doing, Ralph boy?'

"Suddenly I realized Ginny has a whole network of lady friends she can talk with about all this. *Yet the men I've worked with for seventeen years, sixty hours a week, hardly know me. Nor do they want to*" (italics mine). Farrell notes that Ralph's words remain some of the most important he has ever heard concerning the plight of men.[4]

How is it that men can coexist with other men for years—working next to them in an office, eating lunch together in restaurants, strategizing in boardrooms—and never get beneath the surface of life and develop bonds that allow them to talk about the deepest, most difficult, and most important areas of life? There is no single, simple explanation, of course. But there are categories of answers that can help explain why men are natural "loners."

Cultural.

The cycle of growth for men in our culture is relatively well-established and therefore predictable. Sons grow up seeing their fathers leave home for work every day and come home tired in the evenings. Boys don't witness their fathers in intimate friendships with other men (e.g., via a bowling league, a fishing partner, a church committee) because, according to Dad, "there simply isn't time or place." The bonding that is accomplished between fathers and sons, the friendship, is limited by the very fact of sep-aration for ten to twelve hours every day. In high school, young men often form strong friendships, and these are either continued or substituted for equally close male relationships in college. During these years, young men are single, adventurous, out of the house or working, and free to bond and forge deep friendships with other young men. But then they fall in love, get married, become seriously committed to careers, begin having children . . . and the pattern begins all over again.

While holding a men's discussion at the Pentagon, researcher Gail Sheehy had a group of career army officers answer this question: "How many close friends do you have—that is, friends in whom you can confide almost anything?" One officer, who had confidently asserted that his life's priorities were God, then his wife, then close friends who are "absolutely essential," was stopped in his tracks by the question. "I was shocked to real-ize I have not developed a single friend at that level since college," he admitted.[5] There it is—Exhibit A: college is the last great friend-making experience in most men's lives.

The Industrial Revolution is often cited as being complicit in the breakdown of the American family. Prior to that transforming period in our history, fathers often worked at home as farmers or craftsmen, or in nearby shops with their sons as apprentices. The contact between fathers and their children was continual. But when factories began dotting the landscape of the country, men left their farms and shops and began spend-ing the day working away from home. The resulting disconnect between sons and fathers was notable in the cultural evolution.

I recognize what I have just written is a vast oversimplification. I am not suggesting that prior to the Industrial Revolution adult men sat around in barns and shops discussing their innermost feelings, mentoring such behavior for their children. But it is true that men and boys in America spend less time together today than at any time in our history. Compare this cultural norm with what was, and still is, the norm in many other cul-tures of the world: the extended family. Under that model, several genera-tions of men live and work together, sharing the joys and sorrows of life as a way of life. Nothing is hidden. At an early age boys learn from fathers, uncles, and grandfathers what it means to be close to other men.

The fact remains that the American culture promotes living as a loner.

It takes effort for men to overcome that momentum and learn to live a connected life.

Emotional.
Have you ever thought about why college and high school reunions are a fact of life in America? No matter what our life situation or physical location, we'll often make an effort to reconnect with our old friends during those ten-, twenty-, and thirty-year markers. It's telling that the connections formed and emotions experienced during that period of life are worth trying to recapture, if only for a weekend.

The high school and college years, physiologically speaking, are the adolescent and post-adolescent years when hormones are running full tilt. Boys fall in love, become heroes on the athletic field, live the *Animal House* life of Bluto, Boon, and Otter, take road trips, and talk about sex. (I'm drawing on my thirty-year-old college memories. The activities may have changed some since, but the effect is the same.) The memories and experiences that get imprinted on the male mind during that period are like none other in life. And part of that imprinting involves friendships, a bonding that rarely is duplicated in life again. Ask most men today who their best friends are or were and they'll usually point back to the period when they were between ages sixteen and twenty-five.

The fraternal feelings that come from such close ties are instrumental to a man's ongoing development *at any age*. Unfortunately, our culture disperses young men to the four winds following high school and college. They take their wives with them but leave their best friends behind. And the result is an emotional need that is never met, turning adult men inward to placate their longing for male companionship via pseudo-self-fulfilling work, sports, hobbies, gadgets, and the like.

Developmental.
In his famous work on men, *Iron John,* author/poet Robert Bly highlights the practice of the Kikuyu people in Africa. At the age of manhood, a boy is taken into the bush to fast for three days, after which he is brought into a circle of men. Each of the men cuts his own arm and drains a bit of blood into a bowl, from which the initiate drinks. It is a sign to the young man that the nourishment he has previously taken from women he now

takes from men. In commenting on this ritual, Gordon MacDonald notes that, "The milk gives nurture and strength. The blood provides the courage and vision of one's father and the father's father." A girl remains tied to the women of the tribe, even her body telling her every twenty-eight days who she is. "A girl is a woman; her body says so and the women echo the message. *But a boy is a man only when the men say so,*" MacDonald concludes (italics mine).[6]

How many ways are there in our own culture for men to tell their sons that they have become men, that they have entered the circle of their fathers and grandfathers? Unfortunately, most fathers and grandfathers don't have a "circle" into which to invite their sons. And if they did, there are few rituals or ceremonies (such as the Jewish Bar Mitzvah) to serve as rites of passage. It is difficult in Western cultures for a young man to cross over from adolescence to manhood and enter into the embrace and friendship of other men.

Most men fondly remember some experience they had as boys in which they were invited to accompany their fathers and a group of men on an outing. Perhaps it was hunting, perhaps a trip to a sporting event, or even a business trip. The memory of being "one of the men" is indelibly seared into a boy's consciousness and forever serves as the closest thing he can remember to being invited to become a man.

Familial.

Much of a man's practice is simply an imitation of his own father. Like the famous young geese that "imprinted" on an ultralight plane and followed it south for the winter, so young men imprint on their fathers and duplicate their ways in their own lives. If a man's father was gregarious with lots of friends, if a man saw and heard his father openly talk about matters of the heart and spirit, if a man was invited to participate in his father's circle where he witnessed men relating on a personal basis . . . then he will likely reproduce those same traits. Ask any man today how many close friends he has, and the number will probably approximate the number of close friends his father had.

Knowing that the majority of men in our culture were not raised by fathers who had close friends, it will take a conscious choice for today's men to break that pattern and create intimate, personal relationships with other men. The "do it for the children" mentality that pervades our culture today requires men to almost become soccer moms for the sake of their children. Every spare moment is dedicated to attending recitals, games, parties, and parent-teacher meetings, to the degree that fathers and mothers have almost given up lives of their own. The irony is that one of the most important things men could do for their children is allow them to witness their father interacting with other men in healthy, close relationships, and inviting their children to participate in those relationships on occasion.

NEW DIRECTIONS

Dave Phillips, a motivational speaker and former Canadian alpine ski team member, has said that "after the age of forty, men typically have no close friends at all."[7] So what's a man to do? You can do what David Bentall did. When he and his fiancée were planning their wedding, he realized he didn't have a single male friend whom he considered to be close enough to ask to be his best man. This shocking realization became the impetus for change. He identified two men he knew who shared his faith and values and prayerfully approached them about the possibility of exploring and developing long-term friendships. They both responded positively, and the three have continued a deep and trusting relationship for several decades. In fact, out of their relationship came the insights for Bentall's book, *The Company You Keep: The Transforming Power of Male Friendship*, which is a great resource for men on the subject of friendship.[8]

Every man who is without at least one close friend is missing the three advantages Dr. Larry Crabb details that come with having a close friend or group of friends: (1) someone with whom to walk despite failures, (2) someone with whom to explore a vision for life, and (3) someone with whom to face the darkness of our world.[9]

If you have needed reasons to begin seeking and building a friendship with other men, those are as good as any you will find.

God's initial reason for solving the aloneness of Adam has never been improved upon: "It is not good for the man to be alone" (Genesis 2:18). I urge you not to negate it by your choices. A man's wife is the primary solution to his aloneness, but other men are there to do what wives cannot.

NEW CONNECTIONS

A husband having close friends can positively impact any marriage relationship. David Bentall asked his wife, and the wives of his two closest friends, to express whether the closeness of the men's relationships has been a threat to their marriage. The wives' answers were quite to the contrary:

- "I'm not at all threatened by it—in fact, I'm comforted. David's commitment to being accountable to friends indicates that he cares enough about his life to grow, and any personal growth for him will help us in our marriage."
- "I know Bob gets great support from his friends, and that enables him to be able to love me and our children in a better way."
- "I cannot be all things to my husband. I want him to have other people to turn to for accountability and perspective. This doesn't prevent him from being accountable to me, nor does it prevent him from getting my perspective. I appreciate knowing that I am not alone in helping him to be all he can be. I don't know if I've stated it strongly enough, but I really value what happens between the three of you. When Carson comes home from being with you, I can see that he is energized by it and more fulfilled. I just love to see that in him!"[10]

Men's friendships create more connections than simply those between men. As men get healthier, every other relationship in their lives luxuriates in the overflow of growth in maturity. If you are a man reading this and you want your relationship with your wife to be better, build close friendships with other men (which, in time, may well lead to friendships between couples). If you are a woman, encourage your man to make time to become close with other men. Lovingly present to him all the various positive reasons and benefits for male friendships that we've covered in this chapter. And remind him that he may need to take the first step; gaining a friend requires *being* a friend.

It seems odd that a man walking away from his wife to spend time with other men could ultimately draw a couple together, but it can.

Chapter 9

LIVING WELL AND LONG

I magine a man in his twenties, sixty pounds overweight, a smoker of two packs a day, seemingly allergic to exercise, possessing extremely high cholesterol and taking blood pressure medication. He is walking toward the grave. If he does not make some changes, he might never make it out of his forties. In fact, he might not even make it to his forties.

This guy did end up making some changes, but not for the purest of motives. It was vanity, pure and simple, that motivated the adjustment. He was sick and tired of looking like a blob and a slob. He began with small steps that he could keep up for the rest of his life rather than a radical reversal he could only make last a few weeks or months. But the changes stuck— and I'm so thankful they did. Because the he, as you might have guessed, was me.

It was after I began making lifestyle changes that I began to care about changing for the right reasons, for the sake of living a healthy and productive life. I went from vanity to sanity, and the results started adding up. As I began to lose weight I also lost the high cholesterol and high blood pressure. But there were two things that I gained: more energy and the expectancy of more years. At this point, tests and calculations say I will live three years longer than the average male. Regardless of whether that pans out or not, I am not the same man I was in my twenties and couldn't be more thankful for the changes.

I am also thankful for, and encouraged by, the number of men I see who are making similar changes. For men, the thought of checking out early and not seeing their grandchildren becomes all too painful a possibility around midlife.

WHAT WE KNOW ABOUT MEN'S HEALTH AND LIFE EXPECTANCY

This chapter's topic is literally a matter of life and death. Yet it also reflects a degree of naiveté on the part of the men who participated in our survey.

Here's the question we asked: "Are you concerned that physical or health problems may lead to early death?" In response, only 34.4 percent of the 3,600 respondents answered positively. Given the general physical condition of the American population, that number strikes me as being low. Perhaps our surveyors spoke with the third of American males who are exercising daily, are slim and trim, and are eating their recommended nine servings of fruits and vegetables every day. But on a random survey, that's unlikely.

Perhaps we've been lulled into complacency by the general upward trend in life expectancy statistics over time (Neanderthals lived around twenty years, modern Westerners average a lifespan of seventy-seven to eighty-one years).[1] Yes, human beings are living longer. But chronological longevity says nothing about the quality of life we enjoy as we survive. Everyone's goal is to die like Moses did: "Moses was a hundred and twenty years old when he died, yet his eyes were not weak nor his strength gone" (Deuteronomy 34:7). But Moses didn't live in twenty-first century America, where life is much different.

For the one-third of American men who are concerned that health problems could cut short or seriously compromise the quality of their life, they've got good reason to be worried. All you need to do is watch the evening news to come to the realization that health care is the eight hundred pound gorilla in the living room of our lives.

Here's a snapshot of a few critical health indicators:

Obesity.

This has been on the national radar screen during recent years. The Centers for Disease Control (CDC) reports that 68.8 percent of men age twenty to seventy-four were overweight in the period 1999 to 2002 (overweight means a Body Mass Index of greater than or equal to twenty-five). Just over 28 percent of those men were obese (their BMI was greater than or equal to thirty).[2] Though it's come under recent criticism, the Body Mass Index is currently the accepted way of determining a healthy weight since it measures weight as a corollary of height.

There are plenty of BMI calculators on the Internet where you can determine your own Index score. Generally, a person's BMI should be below twenty-five. You may disagree with the results, however—this is a very conservative scale. Yet the original British researchers who devised the Index studied 7,700 men over fifteen years and found that those with a BMI under twenty-five had far fewer health problems.

Smoking.

The CDC also reports that 24 percent of American males smoked in 2003.[3] Do we really need to say anything about smoking? Apparently, because if our survey of random men is a fair representation of the male population, then about 20 percent of them still smoke. Hopefully, all those men were among the 34 percent who said they were worried about their future health—because they should be! Besides the long list of health problems exacerbated by smoking (cancer, stroke, hypertension, and others), the simple fact is that a smoker's life span is dramatically affected as well. Statistics abound regarding the actual number of years shaved off a lifetime when you smoke. Why else would tobacco use be a guaranteed question on all life insurance applications and medical exams? Smoking is a bottom-line issue for insurers because they know you are likely to die sooner if you smoke. Their bean counters fine-tune their actuarial tables precisely to know where the profit and loss expectancy is on insurance policies. And by the way, if you're an obese male smoker, good luck: you can expect to lose nearly seven years off your life after age forty.[4]

Health care.

It comes as a shock to most people to learn that America's health-care system is among the leading causes of death in the United States—possibly the third highest (225,000 deaths occur per year based on doctor and hospital errors, making it the third-leading cause of death after heart disease and cancer).[5] A 2000 *Journal of the American Medical Association* article pointed out that the United States ranked twelfth out of thirteen industrialized nations, based on sixteen health indicators such as life expectancy, infant mortality, and others.[6] When it comes to emergency care, our nation is the best. But as far as overall health care goes, we're close to the bottom among peer nations, despite the fact that we spend more real dollars ($1.7 trillion in 2003) and a greater percentage of GDP (15.3 percent in 2003) on health care than any other nation.[7] What does this have to do with you? Simply this: if you're depending on the American health care system to ensure your longevity, it might be time for a better plan.

Prostate cancer.

I list this issue separately from all other cancers because it is the most common cancer in America except for skin cancer. What breast cancer is to women, prostate cancer is to men—only more prevalent. If you are over age forty and don't have a prostate cancer prevention program in place (i.e., regular prostate exams, diet low in fat—especially animal fats—and rich in zinc and selenium), you're behind the curve. As of 2006, prostate cancer affects one in six men in America. Look what happens to the incidence rate based on age:

Age under 40	1 in 10,000 men affected
Age 40–59	1 in 38 men affected
Age 60–69	1 in 14 men affected
Over 65	More than 65 percent of all prostate cancer cases

If you are an African American male, you are 61 percent more likely to develop prostate cancer than a Caucasian male, and two-and-a-half times more likely to die from it. Any man with a first-degree relative (father, brother, or son) who had prostate cancer doubles his own risk; two or more such relatives quadruples the risk.[8]

Those are sobering statistics. But the good news is that prostate cancer is slow growing when confined to the prostate. Because every death is not autopsied, this general statement can't be proven, but it is accepted as true: more men will die *with* prostate cancer than *from* prostate cancer. However, once it metastasizes (spreads beyond the prostate), it quickly becomes life-threatening.

That's enough doom-and-gloom to establish the fact: the health issues the average American male faces are serious issues. Our lifestyles (sedentary and stressful), vices (smoking and excessive drinking), and diet (processed and artificial) have created negative prospects for good health. Fortunately, health can be impacted by positive changes in lifestyle and diet. If you are a man reading this chapter and you're worried about dying early, you need to make health a priority. If you're a woman and you want to grow old with your man, it's time to get involved with his efforts.

WHAT (THE LACK OF) HEALTH AND LIFE EXPECTANCY MEANS TO MEN

While you're on the Internet using a BMI calculator, look for a life expectancy calculator as well. BMI calculators are standard, so one is as good as another. But for life expectancy calculators, it's best to search only reputable insurance or medical Web sites to find the most accurate ones. Fill out several, and take an average of the readings. They're quick and easy to use; the questions simply ask about your lifestyle and medical history. And while not scientific or (obviously) guaranteed, these calculators will give you an idea of your life expectancy. Better yet, if husbands and wives each use the same calculators you'll have a general look at your life span as a couple.

That brings me to the first consideration of why this subject is important to men: we have a legitimate fear of dying prematurely and leaving our wives and children financially unprotected (as we discussed in Chapter 1). Depending on the source, we already know that women will live, on average, five to seven years longer than men. So even if a man lives an average life span, his wife is likely to spend another five to seven years as a widow, unless she remarries. Hopefully, whatever resources the couple lived on between retirement and the husband's death will be adequate for the wife to survive on until her own death.

But what if the husband dies in his forties or fifties? We are no longer shocked in America when we hear of a young husband and father dropping dead of a heart attack before his fiftieth birthday. While a large life insurance payout can relieve some of the immediate financial stress, nothing can compensate entirely for such a loss, emotionally or monetarily.

Another fear men have is the loss of mobility or mental capacity even if they live a long life. Alzheimer's patients, for instance, often live into their seventies and eighties, but spend their twilight years without consciousness of who or where they are. It's not so much being in that condition that worries men, because they are obviously beyond knowing at that point. Instead, it is the present thought of ending up in such a state in the future that is worrisome. To a man, the idea of losing his mind and returning to an infant-like existence in which he has to have his diapers changed and be bathed by a caretaker is emasculating at best, horrific at worst.

Or perhaps this same fear involves colon cancer—having colostomies and being forced to wear a "bag" for the rest of your life. Or erectile dysfunction. Or type 2 diabetes. Or another form of cancer. Or a Parkinson's-type neurological disorder. All of these conditions condemn a man (in his mind) to a lifetime of incapacitation and, for some, total dependence on others. And that is definitely not what he signed up for. Men stricken by disease can and do still make contributions, and there can be something life changing for many men about learning to live out of weakness instead of strength. But standing back from the forest, men will always want to see themselves as a sequoia, not a pine twisted by the elements. They want the words Eliphaz spoke to Job to apply to them: "You will come to the grave in full vigor, like sheaves gathered in season" (Job 5:26).

Long-term health and disability insurance has become a popular product in recent years. As more and more baby boomers enter their retirement and then sunset years, the prospect of needing financial assistance with nursing homes or other medical expenses has become all too real. With companies cutting back or doing away with medical benefits for retirees, some men and their wives see resources for health care decreasing at the very time when need is increasing.

For the most part, men are not threatened by the normal toll of years on the body—graying or loss of hair, loss of muscle strength, stooped shoulders. These features convey a grandfatherly or "elder" status that most men are proud to carry with dignity (see Proverbs 16:31; 20:29). But when disability sets in—mental or physical—men don't respond as well. They often react negatively if they can no longer think, speak, or act like they believe they should be able to. And by the same token, fear arises in them if they think that day is coming in the future.

NEW DIRECTIONS

In the nineteenth century, Louis Pasteur fought an uphill battle to prove that germs cause some diseases. The medical establishment of his day simply was not ready for such a notion. In a similar vein, the modern medical establishment has only recently begun to acknowledge that many diseases can be impacted by lifestyle factors such as nutrition and the quality of food, exercise, state of mind, and detoxification. As a result, there has been a revolution in preventive health strategies, a holistic approach that puts individuals, not the medical community, in charge of their own health. Instead of curing diseases, the new focus is on preventing them.

Any man can take it upon himself to set new directions for his life when it comes to health. We do not need to be squeezed into the world's mold when it comes to the food we eat or the lifestyle we adopt. But if we're not currently investing time, talent, and treasure into improving our health (and therefore our prospects for longevity), it will require a serious paradigm shift. After all, when considering the importance of health in the grand scheme of things, is any cost too great?

Health needs to become a lifestyle, not a temporary project such as a diet. It must be viewed as an act of stewardship; we are managing something that belongs to God, something that was created for His glory, something entrusted to us to improve and make fruitful for all the time we have on this earth. Biblical stewardship is a matter of waking up in the morning with the attitude that everything depends on me, but then going to bed at night knowing that everything ultimately depends on God. When it comes to health, it's our responsibility to do everything we can to make wise choices, and then trust God's providence if something occurs that is completely beyond our reach to change or control.

This book is not the place for a full-blown presentation on a healthy lifestyle—there are plenty of better resources available for that. But as a place to start, here are the fundamentals that impact the GIGO principle (Garbage In, Garbage Out), based on Adele Davis' 1950s mantra that "you are what you eat":

- **Pure food.** Most commercially grown food is loaded with toxic chemicals (pesticides, herbicides, and fertilizers), some of which are carcinogenic, and none of which are needful for human health. Whenever possible, buy locally grown, organic food. Genesis 1:29 suggests humans were created to be vegetarian. To that end, include as many fresh fruits, vegetables, nuts, seeds, and whole grains in your diet as possible.
- **Pure air.** If you are a city dweller, the amount of toxins you inhale daily is enough to make your kidneys and liver work overtime filtering them out of your system. Even our homes and offices "leak" toxic vapors for years after they are constructed. Filter your air if needed.
- **Pure water.** You should avoid anything that comes out of a chemical plant with a skull and crossbones on it—such as chlorine. Filter or distill your drinking water. It's fine for chlorine to kill bacteria in your city water; just remove it from the water before you ingest it.
- **Pure soul.** Choose not to be angry, bitter, resentful, envious, proud, or despairing. "*Above all else*, guard your heart," Proverbs 4:23 says, "for it is the wellspring of life" (italics mine).
- **Pure environment.** Become conscious of the fact that we live in a physically and spiritually toxic world. It is the petrochemical products we fill our landfills with that leach into the ground water we will one day have to drink. That is a huge "system" to contemplate, and it is challenging to think that any of our individual acts in this regard could impact our health. But when we compare the Bible's image of the Garden of Eden with a modern polluted city, it's not difficult to see how our personal, microhealth might be impacted by the world's macrohealth.
- **Pure body.** Exercise. Work up a sweat. Lift a few weights. Drink lots of water and juices. Cut out the sugar and salt and caffeine and alcohol and tobacco. Get that BMI down to where it should be.

This is a bullet-point list in an outline for healthy living. You can fill in the sub-points by reading and research. But don't forget the most important point at this stage: you can do this. As a man, you do not have to fear the future with regard to health and longevity.

NEW CONNECTIONS

Yes, men can do this . . . but they'll do it better if their better half is encouraging them, helping them, and perhaps pursuing the same goals. For example, imagine that a man decides to gradually switch to decaf coffee, or get off caffeine altogether. If he's been a regular coffee drinker, he'll go through the withdrawal headaches typical of breaking any drug addiction. He'll be miserable and cranky for a few days, and then begin to feel better. (Multiply this by a thousand if he decides to quit smoking.) An understanding and encouraging wife can make the transition less painful.

Likewise, losing weight is a simple matter of balancing calories. But because our busy, stressful lifestyles leave little opportunity for exercise and create great excuses for consuming "comfort foods," we struggle to lose weight. But couples who begin eating light suppers together, followed by a walk through the neighborhood, will encourage one another to achieve new plateaus of health.

I'll refrain from further suggestions because those aren't really what's needed. The most important factor in creating a healthy lifestyle is the "aha!" moment when a man, or a couple, realizes that health is their responsibility and that living well can be achieved. No, everything in health cannot be controlled. But many, many factors can be. And should the unthinkable happen, at least there will be no regrets, no "I wish I had taken more steps to prevent this from happening."

You can age, and even manage disease, with grace—witness Billy Graham, Pope John Paul II, and numerous others. The future does not have to be approached with fear. If men will approach health with the same degree of planning, diligence, and execution with which they approach work, sports, and other ventures, they will create a life that is eminently enjoyable—now and in the future.

So where do you start to find a better way to live? Begin by doing the next right thing. That right thing is often the most difficult step and causes the most short-term pain. Yet if you want to live confidently, you have to live consciously of the choices you are making. Take it from a man who used to weigh sixty pounds more than he does today—you can make a difference in your own life with the choices you start making now!

Chapter 10

ROMANCE AND EXCITEMENT IN LIFE

Cullen was one of the most responsible, hardworking, and predictable men you will ever meet. Year after year he drove 3.4 miles to his office at the bank, where he audited every dollar that came in and every penny that went out. The most exciting part of his job was surprising the occasional teller with the news that she had been caught embezzling bank funds and that the police were on their way to read her rights to her. Other than that, life for Cullen was battleship gray.

Then everything changed.

In the mail one day he received a check for $500,000—the payout on a life insurance policy his recently deceased mother had paid on for years. In orderly fashion Cullen set aside money to pay the taxes on the bequest, gave another 10 percent as a tithe, and put the remaining $350,000 into CDs at his bank—in his name. That deposit was step one in the plan of escape Cullen had dreamed about for years.

For the next six months Cullen made his wife a bit suspicious by spending more time away from home—until the day he pulled up in a gleaming eighteen-wheeler, a tractor trailer rig as long as his house lot was wide. When his wife was finally able to close her gaping jaw, she took a tour of the cab. What she had thought was just "a truck" when she saw one on the freeway turned out to have a bed, refrigerator, microwave, closet, shower, and toilet—all inside the cab!

When they finally sat down to talk, Cullen let his wife in on the plan. He told her about the money, the driver's training he had received, and—this was the shocker—him quitting his job at the bank. He had $150,000 of the money left and wanted to start a new career. He wanted to haul stuff cross-country, and he wanted her to go with him and be his partner. He had been waiting all his life for the opportunity to break out of his accountant's mold and do something that would test his testosterone levels in a new way.

Within a week, they decided together to make the leap. Cullen's wife saw him come alive in a way she'd never seen before. Was it a risk? You bet. But she was willing to take it because of the new lease on life she thought it would provide for Cullen and for their life as a couple.

WHAT WE KNOW ABOUT MEN AND THEIR DESIRE FOR ROMANCE AND EXCITEMENT

Try doing an Internet search for "adventure tours" and you'll face the daunting task of scrolling through more than five million results. You'll find tours available to or in Australia, all parts of Mexico, Polynesia, Belize, British Columbia, Oklahoma (chasing tornadoes), Brazil, Pakistan, the Canadian Rockies, New Zealand, Tanzania . . . well, you get the drift.

What is an adventure tour? In a scholarly article on the subject, author Heidi Sung defined it as "a trip or travel with the specific purpose of activity participation to explore a new experience, often involving perceived risk or controlled danger associated with personal challenges, in a natural environment or exotic outdoor setting."[1] I find the aspects of "perceived risk" or "controlled danger" interesting. For the last couple of years, many of the cruise ship commercials on television have as much to do with activities off the ship—swimming with dolphins and sharks, climbing on glaciers, getting close to ice calving, petting penguins—as on the vessel. It's not until you're halfway through the commercial that you realize what's being advertised is a formerly calm and relaxing Caribbean cruise. Now it's (perceived and controlled) *Thrills! Adventure! Excitement! Danger!*

The Adventure Travel Trade Association notes that in 2000 the Yahoo search directory contained 601 listings for "adventure travel," 36 listings for "eco tours," and 33 listings for "educational or sports tours." Five years later, there were 770 listings for "adventure travel," 335 listings for "eco tours," 499 listings for "cultural tours," and 390 listings for "heritage tours." Cultural and heritage tours weren't even a category in 2000; in 2005 they had 889 listings. Within the five-year period, overall adventure travel listings increased by 28 percent.[2]

What's going on here? Americans are spending hundreds of millions of dollars annually seeking out a way of life that is different from their own. They're leaving the safe confines of their world and traveling around the globe in search of experiences (real, perceived, or controlled) that just a couple of centuries ago would not have been out of the ordinary in their own country. (American pioneers and settlers certainly had their share of roughing it, danger, and risk.) Forced to choose, few people would opt to live permanently in a *Survivor*-type setting. The creature comforts, relative safety and predictability, and standard of living we are used to are not easily given up. Nonetheless, there remains a latent desire for something more exciting than the nine-to-five in the lives of most Americans. In a 2002 report, the Travel Industry Association of America and *National Geographic Traveler* said there are 55.1 million Americans—a fifth of the entire population—who could be called "geotourists," a subset of which is the "geo-savvy" travelers: those twice as likely as the average vacationer to seek outdoor ventures that offer challenge, risk, and excitement, and three times as likely to travel to primitive or wilderness areas.[3]

It comes as no surprise, then, that in our survey of 3,600 men nearly one-third (29.4 percent) said they were "disappointed by the lack of romance and excitement in their lives." "Romance and excitement" brings to mind the covers of pulp fiction paperback novels that are churned out by the hundreds every year, satisfying an insatiable thirst in the lives of their (mostly) female readers. But is that what the men we surveyed are looking for? Are they secretly seeking to fulfill their Fabio fantasy by killing the fiery dragon, rescuing the fair maiden, and restoring order to the kingdom?

WHAT ROMANCE AND EXCITEMENT MEAN TO MEN

It might be, according to John Eldredge, author of one of the most influential books on men in recent years. Culling from his years as a teacher and counselor, Eldredge penned *Wild at Heart* to critique the loss of passion specifically in Christian men, so his comments need to be taken in that context. Yet what he says about Christian men can be applied, to some degree, to men in general:

> When all is said and done, I think most men in the church believe that God put them on the earth to be a good boy. The problem with men, we are told, is that they don't know how to keep their promises, be spiritual leaders, talk to their wives, or raise their children. But, if they will try real hard they can reach the lofty summit of becoming . . . a nice guy. That's what we hold up as models of Christian maturity: Really Nice Guys. We don't smoke, drink, or swear; that's what makes us men. Now let me ask my male readers: In all your boyhood dreams growing up, did you ever dream of becoming a Nice Guy? (Ladies, was the Prince of your dreams dashing . . . or merely nice?)
>
> Really now—do I overstate my case? Walk into most churches in ·America, have a look around, and ask yourself this question: What is a Christian man? Don't listen to what is said, look at what you find there. There is no doubt about it. You'd have to admit a Christian man is . . . bored.[4]

For Eldredge, boredom is the result of spiritual castration whereby men have been relieved of their manhood by the imposition of false standards and stereotypes concerning what it means to be a man. He argues that at the core of every man's life (not just Christian men) are three primal, God-given desires: to fight a battle, rescue a beautiful woman, and live an adventure.

Wild at Heart has, as all best-selling books do, caused no small amount of discussion and disagreement within the author's (primarily Christian) target audience. Because Eldredge is an avid outdoorsman, he has been criticized for suggesting that true spirituality is found only when a man trades in his suit for a flannel shirt, throws away his razor for a week, and learns to live in the great outdoors. One blogger asks whether the solution to true manhood isn't more than entering the wilderness to "hunt grizzlies with nothing more than a pointy stick."[5]

That's an obvious oversimplification of Eldredge's notion, but you get the point. His message and his detractors both raise what is the most important question for this chapter: why are a certain percentage of men disappointed with the level of romance and adventure in their lives? Is it simply because they don't have the time and/or money to take the occasional adventure travel tour to kick-start their adrenalin? Or is there something more fundamental missing? Are adventure travel tours, and the gazillion other things men do to try to spice up their lives, simply dealing with symptoms instead of with a root cause? If so, what is the real disease?

Unfortunately, I don't have *the* answer to those questions, nor does anyone else. Many people have written on the subject, and little that I will say in this short chapter will bring closure to the issue. From my perspective, however, five things ring true concerning the lack of excitement men feel in their lives.

1) Root Causes

Our culture tends to address symptoms in life much better than it does causes. The modern drug industry is built on the idea of dispensing pills that mask symptoms (e.g., ibuprofen for headaches) rather than eliminate a cause (stress that causes the headache). That is not to condemn the drug, adventure travel, or any other industry that provides welcome relief, diversion, or excitement in a man's life. It is simply to say that when we talk about the nature of man, it has to be a discussion of root causes, not symptoms.

2) Long-Term

The major shifts in life almost always happen over an extended period of time. It has taken several hundred years in America to get to the point where most men are exhausted by their work, stressed-out over their debt, lonely though married, fearful about their financial future and their health, worried about the world their children will inherit from them, and frustrated that their lives lack "excitement." Therefore, the men and their wives reading this chapter will have to consider long-term, not short-term, responses.

3) Excitement = Purpose

Though we used the words *excitement* and *romance* in our survey, I believe that translates into "purpose." I don't think the average man is looking for more laughs. Nor do I think the average man will ultimately be satisfied by the occasional white-water rafting trip through the Grand Canyon. Excitement about life is deeper than that and is usually experienced when a man believes he is doing what he was put on this earth to do. Unfortunately, few men live with such a sense of calling. (More on this later in the chapter.)

4) False Images

We live in a culture that sells excitement in a thousand different forms. It might be the 007 image of James Bond, it might be the offer of sexual fulfillment, it might be the appeal of a life of glamour and wealth, or it might be the idea of attaining celebrity status and the attendant lifestyle it provides. All a man needs to do is spend time in any of those venues, or talk to those who do, and he will find that the same problems exist there as in the workaday world. They just have different labels and higher price tags. There is a huge danger of men "drinking the Kool-Aid" and succumbing to the siren song of a culture that promises but cannot deliver excitement at the root level of a man's existence.

5) Change

It stands to reason that if a significant number of men are disappointed with the level of romance and excitement in their lives, then change is in order. It could be that their perception of "excitement" needs to change. They may have bought into the idea that if they just had more money, a trophy wife, or a red Corvette convertible, they would experience true excitement. Such men are immature and will never find real fulfillment as long as they continue searching through the "stuff" of life. No man's heart has a Corvette-shaped vacuum that, once filled, will stop aching.

On the other hand, it may be that a man truly understands that a purpose and mission (life calling) are what make life exciting. In that case, he may want to trade in his corporate lifestyle for an inner-city ministry. Or he may want to go to law school to get the training he needs to run for public office and influence the direction of the nation. Yet changes at those levels are difficult. They require family support, perhaps financial and lifestyle changes, and a reorientation to life that can take months or years to accomplish. Countless things in our culture—mortgage and car payments, college educations, braces for the children's teeth, identity and status in an extended family or community—make it difficult to consider changes. But if a man understands the nature of true excitement in life, and his current life is not producing it, then change will be necessary.

Legendary motivational speaker Zig Ziglar, in his latest book *Better than Good: Creating a Life You Can't Wait to Live*, offers what I believe is a healthy measure of septuagenarian wisdom: true life—what he would call an "exciting" or "better than good" life—is found when passion, peak performance, and purpose converge. This union is not a single point in time, however, but an ongoing process. Ziglar describes how he discovered his own passion (motivating and inspiring people) long before he discovered his purpose (to live a fulfilled life as a child of God). When those two elements merged, his peak performance (his excitement about life) increased exponentially and continues to expand.[6]

He points out that most people understandably begin their adult lives with little overlap between passion, peak performance, and purpose.

THE WAY A LOT OF PEOPLE LIVE

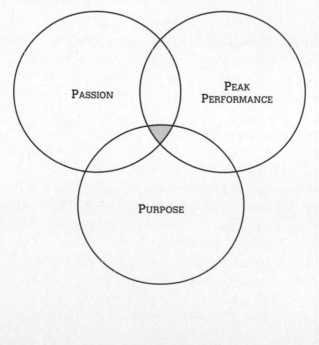

- PASSION
- PEAK PERFORMANCE
- PURPOSE

The small area where the three circles overlap represents how many men live their lives, with little correlation between what they do (passion), why they do it (purpose), and how they do it (peak performance). Again, we all start that way for the most part, searching for the combination of what, why, and how that will bring us satisfaction (excitement) in life.

Ideally, those three elements of life should converge and be a unity, representing a life that is lived full-tilt, on a mission, fulfilling a God-ordained calling.[7]

THE WAY EVERY PERSON SHOULD LIVE

For purposes of illustration, these two diagrams represent opposite ends of the spectrum. Few adults live the disconnected life pictured in the first diagram, and an equally few amount reach the stage of convergence shown in the second. But the latter is still the goal. And if I may put words in Mr. Ziglar's mouth, it is the place where true excitement in life is discovered.

It's important for us to keep in mind that "excitement" is not a point in life. Rather, it is a process whereby we get to know ourselves (and from my perspective, our God through Jesus Christ) so well that we find ourselves merging into a current of satisfaction that eventually carries us through life in an almost effortless fashion. Instead of dreading the prospect of another day, we wake up early without an alarm and hit the ground running in order to not waste a moment of opportunity.

Having stated the above in general terms that apply to both women and men, we still need to return to the subject of "man" specifically. Without quibbling over details, I believe John Eldredge, Robert Bly, Sam Keen, George Gilder, Leanne Payne, Larry Crabb, Gordon Dalbey, and a host of others who have written about men are on-target. I also believe that, without asking any of those authorities to second my own views, they would all agree that men long to achieve something great in life and were made that way by God. But for the most part, men have lost a vision for their greatness. To use Sam Keen's words, they've lost that "fire in the belly" that should send them out into the world every day intent on subduing it and exercising dominion over it.[8] Men have been confronted by a host of enemies—financial, relational, spiritual, occupational, personal—and have been tamed into submission. Many have thrown up their hands at the idea of ever moving beyond merely existing to truly living.

That is not God's plan for any man. No being created in the image of God should be living a passive, dispirited, passionless life. The man who feels he is needs to take stock, to find the root cause(s), and begin making long-term plans to change.

NEW DIRECTIONS

Since man was made in the image of God, I don't believe any man will ever fulfill his ultimate purpose while lacking a relationship with his Creator-God. It is by knowing Him, and discovering our calling in life, that true excitement in life is found. The words of David, the psalmist and king in Israel, are worth considering: "For you created my inmost being; you knit me together in my mother's womb. I praise you because I am fearfully and wonderfully made; your works are wonderful, I know that full well. My frame was not hidden from you when I was made in the secret place. When I was woven together in the depths of the earth, your eyes saw my unformed body. All the days ordained for me were written in your book before one of them came to be" (Psalm 139:13–16).

David had a spiritual sense that his life was no accident, that there was a purpose, a destiny, for him to achieve and experience. To the degree that God is no respecter of persons, I believe the same can be said for every man.

The question is, Where to start? Prayer, reading, conversations with trusted counselors, hard looks at how we define "excitement," counting the costs it might take to implement adjustments and course corrections—all of these are ongoing elements of what it means to finding the life that Zig

Ziglar calls "the life you can't wait to live." Doing nothing will only make life less exciting, not more. I encourage any man to consider himself worthy of a life he would be excited about living—and pursue it.

NEW CONNECTIONS

No wise man would walk in and announce to his wife and children that he was quitting his job and moving to the outback to pursue his dreams. That's a sign of a midlife crisis, not a depth of perception marked by wisdom. When a man has others who depend on him—a wife, family, or extended family members—life is turned like an aircraft carrier, not a ski boat. To that end, wives who believe their husbands are searching for a deeper and more purposeful path can come alongside and offer their support. Unfortunately, many men are not in the habit of sharing their deepest feelings with their wives. A husband might hesitate to do so for fear of creating insecurity or resistance in her, which results in a pullback and entrenchment that only makes matters worse. In that case, wives may need to encourage the conversation.

Within a marriage, these issues require the greatest levels of vulnerability, acceptance, transparency, sacrifice, and understanding possible. But what could be more important to a couple than taking steps that would make life more purposeful, and thus more exciting, for both husband and wife? I can say without a moment's hesitation that God will support and bless the efforts of every couple who starts down such an exciting path.

A man needs adventure and unpredictability. He will never get that from an overly obsessive or possessive wife who takes him for a child that needs to be mothered. If you are a woman and your husband is a dead man walking, it might be time to kick yourself to the curb, let him fend for himself in order to become a man and find the adventure that will bring him back to life. A little encouragement from a wife might result in a man who is free to be all he was meant to be, all he has longed to be, and all God has wanted him to be.

Chapter 11

TOTAL COMMITMENT

Tahisha called the *New Life Live* radio program with a common problem among single women. She was bright and articulate in clearly stating her dilemma. Five years earlier she had met Maurice and fallen in love with him. He was amazingly responsible, considerate, and polite. She had never seen such a gentleman and, in her eyes, his manners were exceeded only by his handsome appearance. She could not believe that at thirty-five no one had snatched him up and walked him down the aisle. It was not long into their dating relationship that she knew that was exactly what she wanted to do with him.

Sadly for Tahisha, Maurice always had an excuse for not moving forward with plans to marry. For a couple of years the excuse was financial. Then he changed it to not being ready emotionally. As Tahisha was planning his surprise fortieth birthday party she realized that she had given him half a decade and was no closer to walking down the aisle with the man she loved than she was when they first met. Because she loved him she didn't regret the many investments she had made in their relationship, but her biological and maternal clocks were ticking louder and faster every day.

Her question when she called the program was a simple one: "Do I fish or cut bait?" Unfortunately, the answer was not as clear-cut. After talking to her, it was obvious that Maurice was a commitment-phobe and probably was afraid of losing himself if he ever totally gave himself to a woman in a committed relationship. We suggested an ultimatum: give him three months—ninety days—to make up his mind about their relationship. At the end of three months there would either be a ring and a wedding date, or there would be a painful ending of the relationship. She said she would follow our recommendations, but we never heard back from her and don't know what happened.

What we do know is that Tahisha is not alone. Many men are afraid to make a commitment to one woman for a lifetime. Even more common are the men who commit parts of themselves but leave a few compartments tucked away—just in case.

WHAT WE KNOW ABOUT MEN AND COMMITMENT

The phrase "men and commitment" is deceptively broad. In this chapter we'll talk not about commitment in general, as if the inability to commit to anything was a genetic deficiency in men, but about men's hesitancy to make a total, lifetime commitment to women.

A quick scan of the horizon of men's lives reveals that they have no problem with commitment. Without the commitment of men, the NFL, NASCAR, breweries, pornography, bass-fishing equipment suppliers, and various other industries would soon be out of business. Men *can* commit. But it seems that the ultimate commitment—the one whereby they lock in for a lifetime with one woman—is increasingly a challenge for men. This is evidenced not just by the median age of first-time marriage for men (currently twenty-seven—the highest in the nation's history), but also by divorce rates. In other words, men are waiting longer to make a commitment to a woman, and when they do they have a hard time keeping it.

In our survey of men across the country, we found 19 percent of the respondents agreeing that men are either always or often "uncomfortable with the notion of total commitment." (Christian men were slightly more comfortable with the idea than non-Christian men.) If you add the "sometimes" respondents, the total percentage increases to a startling 77 percent of men who are uncomfortable with the idea of total commitment. That leaves 23 percent of men who are "rarely" or "never" uncomfortable with the idea. For women who are looking for "Mr. Total Commitment," the neck of the funnel is so narrow that only one out of every four men is dropping into the selection pool.

The National Marriage Project is a nonpartisan, nonsectarian, and interdisciplinary initiative located at Rutgers, the state university of New Jersey. Its mission has been "to provide research and analysis on the state of marriage in America and to educate the public on the social, economic, and cultural conditions affecting marital success and well-being." In summarizing the project's findings on single men's attitudes regarding the timing of marriage, a report says that "men experience few social pressures to marry, gain many of the benefits of marriage by cohabiting with a romantic partner, and are ever more reluctant to commit to marriage in their early adult years."[1]

A number of statistics from the National Marriage Project report are helpful when considering the idea of commitment:

- Americans have become less likely to marry. From 1970 to 2000, the annual number of marriages per one thousand unmarried adult women declined by one-third.
- The trend is to delay first marriages. In 1960, the median age for first marriages was twenty for females and twenty-three for males. In recent years, those numbers have risen to twenty-five for females and twenty-seven for males.
- The percentage of adults in the population who are married has diminished. In 1960, 69.3 percent of men and 65.9 percent of women were married. In 2000, only 57.9 percent of men and 54.7 percent of women were married.
- From 1960 to 2000, the percentages of individuals aged thirty-five to forty-four who were married fell from 88 to 71.6 for men and 87.4 to 69 for women.[2]

As telling as these statistics are concerning marriage, they don't say anything as definitive about commitment as does the following paragraph from the report:

It is important to note that the decline in marriage does not mean that people are giving up on living together with a sexual partner. On the contrary, with the incidence of unmarried cohabitation increasing rapidly, marriage is giving ground to unwed unions. Most people now live together before they marry for the first time. An even higher percentage of those divorced who subsequently remarry live together first. And a still small but growing number of persons, both young and old, are living together with no plans for eventual marriage.[3]

There's the kicker for commitment: *marriages are declining but cohabitation is rising.* In other words, people want the romance (sex, fun, partnership, shared income, even children) without the responsibility (legal entanglement, binding marital status, implied loss of freedom, and [for men] fear of financial ruin in case of divorce).

It's impossible from the above statistics to tell who's less willing to commit. But all indications are that it's the male sector. Men see themselves as having more to lose and less to gain from commitment than women.

WHAT COMMITMENT MEANS TO MEN

As with all the chapters in this book, we're trying to step away from the trees and look at the forest. Trends develop over decades in any society, and it's easy for individuals to be influenced by slow-growing trends without even knowing it.

For example, anyone who thinks the modern feminist movement has not affected a man's willingness to commit to a woman is living with his or her head in the sand. The traditional culture of the 1950s, in which a man provided for his family and a woman nurtured their children in the home, has given way to the culture we now know: two-income families, dual (competing) salaries, separate checking accounts, and egalitarian views on leadership and decision-making. Without supporting one trend over the other, we can say that these two cultures have clashed since the 1970s. Men have had to figure out where they fit in the new scheme of equal-everything, and many are questioning whether the payoff for total commitment is the same as it used to be. For many men, risk/reward analyses have resulted in fewer rather than more reasons to make a total commitment to women (for reasons outlined below).

All of us are influenced by "cultural osmosis"—the tendency to let "the

world around [us] squeeze [us] into its own mold," as J. B. Phillips rendered
Paul's words in Romans 12:2. It's hard to say where, how, and with whom
trends start, but men in general definitely seem less willing to make a lifetime commitment to one woman than they did in decades past. Here are
ten reasons cited in the Rutgers study for why men won't make such a commitment (the comments under each point are my own):

1. They can get sex without marriage more easily than in times past.
If a man does not have a spiritual/moral reason for limiting his sexual pursuits and subsequent activity, then total commitment to a woman becomes
a self-limiting constraint on what is his strongest physical drive. Add to this
the perception (which, sadly, is often true) that sexual satisfaction declines
predictably and irreversibly the longer one is married, and total commitment for a man seems to be a shot in his own sexual foot.

**2. They can enjoy the benefits of having a wife by cohabiting rather
than marrying.**
Many men today rationalize cohabitation by claiming that it requires a
commitment equal to marriage, that a legal marriage is nothing more than
the receipt of a piece of paper. But that is clearly not the case. A legal marriage obligates one to far more than cohabitation, especially in the case of
the dissolution of the marriage. It is the avoidance of those obligations
that no doubt augurs in favor of cohabitation for some men. (An interesting note regarding this from the Rutgers study: In 1960, there were
439,000 heterosexual cohabiting couples in America; in 2000, there
were 4.736 million.)

3. They want to avoid divorce and its financial risks.
If a man has been the chief provider in a marriage, then he stands liable to
pay alimony and child support in case of divorce. Since child support normally runs through a child's eighteenth birthday, if a divorce occurs when a
child is young, a man's earnings will be seriously impacted for a decade or
more. Not that they shouldn't be. Still, many men believe that courts are
predisposed toward women and children, and are assumptive of blame
toward men in the case of divorce and financial settlements. Whether true
or not, that perception works like a reality in making men want to avoid
getting into that predicament.

4. They want to wait until they are older to have children.

There is definitely a trend toward having children later in life. Men have picked up on this trend and said, "What's the rush?" For most men, having children signals the end of life as they once knew it. Discretionary income once spent on man-toys and entertainment will now be directed toward day care, private schools, and college funds.

5. They fear that marriage will require too many changes and compromises.

This is the self-centered male at his best, wanting sex and good times without "changes and compromises." There is nothing mature about this position at all, though that's not the point. The point is that it is out there in our culture, and *all* men are absorbing it to one degree or another absent any defensive shield with which to protect themselves.

6. They are waiting for the perfect soul mate, and she hasn't yet appeared.

This perspective only encourages the shopping mentality that postpones commitment. Airbrushed models and surgically enhanced celebrities have given men the idea that the "perfect ten" actually exists, and that if they wait long enough, they'll find her. This kind of fantasizing can go on forever (see Proverbs 12:11; 28:19).

7. They face few social pressures to marry.

Young men today discover few social impediments to failing to commit. Even so-called Christian young people find that parents and churches, while possibly disapproving of cohabitation, will do little to make the choice difficult for those who choose it. There is absolutely no social stigma attached to being single or cohabiting today. This is not only a radical departure from traditional American culture, but also other cultures around the world where early marriage was a sign of desirability, stability, and maturity. *

8. They are reluctant to marry a woman who already has children.

Divorce rates in America have produced an inordinate number of single women with children. Not only do men not want the immediate responsibility of children or the notion of giving up the "honeymoon" stage of marriage, they fear that they may be used by women who are desperate to find a stable provider and father figure. The marriage becomes less about the man as a person and more about what he brings to the table in terms of assets and long-term security for the woman and children. (Again, some interesting findings from the Rutgers study: The percentage of children under the age of eighteen living with a single parent increased from 9 percent in 1960 to 27 percent in 2000. In the same period, the number of cohabiting, unmarried adult heterosexual couples living with one or more children under the age of fifteen soared from 197,000 to 1.675 million. The key here is "cohabiting, unmarried.")

9. They want to own a house before they get a wife.

Why is it that men will commit to a thirty-year mortgage more easily than a marriage? Because they can unload the house at any time with no negative ramifications. Fortunately, wives are not considered property in our culture. If they were, there probably wouldn't be a chapter in this book on commitment.

10. They want to enjoy single life as long as they can.

It's only natural to pursue those things that bring the greatest pleasure. The question to answer in this discussion is, Why do men view the single life as more pleasurable than marriage? Is it possible that a marriage relationship could provide more pleasure than single life for a man? Women who are frustrated with men's hesitancy to commit ought to examine their answers to this question and what they think they could do to turn the pleasure tables in their favor.

Finally, it is obvious that the fruit is not falling far from the tree. The Rutgers study showed that the percentage of high school seniors who believe it is a good idea for couples to live together before marriage to see if they are compatible is increasing. In the late 1970s, 32.3 percent of girls believed this, yet this figure jumped to 59.1 percent by 2000. For boys, the numbers increased from 44.9 percent to 65.7 percent.[4]

I have seen no one summarize more succinctly the difference between a man's unwillingness to commit and a woman's willingness to do the opposite than Dr. Warren Farrell, author of *Why Men Are the Way They Are*. He identifies man's primary drive in life as sexual, which he means as the ability to play the field and maintain access to a pool of beautiful women.

Women's primary dream is not sex but security: a relationship with one man who has the present ability or the future potential to provide economic security. "*So commitment often means that a woman achieves her primary fantasy, while a man gives his up.* Commitment, then, means almost exactly the opposite to a woman as it does to a man. And legally, once a man commits to marriage, if he tries to achieve his primary fantasy he breaks the law (adulterer). Women's primary fantasy *is* the law" (all italics his).[5]

Even if they haven't read Farrell's book, men maintain this suspicion about women. It is a great offense to a man who suspects that a woman is more in love with his assets than with him (just as it is an offense to a woman who believes a man loves her body more than her soul).

NEW DIRECTIONS

Dr. Scott Stanley of the University of Denver has pointed out that commitment involves holding a long-term view of life and "making a choice to give up choices." Neither of these two aspects is characteristic of the American culture at present. We are the world's greatest consumer-debtor nation because of our commitment to having everything now. We don't like to give up choices, and we don't like to measure immediate gratification against long-term benefit. Stanley says we are like the proverbial monkey that has reached in the jar to grab a handful of food but then can't extract his balled-up, greedy fist. His unwillingness to give up the immediate gratification from the food for the long-term use of his hand is the dilemma of the modern man who won't commit. It's easy to tell men to "let go of the food," yet when no one else around you is making that choice, it's hard.

Stanley illustrates the danger of never choosing, of never deciding to commit, via a paradox posed by the Greek philosopher Zeno: Suppose you're standing in the center of a room and you walk halfway toward a wall. Then you do the same thing again—walk halfway to the wall. Then again, and again, and again. While continually decreasing your distance from the wall by half, mathematically you never reach the wall. If the wall is commitment, you never get there despite continually moving closer to it. The only way you get to the wall is by choosing to walk to the wall once instead of going halfway there an infinite number of times.[6]

Obviously, the analogy breaks down because we can't always look at a man and tell whether he's at the wall or not. At some point "98 percent committed" starts looking like 100 percent. But a man who continually takes half steps is a man who is holding out a portion of his heart, however small it might be, for "something better." This kind of holding back will hurt a marriage in the same way that keeping a portion of our hearts open to carnal pursuits will hamper our maturation in God. It is ultimately a sign of immaturity. It is the perspective that says "I do" at the altar, but says "Maybe I do, maybe I don't" secretly in the heart.

As men, the first new direction we need to take is to break away from the mentality that says making choices and promises inherently shows maturity. While these are certainly *steps* toward maturity, Ecclesiastes 5:4–7 has some strong words for those who make promises carelessly: "When you make a vow to God, do not delay in fulfilling it. He has no pleasure in fools; fulfill your vow. It is better not to vow than to make a vow and not fulfill it. Do not let your mouth lead you into sin. And do not protest to the temple messenger, 'My vow was a mistake.' Why should God be angry at what you say and destroy the work of your hands? Much dreaming and many words are meaningless. Therefore stand in awe of God."

Unfortunately, as one Web site states, "'Till death do us part' no longer holds the same significance [as it once did]. This wedding vow phrase is now understood to mean 'Til the death of our relationship takes place and we divide our assets.'"[7] Any of us guys who said "I do" or "I will" or "I promise" or "I swear" at the beginning of our marriage—or at any other point in it—needs to know those are words of commitment. That is not a judgment upon those among us who have failed to keep a vow. But it is a reminder that on the front side, we need to count the costs and be willing to give up "options" when we commit.

NEW CONNECTIONS

Many men carry in their hearts a secret fear of commitment. Even men who have made commitments are fearful of not being able or willing to see them through. Some men carry the guilt that comes with failing to keep a moral

commitment. Other men know they live with one or more of the ten reasons mentioned earlier for why men won't commit.

All of these are fertile grounds for discussions between husbands and
wives. But like all the secrets discussed in this book, this is a flammable
subject that must not be approached with a spark of resentment or anger.
There is no hope for any marriage in which commitment is an issue if forgiveness, mercy, and grace are not extended.

I strongly encourage couples to talk together about commitment, albeit
carefully and prayerfully. Using wisdom and discernment along the way,
address the following questions:

- How does each of us define commitment?
- What are the hardest choices for us to make?
- With which of the ten reasons discussed earlier do we most
  identify?
- What failures of commitment have there been in our past?
- What should we do about those failures?
- Where do we stand today in terms of commitment to our
  relationship?
- What could each of us do to make married life more desirable than
  single life?
- To what degree does this statement define us: "For a man, commit-
  ment means giving up his chief desire, while for a woman it means
  gaining hers"?

Commitment is a choice, but it is also a work in progress. As new
evidences of shaky commitment surface, they can be dealt with so that
progress is made and maturity gained.

SECTION 3

SECRETS ABOUT
SPIRITUALITY

Chapter 12

WAKE ME UP WHEN
CHURCH IS OVER

I moved to Southern California when I was twenty-eight years old and did not rush to find a church home. I had attended church faithfully out of a sense of duty for years, but couldn't say that I really enjoyed it. Even though I'd been a music major for a couple of years in college and loved great music, church music was a turnoff. I could never quite figure out why we were singing songs in the late twentieth century written by people who lived in the previous three centuries. The preaching was formulaic, predictable, boring, and rarely touched on anything related to where I was in my life. (If that sounds negative and critical, trust me, it's how a lot of men feel about church—just keep reading.)

Fortunately for me, a secretary at the John Wayne Tennis Club in Newport Beach told me about a great church that met in a school gym nearby. I checked it out the following Sunday and could not believe what I found. The music was amazing and really alive. The preacher was funny and relevant and preached like a man who'd been reading my mail. I never lost interest during the entire service, which was amazing for a guy who was suffering from ADD and didn't know it.

That church is still going strong in Newport Beach and attracts big crowds—crowds that include lots of men. Churches like that one are found all across the country today. They're "user friendly" and full of life. But there are still lots of men who profess to be Christians who haven't found a reason to attend. Not only is this a detriment to their spiritual lives, it creates a disconnect in their home when wives are the ones taking the children to church and related activities. And it's an unsolved problem.

WHAT WE KNOW ABOUT MEN AND CHURCH

If you are a churchgoing man, past or present, you could probably write this chapter—the opinion parts, anyway. I've never met a man yet, including the one in my mirror, who doesn't have strong opinions about the church. Those views aren't all negative, but they are all energetic and heartfelt. For the most part, the church in America has fallen on hard times when it comes to men: they don't like it. That's a sad fact, given that the founder was a man and His first "board of directors" were all men.

There are a lot of men who currently attend church who, if they had the chance to stop, probably would. A large number already have. Many of the men who do attend church regularly do so more out of a sense of obligation to God and family than because they really want to. Is church supposed to be like castor oil—something you hold your nose and swallow because your mother said it was good for you? Or should it be something a man needs for replenishment like a parched runner gulps water?

I'm going to identify the trend regarding men and church (and related church activities) from our own survey because it's the simplest number to report. Then I'll share a few more statistics that paint the sad picture: men are bored with church.

In our survey of 3,600 men, 34.1 percent said they were either often (29 percent) or always (5 percent) "bored by the idea of church and church activities." Among the Christian men, 27.9 percent responded that way; of the non-Christian men, 51.3 percent (not surprisingly) agreed. With all the men surveyed, if you include those who answered they were "sometimes" bored, the total shoots up to almost 88 percent. Only 12 percent of those surveyed said they were "never" or "rarely" bored with church. (The "sometimes" category is not critical. After all, church doesn't exist to entertain.

If men get bored "sometimes" in a non-entertainment venue, that's probably to be expected. It's the one-third who are often or always bored that worries me.)

From David Morrow, author of *Why Men Hate Going to Church*, come these additional snapshots:

- The typical American congregation draws an adult crowd that's 61 percent female, 39 percent male. This gender gap shows up in all age categories.
- On any given Sunday there are thirteen million more adult women than men in America's churches.
- This Sunday almost 25 percent of married, churchgoing women will worship without their husbands.
- Midweek activities often draw 70 to 80 percent female participants.
- The majority of church employees are women (except for ordained clergy, who are overwhelmingly male).
- As many as 90 percent of the boys who are being raised in church will abandon it by their twentieth birthday. Many of them will never return.
- More than 90 percent of American men believe in God, and five out of six call themselves Christians. But only two out of six attend church on a given Sunday. The average man accepts the reality of Jesus Christ but fails to see any value in going to church.[1]

The guru of data-gathering for the Christian faith, George Barna, published results of a 2005 survey concerning eight measures of religious commitment among American Christians (such as commitment to Christ, spirituality, priority of religious faith, and others). He found that women were 36 percent more likely to express a higher level of commitment for all eight factors. A majority of women expressed commitment to six of the eight factors, while men expressed commitment to just three of the eight.[2]

I could go on, but additional data would only reveal the same truth from yet more directions. There is no hiding the fact that men are not as spiritually engaged as women; that they are turned off by church and its related activities.

WHAT CHURCH AND SPIRITUAL ACTIVITIES MEAN TO MEN

What's fascinating about men and church in recent years is that while their church attendance has waned, their involvement in small groups has actually increased. It's as if men have left the church and found other ways to seek out Jesus. Author, artist, and documentarian David Murrow has reported a finding of George Barna that "between 1994 and 2004, men's church attendance was flat, *but men's participation in small spiritual groups doubled!* During that decade about nine million additional men joined a small group that meets during the week for the purpose of prayer, Bible study, or spiritual fellowship, apart from Sunday school or other church classes" (italics his).[3]

When I see what's happening with Christian men I think of the lyrics to the U2 song, "I Still Haven't Found What I'm Looking For," in which frontman Bono sings explicitly about a faith in Christ's redemptive work. After all is said and done, however, he still admits that his search for this "Kingdom come" continues.[4] I'm not suggesting that Bono is singing about his search for the church, nor am I saying he's not.[5] But there are many men who believe what he describes—sound biblical theology—who nonetheless continue to search for a place to experience the reality of what they believe.

Is that possible apart from the church? "Absolutely," Murrow writes. "I know a number of men who are intensely devoted to Jesus, but who do not attend organized worship services. Robert Lewis estimates that his Men's Fraternity meetings regularly draw 100 to 150 men who do not attend church. Men are taking a Costco approach to faith, going factory direct, cutting out the middleman."[6]

One place that is happening is in New Canaan, Connecticut. Early every Friday morning up to 250 men, from Wall Street bankers to blue-collar workers, meet in this tiny community in a gathering known as the New Canaan Society. They eat, worship, hug, laugh (a lot), and hear distinguished Christian leaders challenge them with a biblical message that has a masculine ring. Cigars are okay, as are tears. There are dinners once a month and a men's retreat once a year. And to hear the men tell it, it's the most important part of their spiritual life. The core values of the New Canaan Society are honesty, humility, humanity, holiness, hope, and humor. Their "resolves" and statement of faith would pass muster in any evangelical gathering. And it's all being done outside the church.[7]

This is not the only such group, of course. The general trend all over the country is that men haven't stopped believing in Jesus, they've just found more meaningful ways to express that belief than in a church building at 11 a.m. on Sunday mornings. At the same time, it must be noted that groups like the New Canaan Society and others are not *anti*church. Instead, they see themselves as parachurch, coming alongside the church to do something it is apparently not capable of doing itself.

In a video about the New Canaan Society on its Web site, one of its members says the group is especially for "men who might have difficulty going to church because it's off-putting for them. They're finding a whole group of men just enthusiastic about serving God." A statement on the Web site reads, "For many, NCS bears a striking resemblance to a Christian fraternity house, if there were such a thing. For others, we are a 'Young Life' group for men. For still others, NCS is a twelve-step program for 'recovering sinners.'"[8]

What do men find in a fraternity house in college or a fraternity-like atmosphere after college that they don't find in church? The same thing that C. S. Lewis, J. R. R. Tolkien, and their colleagues, The Inklings, found when they met together at the Eagle and Child pub in Oxford, England, for a pipe and a pint: collegiality, stimulation, acceptance, camaraderie, and good humor. Fortunately, many churches have discovered that men respond to settings like these far more than the Sunday morning hour.

I was amazed—though not surprised, since I've felt the same way—when I read Chuck Colson's confession of his own Sunday morning frustration. There is no greater supporter of Christ and His church in our day, but this hard-boiled former White House counsel to the president had reached his limit with what many are calling the "feminization of the church." Here's Colson's account of what happened:

> When church music directors lead congregations in singing contemporary Christian music, I often listen stoically with teeth clenched. But one Sunday morning, I cracked. We'd been led through endless repetitions of a meaningless ditty called "Draw Me Close to You," which has zero theological content and could just as easily be sung in any nightclub. When I thought it was finally and mercifully over, the music leader beamed. "Let's sing that again, shall we?" he asked. "No!" I shouted, loudly enough to send heads all around me spinning while my wife, Patty, cringed.[9]

Unfortunately, Colson doesn't say what happened next. But it's my bet that more than one man approached him after the service to thank him for saying what he was feeling. The "endless repetitions" of warm and fuzzy choruses so popular in churches today is not something that is going to draw men to church. For the most part, men don't do "warm and fuzzy," yet that is what characterizes most church services.

Some scholars have traced the "feminization" of Christianity back to the Middle Ages in Europe; and, in America, to transitions such as the Industrial Revolution in the 1800s, when men left farms and villages to work in cities, leaving women behind who proceeded to populate and shape the church.[10]

Regardless of the cause, there has been a significant shift in perception about the nature of the church.

Consider an exercise set forth by Murrow. He has shown the following two lists to hundreds of people, Christians and non-Christians, asking them to identify which best characterizes Jesus Christ and His true followers:

LEFT SET	RIGHT SET
Competence	Love
Power	Communication
Efficiency	Beauty
Achievement	Relationships
Skills	Support
Proving oneself	Help
Results	Nurturing
Accomplishment	Feelings
Objects	Sharing
Technology	Relating
Goal-oriented	Harmony
Self-sufficiency	Community
Success	Loving cooperation
Competition	Personal expression

More than 95 percent of the time, Murrow says, people choose the Right Set as the best representation of true Christian values. The shocker is that Murrow created the two lists using words culled from John Gray's classic book, *Men Are from Mars, Women Are from Venus*. The Left Set are the values of Mars (men), and the Right Set are the values of Venus (women). Murrow's point is that "when most people think of Christ and His followers, they think of feminine values."[11]

I would have to say that most churches I've been in promote values from the Right Set far more than the Left Set. When men pick up on this, even subconsciously, what do you think their reaction is? It's similar to being invited to a bridal shower or other "sugar 'n' spice" events. Men are looking for masculine environments in which to spend time. That's why they go into the outdoors, to physical sporting events, to pubs and bars, to lumber yards and hardware stores. It's no secret that men want to be men. But it's a secret for a lot of men that they don't feel like they can be men at church.

Men spend their working life actively solving problems and accomplishing tasks and goals. But when they get to church, they're asked to become passive—to sit in a pew or chair and listen to someone deliver a sermon or lesson. And often when they do see a problem that needs addressing, they give up rather than navigate the layers of bureaucracy from which they must get approval to undertake the ministry they're interested in starting. Men who are decision makers and achievers six days of the week are asked to "take a number" and wait their turn on the seventh. I sometimes wonder if pastors know who they're seeing when they look out over their congregations on Sunday mornings. Do they recognize the men who know how to get things done, but who are often asked to serve only in capacities outside their giftings and calling?

I love the attitude expressed by Pastor Ted Haggard, leader of New Life Church in Colorado Springs, Colorado, and president of the National Association of Evangelicals. His church offers hundreds of small-group ministries and activities that are not conceived by the pastors. If someone wants to begin a new ministry and passes a basic screening, the church will help promote the group. "New Life organizes the marketplace but leaves the details to the people, who write their own programs," says one writer describing the church's unique approach.[12]

Such a strategy would strike fear in the hearts of many church leaders. The fear of losing control, of seeing gifted men besides themselves ascend to prominence in the church, would be too much. Yet the result is that those gifted men often leave and go places on Sunday where they can compete, reason, challenge, build, solve, and do all manner of masculine things.

Steve Sonderman, a minister to men at a large church in Wisconsin, had seen a Saturday morning men's gathering grow to more than 150 men in January 1996. The leadership team anticipated they'd likely have 175 in February and began making plans accordingly. But the first week of February had seen subzero temperatures with wind chills of minus-seventy-five degrees. Schools and all unnecessary activities were being closed because of the weather. That first Saturday in February ended up being officially the coldest day of the year, and Sonderman considered not even making the trip to the church, figuring no one would brave the weather. But he ended up going, thinking he'd at least lead a small Bible study for the handful that would come. When he came down from his office to the fellowship hall, he was shocked to find 220 men eating, laughing, sharing—all on the coldest day of the year.[13]

Men will pay a high price for something that pays an even higher dividend, if only the dividend is offered.

NEW DIRECTIONS

For the sake of completeness, I need to mention the biblical imperative for the members of Christ's body not to forsake the assembling of themselves together. As Hebrews 10:24–25 states, it's for the purposes of encouragement and motivation to pursue love and good deeds. It should go without saying that men have a biblical responsibility to be active participants in the communal life of the church. To wait to go to church until you find the perfect church is an exercise in vanity and futility. Bad churches don't get better when good men fail to attend.

If you are a man who is not attending church, I encourage you to begin. And if you're a man who attends church but wishes he didn't have to, I encourage you to talk to your church's leaders about what would make church more compelling for men such as yourself. You may think nothing will change—and it might not. But you need to do your part as a change agent by showing up and getting involved.

The number of wives across America who struggle to get children to church alone every Sunday is disheartening, especially considering that their husbands are often sitting in front of the television, on the lake fishing, on the golf course, or in their workshop. There is not a good answer for children—especially young boys who want to be like their dads—who ask, "Why do I have to go to church? Dad doesn't have to!" An amazing study based in Switzerland (where census figures include religious activity in households) shows the effect of fathers on children's future religious interests when the fathers either do or don't attend church. The numbers are enough to scare any of us fathers off the golf course and into church for the sake of our children.[14]

NEW CONNECTIONS

"Almost everything about today's church—its teaching style, its ministries, the way people are expected to behave, even today's popular images of Jesus—is designed to meet the needs and expectations of a largely female audience. Church is sweet and sentimental, nurturing and *nice*. Women thrive in this environment. In modern parlance, women are the target audience of today's church."[15]

Do you agree? Husband and wife, dig into this idea together and see what you conclude. You may both be perfectly happy with your church experience. But there are likely some men in your church who are not—and some women who are unhappy as a result. Do what you can to make this men's secret a part of your life and conversation.

The numbers don't lie; there are a lot of men who are keeping church-avoidance a secret. Yet the church can only be strengthened when they return.

Chapter 13

BEING A TRUE SPIRITUAL LEADER

It is no exaggeration to say that everything I ever needed to know about spiritual leadership I learned from Fred Stoeker.

I was raised in an era and in a theological neighborhood that did not understand true spiritual leadership, that is, servant leadership. I learned principles that sounded reasonable—lists of dos and don'ts—but they were somewhat detached from reality. Husbands are the head of the home on all matters spiritual, I learned, and the tiebreaker on everything. Like a corporate CEO, he listens and then decides. The husband rules the roost.

Then I met Fred—the real deal when it came to husbanding and fathering. He was the spiritual leader in his home, but he led in such a way that won the affection of his wife and children. I wondered what made his style of leadership so unique. As we worked on a writing project together, ultimately published as *Every Man's Marriage*, he began to teach me how to lead. Fred showed me that the spiritual leader in the home is the first one to say, "I'm sorry," the first one to ask for forgiveness, and the first one to forgive. He's also the first one to rise to pray in the morning for his family, and the first one to study and obey God's Word. He is the first one to sacrifice his agenda if doing so would mean a lot to his wife or children. First to worship, to serve, to sacrifice, to fight for what's right and good, and the first to love.

Fred Stoeker is a living book when it comes to servant leadership in the home. By the grace of God I was allowed to spend time with him and study the pages of his life. I'm not the leader Fred is, but I want to be.

WHAT WE KNOW ABOUT MEN AND SPIRITUAL LEADERSHIP IN THE FAMILY

There is no lack of issues—secrets—in a man's life to keep his guilty conscience occupied. And one subject that he is not allowed to forget, due to reminders from church and spouse, is that of spiritual leadership in the home. Men know they should be good leaders for their children, even for their wives, but many men aren't sure what that means. Influence? Modeling? Instruction? Discipline? All the above?

In our survey, we found that 18.1 percent of the men surveyed always or often "feel awkward about being the spiritual leader in the family." Even 16.2 percent of the non-Christians feel that way. Perhaps they are responding within the context of a different faith—Muslim, Jew, or other. But even those who are not religious feel some sense of unease about the task of instilling morals, values, and ethics—spiritual direction—in their children's lives.

Christian men especially feel this way due to the extra-biblical expectations that accompany the modern notion of the father being the priest of the home. Granted, there are Bible passages that direct fathers to bring up their children in "the training and instruction of the Lord" (Ephesians 6:4). But there are also verses that suggest equal responsibility and participation by mothers (Proverbs 1:8). Nonetheless, an entire industry has developed around equipping fathers to be the spiritual leaders of their home. Along with the useful resources come the pangs of guilt for those fathers who are reminded of how much they are not doing.

In the last chapter, I alluded briefly to a study in Switzerland on the effects of a father's spiritual leadership on his children. The focus was primarily on church attendance, but the findings can be interpreted more broadly. In the Swiss decennial census, information is gathered about people's religion, along with other expected information. But in 1994, the Swiss took an extra survey to determine whether a person's religious beliefs and practices carried through to the following generation—and why or why not.[1] Here is the critical summary of what was found: "It is the religious practice of the father of the family that, above all, determines the future attendance at or absence from church of the children."[2]

America has never had state-sponsored churches; Europe has. So the idea of "church attendance" on a continent where Christianity has declined significantly in the post-World War II era has a different meaning at the national level there than here. In America, generational influences on church attendance are not a concern of the census. Yet this does not mean the findings of another country cannot or do not apply to us.

The data from the Swiss study summarized by Church of England vicar Robbie Lowe is voluminous, but several key points are worth noting. While some of these percentages may seem low, keep in mind the point made earlier regarding Europe's considerable decline in church attendance and largely secular culture.

- If both a father and mother go to church *regularly*, 33 percent of their children will follow in their footsteps, while 41 percent will become irregular attendees.
- If a father attends *irregularly* while his wife goes regularly, only 3 percent of the couple's children will become consistent church-goers, while 59 percent will become irregular. (Interestingly enough, if a father doesn't go to church at all yet is married to a consistent churchgoer, that first statistic is only slightly different: 2 percent of the couple's children will become regular attendees, while 37 percent will attend irregularly.)
- If a father is a *regular* at church but his wife either is sporadic in her attendance or doesn't go at all, the percentage of children who will become regular churchgoers actually goes up to 38 percent, while 44 percent will become irregular worshipers as adults.

Regardless of the unimpressive percentages of children-turned-adults who end up in church, the father's sway in spiritually shaping his children is undeniable. Lowe summarizes:

> The results are . . . about as politically incorrect as it is possible to be; but they simply confirm what psychologists, criminologists,

educationalists, and traditional Christians know. You cannot buck the biology of the created order. Father's influence . . . is out of all proportion to his allotted, and severely diminished role, in Western liberal society.

A mother's role will always remain primary in terms of intimacy, care, and nurture. . . . But it is equally true that when a child begins to move into that period of differentiation from home and engagement with the world "out there," he (and she) looks increasingly to the father for his or her role model. Where the father is indifferent, inadequate, or just plain absent, that task of differentiation and engagement is much harder. When children see that church is a "women and children" thing, they will respond accordingly—by not going to church, or going much less.[3]

Again, it's Switzerland, not America. But I would not personally bet against the data. Apparently, the noninfluential doofus that Dad is portrayed to be on American television is inconsistent with the findings. No one has a greater impact on children than fathers, at least when it comes to spiritual matters.

A letter from a woman received by psychologist and author Sam Keen may put the urgency of the issue in proper perspective: "Perhaps the real shift will come when men fully realize, in the gut and not just in the head, that they are equally responsible, with women, for the creation, nurturing, and protection of children—that children are not simply sex objects, ego trips, or nuisances, but their first responsibility—before war, money, power, and status."[4]

WHAT SPIRITUAL LEADERSHIP MEANS TO MEN

Men and power go hand-in-hand. We thrive upon seeing our own influence among others, especially our offspring. Yet if this is the case, then why are we uncomfortable with the spiritual leadership role in the home? Why do men, who don't hesitate to lead on the job, suddenly become passive and unable when it comes to providing spiritual leadership at home? Here are some reasons:

1. Knowledge and Skills

Men lead and accomplish at work because they know what to do. Contractors build, accountants count, lawyers argue, and doctors diagnose and prescribe. Doing the same thing eight hours a day for a decade leads to competence and confidence. Think how incompetent and insecure anyone would feel about something they attempt to do for five or ten minutes a couple of times a week. And therein lies part of the problem: we have communicated to fathers that spiritual leadership consists of a daily devotional hour for the family consisting of Bible reading, a story, a game, Bible memory, prayer, and related activities. Fathers feel like they need a seminary education to pull off such an assignment. (More on an alternative perspective below.)

2. Time

This hardly needs an explanation. Given the frenetic pace that most families operate at today, families (especially with teens) are lucky to find themselves in the same room at the same time more than a couple times each week. A meal together is considered a major accomplishment. Talk to a father about leading his family spiritually and you'll likely get a one-word response: "When?" Again, this is evidence of the compartmentalization of spirituality, like it's an entry in an already-full Day-Timer.

3. Perspective

Many fathers bring their vocational mentality to the issue of spiritual leadership. At work they're used to giving people resources and responsibility—delegating—which leads to results. Without even thinking about it, they apply that same perspective to spiritual leadership: "I give generously to my church in order that my kids, from kindergarten through graduation, will have competent spiritual training and development. I'm doing my part by writing the check. They should do theirs by training my kids." You won't find many fathers saying that, but you will find more than a few of them thinking it.

4. Guilt

If a father drives in from work in the afternoon after battling rush-hour traffic and speaks harshly to his children for leaving their bikes in the driveway, it doesn't exactly set the stage for a family Bible lesson on love. Fathers know their own spiritual lives aren't perfect, and so they are hesitant to put themselves forward as teachers (examples) to their children—or to their wives, who know their failures even better. Yet the truth is, if perfection were required, none of us would do anything in life. Fathers have to learn to practice the confession-forgiveness cycle with their children as well as they do with God. Indeed, that cycle becomes one of the most powerful tools in the father's spiritual leadership tool kit.

5. Lack of Support

Though it happens in the minority of cases, there are times when a husband lacks the spiritual and emotional support of his wife. He may be trying to be a spiritual leader and influencer in his home, only to find that there is no rein-forcement from his wife. If he's out of town on business, his wife doesn't take the children to church or have family devotions. Dad's absence becomes the equivalent of a vacation from God. There is nothing more dangerous for children than having parents not united spiritually. And contrary to popu-lar opinion, sometimes it's the wife who is unsupportive of her husband's efforts to strengthen the faith of their children.

Spiritual leadership means a lot to most men who are Christians. It's not that they don't want to be spiritual leaders, it's just that a day, a week, a month, a year goes by and the status quo goes unchanged for any or all of the reasons I listed above. Counselor Willard Harley summarizes how most wives innately feel about their husband filling this role: "Above all, wives want their husbands to take a leadership role in [the] family and to commit themselves to the moral and educational development of their children. *The ideal scenario for a wife is to marry a man whom she can look up to and respect and then have her children grow up to be like their father*" (italics mine).[5]

And as Jim Conway points out, the older children get the more important their foundational years are when it comes to their own spiri-tual maturity and closeness to their parents:

> By midlife, a shift has happened in our thinking process. We feel a strange conflict of emotions. Only yesterday we had been eagerly looking forward to greater and higher achievement. Now we're beginning to look back. Our adolescent children are the ones

looking forward with great anticipation to the future. For them it means independence and their own lifestyle. For us there is a growing melancholic reflection of days forever gone—and perhaps guilt for delayed or wasted opportunity.

Sadly, it isn't that fathers want to spend more time with their children now, but they want to move the clock back and relive those years when the children were younger. They can't seem to cross that chasm—the lost years of communication. Men keep waiting for their teens to make the first move, but it's the dad's place to be a "man" and make the connection.

Very few men realize that if they would apologize to their teens or young adults, many bridges could be quickly rebuilt and wonderful relationships started. Most teens and young adults are eagerly waiting for Dad to reach out and to say, "I'm sorry! I put my time into getting material stuff instead of connecting with you."[6]

Unfortunately, young children can't tell their dads how much they need spiritual leadership at the time they need it. But when they are older, the lack of such leadership can become a painful reality. Not unredeemable, but painful nonetheless. Which leads to the elephant in the spiritual-leadership room: divorce. What are fathers to do spiritually for children they no longer live with or even see on a regular basis? The simple answer is: everything they possibly can. I want to quote an extended passage by Sam Keen on the subject because it is one man's experience that will hopefully connect with thousands. While he doesn't speak from a typical evangelical perspective, his words are easily applicable to fathers concerned with spiritual leadership:

I had been divorced for five years when I saw a billboard, smack in the middle of the smoggy, industrial section of Richmond, with the dire message: "Nothing makes up for failure in the family." My immediate reaction was to start an argument with the billboard evangelist, to defend myself and the multitude of my fellow divorcés who had broken up families for what we considered the best of reasons. "That's asinine! What a guilt trip! A good divorce is better for the kids than a bad marriage. And, anyway, divorce is not necessarily the sign of 'failure.' And besides that, my kids are living with me and I am 'making up' their loss to them.

And, and, and . . . ." Not until I had exhausted my self-defense did I simmer down and let the full weight of the proposition sink in and think about it in a calm manner.

It has now been twelve years since I saw the billboard. My daughter and son from my first marriage are grown and lovely. I am remarried and I have a ten-year-old daughter. After considerable meditation on the matter, I have come to believe that the message of the billboard is both true and prophetic. In watching my children struggle with the hurts and discontinuities that are the inevitable result of the irreconcilable differences between their parents, I have learned what many men learn only after divorce. There is nothing more precious than our children. In the quiet hours of the night, when I add up the accomplishments of my life in which I take justifiable pride—a dozen books, thousands of lectures and seminars, a farm built by hand, a prize here, an honor there—I know that three that rank above all the others are named Lael, Gifford, and Jessamyn. In the degree to which I have loved, nurtured, and enjoyed them, I honor myself. In the degree to which I have injured them by being unavailable to them because of my obsessive preoccupations with myself or my profession, I have failed as a father and as a man.[7]

NEW DIRECTIONS

If spiritual leadership in the home is not a compartment, not a Day-Timer entry, not a schedule, not a meeting, then what is it? I'm not saying those are not parts of the process, but they are definitely means more than ends.

Let's start with the big picture. I like the three spiritual goals David Bentall and his wife established for the spiritual development of their children. (The points are his, the comments are mine.)

1. Endeavor to live a life worthy of your children's imitation.
The focus here is on parents, not on their children. The principle of modeling and imitation says that spiritual truth is more likely to be caught than taught. Children are masters at separating truth from fiction

in their parents' lives. As a father, if you want to instill biblical values, truth, and disciplines in your children, those elements will have to become realities in *your* life first. If you want to point your children in the direction of the kingdom of God, the first thing you need to do is be headed there yourself.

2. Correct and discipline your children with love.

Note: Bentall didn't say "punishment." The New Testament word for discipline means "training" and "correction" and makes little mention of punishment. Punishment looks back at sins committed, while training and correction look forward to character developed. Discipline-as-training involves teaching, explaining, modeling, revising, correcting, implementing— all of it on-the-job. Being a spiritual leader for your children means you become a life coach from a godly perspective. And while your role transitions from trainer to counselor when your children reach young adulthood, the process of imparting life and wisdom never ends.

3. Affirm and encourage each child as a unique and special gift from God.

The greatest gift any father can give his children is the blessing of welcome and worthiness. If God the Father said to His Son, "This is my Son, whom I love; with him I am well pleased" (Matthew 3:17), how much more should an earthly father tell his children the same thing? Our culture is presently reaping the seeds of absent fatherhood we have sown in recent decades. There are millions of young adults wandering the landscape of America in search of themselves, looking in every dark cultural hole for an identity to claim—young adults for whom there was no father to pronounce a unique blessing and benediction upon them when they needed to hear it.[8]

The Bible's best paradigm for how to accomplish the above is Deuteronomy 6:6–9: "Write these commandments that I've given you today on your hearts. Get them inside of you and then get them inside your children. Talk about them wherever you are, sitting at home or walking in the street; talk about them from the time you get up in the morning to when you fall into bed at night. Tie them on your hands and foreheads as a reminder; inscribe them on the doorposts of your homes and on your city gates" (MSG).

This passage reminds me of the phrase coined by Tom Peters and Bob Waterman in their classic book on business, *In Search of Excellence*. They discovered that the best companies' leaders practice what they called "management by walking around." Instead of putting people into classrooms and drilling principles into their heads, these directors got out on the factory floor and communicated company practice and philosophy on a heart-to-heart and hand-to-hand basis.[9] As fathers, we would do well to view our role of spiritual leadership the same way: leading by walking around with our children.

I've heard through the years several things that Dr. Howard Hendricks, legendary Christian educator and professor, used to tell his (originally all-male) seminary students about parenting. Yet three of his pearls of wisdom in particular fit the Deuteronomy 6 paradigm:

First, never go anywhere by yourself. Every time you can, take one of your children with you. An errand, a trip, a sporting event—wherever a father goes with his children, opportunities will arise to communicate spiritual truth. You have to be in their presence to influence them.

Second, don't buy the lie that "quality" makes up for "quantity" when it comes to time spent with children. Quantity of time is equally important. When a man becomes a parent he can write off the majority of the next twenty years' worth of "free time." The majority of that time needs to be spent with his children.

Third, the best way a father can love his children spiritually and emotionally is by loving their mother spiritually and emotionally.

In other words, being a spiritual leader for a man is more about lifestyle than specific, scheduled events. Granted, events like family devotional times daily or weekly or whenever are important; church attendance is important; Bible reading and memory are important. But so is infusing a deep and pervasive love for God into the everyday events of life: meals, walks after supper, bike rides, games, earning and saving money, serving those less fortunate, healthy competition, rewards for responsibilities fulfilled, family councils, discovering and developing talents, and celebrations of achievement. All of those events—every aspect of life—has a spiritual dimension to be "exploited" for the benefit of spiritual development if only dads will take advantage of the opportunities.

NEW CONNECTIONS

Spiritual training in the home is a team effort. But every team needs a leader, and it appears from Scripture that God expects men to set the pace. As is true in every well-oiled team, leadership is a shared process of discovery and implementation. A wife who puts books or pamphlets on spiritual leadership in her husband's briefcase, or who complains that her husband is not exercising the leadership he should, will see few results. Most men don't respond to such tactics. But most men will react to conversation and dialogue about making changes, especially when it is coupled with an understanding of how difficult that process—and the role the husband must play in that process—can be.

Men don't want their children to fail in life. But if they haven't been exercising spiritual leadership in the home, it will take time to implement new ways of doing so. The best place for any husband to begin is by asking God for the wisdom and will to lead his wife and children toward the kingdom of God, to create a generational process that will continue to bear fruit long after he is gone. I love the way Sam Keen envisions men passing on spiritual strength from one generation to another:

"At the center of my vision of manhood there is no lone man standing tall against the sunset, but a blended figure composed of a grandfather, a father, and a son. The boundaries between them are porous, and strong impulses of care, wisdom, and delight pass across the synapses of the generations. Good and heroic men are generations in the making—cradled in the hearts and initiated in the arms of fathers who were cradled in the hearts and initiated in the arms of their fathers."[10]

All it takes for that process to begin, or to be derailed, is for one man to choose to lead—or to abandon his role—in his home.

Chapter 14

SPIRITUAL INADEQUACY

Paul and Lily's love survived the rush of high school hormones. They stayed together and married young with the support of their extended families. Spiritually, they were a good match in that they were both searching. They tried new churches almost every Sunday, looking for a place to fit in. When Lily became pregnant, she began to think about the spiritual responsibilities involved in raising children and the positive influence of having a church home. Her church search became more serious.

At church one Sunday she heard about an upcoming meeting of MOPS—Mothers of Preschoolers. Since she was about to have a preschooler of her own she attended the meeting and was warmly welcomed. She had never experienced this kind of energy with anything having to do with church, and she continued attending the MOPS meeting regularly. That led to her joining a Bible study group of women, where she made a life-changing discovery: God was holy and she was not. She came to understand the difference between church attendance and having a relationship with God through Christ. It wasn't long before she had experienced a genuine spiritual rebirth.

At first Paul was happy for her—a bit confused and a bit envious at what she had found, but happy for her nonetheless. But soon that changed.

As Lily grew spiritually, she began prodding him to do what she had done: accept Christ and begin to grow spiritually with her. The more she pushed and prodded, the more irritated he got. Finally, he declared his spiritual independence. She could keep going to church but he wouldn't, thank you very much.

Paul said later he realized his digging in his heels was an attempt to hold onto who he was, to not be forced into his wife's mold. But he also realized that his wife was moving into the distance spiritually and leaving him behind. He felt weak and spiritually inferior, and didn't like how it felt. She had become the leader, not yet understanding that the best way to win someone to any new venture is by example, not by browbeating.

Sadly, Paul never did start going to church, and a spiritual chasm remained between the two of them. Handled differently, the outcome could have been more positive for both.

WHAT WE KNOW ABOUT MEN'S FEELINGS
OF SPIRITUAL INADEQUACY

This is the third chapter in the "spirituality" section of the book, all three of which deal with the secrets men keep concerning spiritual issues. Chapter 12 addressed men's boredom with church and related activities, while Chapter 13 looked at men's awkwardness about spiritual leadership in the family. These two chapters by necessity raised the concerns of both men and women: the feminization of the church and how women want men to be stronger spiritual leaders in the home. This chapter continues that theme.

In our survey, a whopping 68 percent of the men said they don't measure up to women spiritually either some of the time (53 percent), often (14 percent), or always (1 percent). But what exactly does it mean to "not measure up to women spiritually"? By their very nature, surveys ask brief questions that get sorted through the grid of those asked—in this case, 3,600 different grids. When that particular question hits the receptors in a man's brain, something emotional happens. Man versus woman is not an intellectual issue; it's an emotional one. And throw in the subjective "spiritual" component and it muddies the water even more. More than two-thirds of the men are saying that, in some way, they feel inadequate spiritually compared to the women they're around. Who are these women—their wives, the women they know at church, their wives' friends, women in general?

WHAT SPIRITUAL INADEQUACY MEANS TO MEN

Based on my own experience and the experience of men with whom I have interacted over my years in ministry, here's what I think men are saying regarding their sense of spiritual inadequacy: "My wife and other women I know are better Christians ('more spiritual' for those who are not Christians) than I am. They know more about the Bible, they do more spiritual stuff with children, they're more involved at church, they pray more, they go to Bible studies, they talk about 'deep' stuff with their friends, they buy and read more Christian and religious books. Compared to them, I'm a hacker—okay, a slacker. I admit it. I feel intimidated by women when it comes to spiritual things."

When we say something or someone is inadequate, we usually follow the statement with "*for*" (e.g., "Our funds are inadequate for the project we've outlined"). What exactly, then, do men feel inadequate "for"? It has to be those things they consider to be the practices of the Christian life. If a businessman feels adequate for the demands of his business, it means he feels competent to manage people, negotiate, solve problems, balance the books, manage inventory, buy and sell products, and a host of other tasks. But if that same man feels inadequate spiritually—compared to women—it means he thinks women would be better, or more competent, at the "tasks" of the Christian life than he would: leading others (including his own children) to spiritual maturity, caring for the souls of people, communicating the truths of the Bible, counseling others, praying with people, sharing the gospel with non-Christians, worshiping God, and others.

What does a man truly mean when he says he feels *inadequate*? Here are the synonyms for *inadequate* found in a couple of thesauri I checked: incapable, incompetent, unequal, unfit, unqualified, helpless, impotent, ineffectual, powerless, weak, deficient, insufficient, scarce, short, shy, wanting, poor, scant, scarce, sparse, paltry, meager, limited, pathetic, unsatisfactory, unacceptable, ineffective, inefficient, unskilled, inept, amateurish, inferior, lame, and shabby.

That collection of words is what linguists call a "semantic range"—a group of words that fall into the same family of meaning. Somewhere in that collection are two words that go at opposite ends of the range, with all the rest falling in between. At the middle of the spectrum would be the words closest in meaning to *inadequate*. A group of synonyms is helpful in that it provides an assortment of ways to say what we feel. If you sat down and had a conversation with the men who took our survey and asked them how they would compare themselves spiritually to the women in their lives, not everyone would use our word *inadequate*. They would say, "I'm helpless . . . pathetic . . . ineffective . . . amateurish . . . shabby . . . incapable when it comes to my spiritual life compared with that of Christian women I know."

What's going on here? Why do these men feel so badly about themselves spiritually compared to women? I believe this is a significant secret men keep, and one that's important for church leaders to recognize—and for wives as well. It can't be a healthy situation for men to feel inadequate or weak about their relationship with God, especially in relation to those people whom they are often called to lead spiritually.

This issue dovetails completely with those of the previous two chapters: men in church and men in the home. Whether Protestant or Catholic, men show up in church far less often than women do as illustrated by this ABC News poll:

WEEKLY CHURCH ATTENDANCE

All men	32 percent
All women	44 percent
Catholic men	26 percent
Catholic women	49 percent
Protestant men	42 percent
Protestant women	50 percent[1]

This kind of evidence points to a self-fulfilling prophecy of sorts: men feel inadequate spiritually, so they don't go to church; they don't go to church (or participate in related activities), which contributes to their spiritual incompetence. And on and on. Where the cycle begins or who is at fault is not the point of this chapter. Instead, we will talk more about a way to break the cycle.

Whether the issue is spiritual competence or another area of the male-female relationship, most men live with some amount of intimidation when it comes to women. Where did the expression "the old ball 'n' chain" come from? Why did the English playwright William Congreve write that "hell hath no fury like a woman scorned"? Why do we see T-shirts that read, "If Mama Ain't Happy, Ain't Nobody Happy"? Why do we equate crossing a woman with getting between a mama bear and her cubs?

Maybe it starts when men are little boys who are raised predominantly by their mothers at home or by other women in daycare settings. Wherever it starts, men learn early not to cross women. Or if they do, they do it on their way out of Dodge. I know, there are some macho guys out there who say they are the rulers of their domain. Fine—they are the exceptions that prove the rule. This is not to say there aren't plenty of men who relate happily and successfully to women. But I believe those are men who have earned their peace with wisdom, guys who have learned to implement a servant leadership style that yields harmony as a by-product.

There is evidence that a man's feelings of inadequacy have ancient roots. In Chapter 7, I alluded to Dr. Larry Crabb's notion of Adam remaining mute during a pivotal moment for him and his wife—and all humanity. In his book *The Silence of Adam*, Crabb goes into great detail about Adam's failure in the garden of Eden to confront the serpent who was tempting Eve. Crabb's point is to say that Adam was silent when he should have spoken up. He was silent when he didn't rebuke the serpent and stand between his wife and the tempter, and he was silent for not speaking to his wife and challenging her contemplation of sin. Crabb writes:

> Adam was not only silent with the serpent, he was also silent with Eve. He never reminded her of God's word. He never called her to a larger vision. He did not join his wife in battling wits with the serpent. He passively listened to her speak, rather than speaking with her in mutual respect.

I am not saying that Adam should have spoken for Eve—or to her, as a father speaks to a child or as a superior speaks to an inferior. Many men make that mistake. Nor am I suggesting that men are to speak and women are to keep silent. Both men and women are created in God's image to speak. This is just where the first man sinned.

Adam . . . was absent and passive. His silence was symbolic of his refusal to be involved with Eve. . . . God punished Adam for eating the forbidden fruit. But he also punished him for listening to his wife. Adam's disobedience was a process. Adam was silent and then he ate from the tree. His disobedience did not begin with his eating but with his silence. Disobeying God was a result of retreating from his wife. It was a silent man who eventually broke God's clear command.[2]

Apparently Adam felt inadequate to speak up in that situation. Did he feel intimidated by his wife? Was he afraid of getting "the look" if he interrupted and said, "Ahem, uh, Eve, do you think we should talk about this? Do you really think this is such a good idea?" I'm sure my vision is inaccurate, but I can just picture Adam in a Bob Newhart mold, playing the hesitant, apologetic husband, clearing his throat and taking his life in his hands in this, the world's first instance of a man attempting to change his wife's mind.

Whatever Adam was feeling—inadequacy, intimidation, fear—he shouldn't have been. God created Adam first and then created Eve to be his helper—not vice versa. As politically incorrect as that may be (I'm amazed at my own temerity in saying so), it is the record of Scripture. Adam had experienced the success of spiritual and practical accomplishments—he named all the animals of the world—before Eve came on the scene. He was comfortable in taking instructions from God and carrying them out. Though there was no one to lead except himself, he at least had participated in the inner dialogue that comes when one knows the right thing to do and decides whether to do it or not. He had led himself to a place of *spiritual adequacy* with God in the Garden of Eden.

Don't worry, I'm not now going to say, "And then Eve came along," as if to infer Eve spoiled Adam's perfect party with God. Not at all. Eve was a beautiful gift of God to Adam who likely enjoyed the same spiritual success Adam did until that fateful day in the garden. But the point is this: Adam had no reason to feel inadequate in his relationship with Eve, nor did he need to be intimidated by her. He certainly should not have been silent. He should have intervened. Why he suddenly chose to clam up and stand by while his wife disobeyed God—*and then join her in that disobedience*—is a mystery unsolved.

The curse of God upon the pair—as well as the serpent and the earth—is indicative of the tension that has existed between man and woman ever since. Genesis 3:16 is the key verse: "To the woman he said, 'I will greatly increase your pains in childbearing; with pain you will give birth to children. *Your desire will be for your husband, and he will rule over you*'" (italics mine). Consulting the authorities on this verse, it's obvious the interpretations are varied. The key word is "desire." It could mean a romantic, sexual desire, the way it is used in Song of Solomon 7:10. Or it could mean the "desire to rule over" as in Genesis 4:7. These are the only other two places in the Old Testament this word is used. Because of the proximity of the two Genesis occurrences, there is good reason to believe that "'desiring' in 3:16 should be understood as the wife's desire to overcome or gain the upper hand over her husband."[3] If that view is accepted, it sets the wife's desires against the husband's "rule over" his wife.

If Old Testament scholars are unsure of the meaning of Genesis 3:16, it behooves us to tread lightly in building a practical paradigm for male-female relationships eons after the fact. Still, we know *something* strained happened in the Garden of Eden between the first man and woman. Eve was created for man, yet she took matters into her own hands without consulting Adam. Adam was passive when he should have actively stepped into the breach and possibly saved Eve from succumbing to temptation. Who was innocent and who was guilty? Both were, and everybody is. Men and women today walk a thin line balancing respect and responsibility, freedom and obligation. On the best days, it's a challenge. On the worst, a catastrophe.

Inject into that balancing act the modern women's movement and you have the potential for men to become silent once again. The feminist movement has been a challenge for Christians, men and women. Many women have liberated themselves from what they perceived to be generations of male dominance. In response, men have acted almost like Adam in the garden by retreating into silence. Not knowing how to respond spiritually or biblically to their wives' self-declared emancipation, they have thrown up their hands and said, "Fine. I'll go back to what I do understand: work and the world of men."

The men in our survey who said they don't measure up to women spiritually are men who were born into this modern male-female milieu we live in. They are probably no less confused than Adam was the day he saw his wife step up and give away their world. This is not an easy issue to resolve in the hearts of men. Asking a man to explain why he feels like he doesn't measure up to women spiritually is akin to asking a child to explain the discomfort of an illness. All they know is that they don't feel good; they know something isn't right.

NEW DIRECTIONS

In a September 1995 article in *Psychology Today*, psychiatrist Theodore Dalrymple wrote that twenty years earlier, when he first began to practice, no one ever complained of a lack of self-esteem or of hating him- or herself. Now, he wrote, hardly a week goes by without a patient making that complaint as if it they expected him, the doctor, to fix it. One young man came to visit him concerned about his low self-image, a condition his mother agreed he suffered from. It was this condition, the patient and his mother said, that caused him to beat up his pregnant girlfriend, which resulted in a miscarriage. The following exchange ensued:

Doctor: "It couldn't be the other way around, could it?"

Patient: "What do you mean?"

Doctor: "That your behavior caused you to have a poor opinion of yourself?"

This possibility, of course, was rejected out of hand by the patient.[4]

I like Dalrymple's question to the low-self-esteem young man and think it bears considering in this discussion. Whenever a man sees himself as inadequate, it is for one of two reasons: he literally doesn't have the ability necessary to be adequate (for example, I am inadequate for the task of brain surgery), or he has the ability but has retreated into a passive place. I believe there are many of us men who, as the doctor suggested, have allowed our passive behavior to create a self-image of inadequacy in our own minds. If I'm right, then a change of behavior would go a long way toward dispelling such an image.

A change of what behavior? A change *to* those behaviors consistent with adequacy in the spiritual life—those I mentioned earlier in this chapter. We all get into downward cycles—blue funks, we call them—that may last a few days or weeks. But I also believe it's possible for an entire gender to get itself into a blue funk that lasts for generations. And that may be where the American male is at present with regard to spiritual leadership. We have pulled back and left a spiritual leadership void. As a result, the women around us have stepped in to fill that empty spot. Each of us has concluded, "I don't measure up." But all we need to do to measure up is begin practicing behaviors consistent with adequacy. Sometimes the head and hands have to lead, to show the heart where to go.

NEW CONNECTIONS

If you have read this chapter and concluded it is a call for men to step up and put women in their place, then I've either written poorly or you have read with an agenda. That's not my point. I believe one of the noblest passages of strength in the Bible is Proverbs 31:10–31. I believe it is noble because it shows a wife and a husband personifying strength and adequacy in their own domains, as inseparable as the two sides of a coin. The wife is the CEO of a multifaceted business that includes agriculture, real estate, textiles, and philanthropy. All the while, her husband "is respected at the city gate, where he takes his seat among the elders of the land" (v. 23). Both combine spiritual and intellectual prowess, each taking the lead in their respective arenas, each yielding to the other's adequacy where he or she is lacking.

As a counselor I long to see modern men and women throw off the yoke of cultural confusion they labor under today, to stop competing for ascendancy and power, to serve and love and lift up one another so that the adequacy God gives in Christ becomes the adequacy they have individually and for one another. May God grant it for the sake of His people and His church.

SECTION 4

SECRETS ABOUT RELATIONSHIPS WITH WOMEN

Chapter 15

COMMUNICATING WITH WOMEN

When Esther started dating Robert, she felt there was something different about him from the beginning. He was quiet and stoic, never really getting excited about too much of anything except when it came to his favorite West Texas football team. When they were playing, he became a different person, full of energy and expression, yelling his lungs out whether they were winning or losing. But other than those games, very little sound came out of Robert.

It was his lack of expression that caused his proposal for marriage to mean so much. Robert planned the evening out on a ski boat in the middle of a lake. He had flowers, wine, and fried chicken he had picked up at a local diner. After they ate, he held her hand and said three words she would never hear again: "I love you." Then he asked her to marry him and she said yes. She was saying yes to a life of quiet devotion.

Over the years that followed, Robert was faithful to Esther and provided her with a comfortable living. He worked hard, took her on two vacations a year, and was generous with how much he budgeted for her clothes and other personal needs. When she was sick, he took care of her, and when she was excited about something that had happened that day, he listened intently. But up until the day he died, he had only said "I love you" one time—the night he asked Esther to marry him.

Esther and Robert are an extreme case of a man's difficulty in expressing himself—and in particular his feelings—to his spouse. Their story is radical in terms of Robert never telling his wife he loved her, but it is not that far out when we consider the number of men who struggle with how to communicate with women. In fact, it seems to be more the norm than the extreme. Like Robert, many men choose to express their feelings by working hard, remaining sexually faithful, and being a good father and husband. And while wives appreciate those efforts, they still long to hear their husbands verbalize not only their love, but also what they think about and feel. Unfortunately, that doesn't happen as much as it should.

WHAT WE KNOW ABOUT MEN COMMUNICATING WITH WOMEN

In her excellent book on what women need to know about men, *For Women Only*, author Shaunti Feldhahn asked the men she surveyed this question: "What is the one thing that you wish your wife/significant other knew, but you feel you can't explain to her or tell her?" She was "stunned" (her words—remember, she's a woman) at the response. Out of the hundreds of answers she received, one was dominant above all the others. Thirty-two percent of the men said, in so many words, "I want her to know how much I love her."[1]

The reason I point out that Feldhahn was both stunned and a woman is because I wouldn't be surprised if she thought, "Well, if you want your wife to know how much you love her, why don't you just tell her?" When she told a male colleague about the men's answer to her question, he said, "Men really do have an unspoken longing to be able to say or show 'I love you,' but they rarely feel successful at accomplishing it."[2]

Therein lies the problem—and the subject of this chapter. One of the secrets men harbor (and it's not really a secret; women are all too aware of it) is that they "feel frustrated trying to communicate with women." That question on our survey of 3,600 men received the fourth-highest positive response out of the twenty-five topics on the survey. Here are the numbers: 94 percent of the men said they are sometimes (47 percent), often (39 percent), or always (8 percent) frustrated in their efforts to communicate with women. Even if we take out the "sometimes" responses, that leaves nearly half (47 percent) the men who are often or always frustrated when they attempt to communicate with women.

This isn't anything new, of course. Men and women who have been in a relationship with each other of any depth at all have quickly discovered that "exchanging meanings" with each other is a challenge. *Redbook* magazine commissioned a survey of more than 2,100 men and women who had been married between ten and twelve years. Though all the respondents believed that communication was important, 31 percent of the women and 26 percent of the men thought their marriage was barely scraping by in that department. Out of seventeen components graded by respondents as to their necessity in marriage, these were the top four:

	WOMEN	MEN
Respect for each other	100 percent	99 percent
Trust	100 percent	99 percent
Honesty	100 percent	99 percent
Communication	99 percent	98 percent[3]

Obviously, everybody thinks communication is important, but not everybody thinks they're very good at it—an opinion shared by professional marriage counselors. A survey of 730 marriage counselors revealed that the number one cause of marital breakdown is "poor communication or the lack of meaningful communication." In fact, the first five out of the top ten factors in marital breakup were issues that could have been dramatically impacted by better communication.[4]

I believe that the reason this is such a hot-button issue in men's lives—women and wives, take note—is twofold: first, men don't think they have a problem communicating. If they believed this, how could they be successful in anything? In Chapter 7, we discussed the secret that men have a hard time talking about their feelings. But that's only one part of communication. When men are communicating at work, they do fine—or fine enough. It's at home where they seem to struggle. Which leads to the second reason: men are frustrated that they are perceived to be the "bad guys" in the communication process. The perception is that women are good communicators and men are not. They want to know why a woman's way of communicating is the "right" way and a man's is the "wrong way."

Here's how one man put it: "My wife is an expert on what is a 'feeling' and what isn't a 'feeling.' I have tried to tell her what is going on inside of me, and she tells me, 'But that's not a feeling.' Where is the book she uses to tell herself what is a feeling and what isn't? I feel like giving up if I'm never going to get it right."[5]

When men perceive that women and culture in general have already decided that they are the problem, they pull back with a "what's the use?" attitude.

WHAT COMMUNICATING WITH WOMEN MEANS TO MEN

It seems women want from men what America had in Ronald Reagan, our fortieth president: the Great Communicator. He gained that moniker by speaking simply and clearly, in a folksy, optimistic manner. He almost always spoke with a smile and loved to tell stories, share anecdotes, and use illustrations. Granted, Ronald Reagan had a career in radio, movies, and public speaking before becoming president. But that doesn't mean he was born knowing how to communicate. When he was a college student at age twenty-two, he memorized Franklin D. Roosevelt's (another great communicator) 1933 inaugural speech, the one in which FDR had said, "The only thing we have to fear is fear itself." He would practice delivering the speech using a broomstick for a microphone. And he loved Roosevelt's phrases like "rendezvous with destiny." Reagan biographer Lou Cannon said about the president, "The greatness of Reagan was not that he was in America, but that America was in him."[6]

That may be the key to any successful communication—that it is, first and foremost, a matter of the heart, a matter of wanting to be understood.

Communication skills can be learned and improved upon. Who hasn't heard the (probably apocryphal) accounts of Greece's greatest orator, Demosthenes? Suffering from a speech impediment as a youth, he was determined to be understood. So he filled his mouth with pebbles and forced himself to speak clearly. He recited verses while running. He spoke on the seashore over the deafening crash of the waves. Granted, at this point Demosthenes was learning to speak, not communicate. And there is a difference, as wives are quick to point out. But eventually Demosthenes became a communicator—the greatest orator in the land.

Any man who wants to learn to communicate with those who are important to him can do so. It's a matter of thinking in terms of foreign languages. All the effort, mistakes, experiences, embarrassments, dead ends, and frustrations one experiences when visiting a foreign country and attempting to communicate with the natives . . . that's what men and women learning to communicate is like. That's why Dr. John Gray named his best-selling book on male-female relationships *Men Are from Mars, Women Are from Venus*. The fifth chapter of his book, "Speaking Different Languages," may be the best single summary in print of the differences in how men and women communicate.

Here's a good example from the experience of psychiatrist Scott Haltzman. (If you don't laugh when you read this, then you're not normal.) When in college, Haltzman had just ended a serious relationship with a girlfriend in Booton. His best friend was giving him a ride back to their college town, and as they drove Haltzman was pouring out his heart to his friend. After several painful minutes of baring his devastated soul, his friend interrupted with a question: "Have you bought the textbooks for our histology class?"

What a classic guy move! It's the equivalent of a newly married young couple splurging on a big night out at the local burger joint. The wife is starry-eyed with romance, reveling in their lovesick-but-dirt-poor place in life, telling her new husband how much this night and their future mean to her. In the midst of her moist-eyed monologue, he interrupts, pointing to her plate: "You gonna eat that pickle?"

Haltzman was devastated by his friend's lack of compassion for his situation, but kept his feelings to himself. Later that week, he had a chance to relate the same story to another college friend—this one a female—as they sat on a park bench. This friend listened quietly to the story, barely speaking a word, as she heard how special the relationship had been and how difficult it was for it to end. When he finally finished, the young woman affirmed that he had indeed lost something special and that his pain was definitely understandable. That's all she said. But it was enough to introduce the future psychiatrist to the power of listening and communicating at the level of empathy and meaning—and how women by nature get it, while men often don't.[7]

I can identify at least nine reasons why communication is a challenge for men and women. Keep in mind, these are general differences, not faults in men or faults in women. But for any man who wants to communicate better with women, these ought to be considered.

1. Male-Female Differences

I'll let Haltzman summarize this point with a fascinating piece of research:

"Biologically, women are more attached to expression through words. Right from birth, girls are more attuned to verbal sounds and learn to speak earlier and have larger vocabularies than little boys. As they grow, the imbalance continues: The average woman uses seven thousand words in a day, using many gestures and up to five tones. Compare this to a man's paltry two thousand daily words with only three tones, and you can see the attachment women have to speech."[8]

This, of course, conjures up the stereotype of grunting and chest beating that has been applied to men by the satirists. But the fact remains: there are differences in how men and women communicate, *and for what purpose*. This latter difference underlies most communication problems between men and women. As Gray explains in numerous ways in his book, women use (lots of) words to communicate feelings, while men use (a few) words to communicate information. (If you want to take one thing from this chapter that could change your life, that's it.) For women, communication is a journey with no set destination; for men, communication is a straight-arrow freeway from Point A to Point B.

2. Personality Differences

Most adults have taken one kind or another of temperament or personality profiling test (e.g., Myers-Briggs, Performax, Keirsey™ Temperament Sorter®-II, and others). The Performax DISC test, for example, clearly reveals different communication styles: High-D types like to get to the bottom line as quickly as possible. High-S types like to savor the conversation. And High-C types like to cover every jot and tittle (driving High-Ds crazy). Whether you are male or female, personality type plays a part in how you communicate. Couples who take these kinds of tests together often shake their heads in amazement over the findings: "So *that's* why we talk so differently!"

3. Spiritual Differences

For the most part, a Christian should have a completely different perspective on relationships and character than a non-Christian. The New Testament says that qualities such as love, kindness, gentleness, self control, and patience should characterize the Christian—and presumably how a Christian communicates (Galatians 5:22–23). If there are marked spiritual differences between two people, those differences can definitely impact communication.

4. Background Differences

It's not rocket science to know that the communication patterns of our parents or guardians are likely to become our own default patterns. Since the majority of communication in life is done in "default" mode—that is, without thinking about it or planning exactly what we're going to say and how—our upbringing becomes a major factor in how we interact with others. Someone whose parents communicated openly and respectfully is going to bring an entirely different expectation about communication to marriage than someone who grew up in an environment where the parents communicated with monosyllabic utterances and the TV provided the only complete sentences.

5. Maturity Differences

A simple fact of life is that some people are more mature than others. Mature people don't fly off the handle, don't criticize, and don't clam up when conversations aren't going their way. Maturity is a subjective measure, to be sure, and people can be mature in different areas of life. Individuals can handle finances in a mature manner yet be immature in their communication skills; they can be diligent and responsible when it comes to work, but immature when it comes to expressing feelings, desires, concerns, and preferences. As people grow up in years, it should be expected that they'll also develop in communication skills (though this obviously isn't always the case).

6. Intentional Differences

Unfortunate as it is, people can use communication as a weapon or tool to inflict harm on others. If a wife suspects her husband of inappropriate behavior, she may intentionally communicate her suspicions in a hurtful way. Her husband may then intentionally close his communication door as a way to retaliate and defend himself against her attacks. Communication—or the lack of it—can be a symptom of underlying problems in a relationship.

7. Interest Differences

There was a time in this country when married couples' worlds were the same. They shared one goal on the homestead or family farm: survival. They each worked hard and contributed their skills to the same task, communicating all day about family and work matters. That doesn't mean they were great communicators, but it does mean that their interests overlapped almost completely.

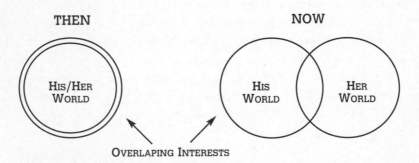

THEN   NOW

His/Her World   His World   Her World

OVERLAPING INTERESTS

Consider how times have changed. Today, the husband—or more likely, the husband and the wife—both leave home and are separated all day. They likely work in totally different worlds. They may have college degrees, even graduate degrees, in different subjects and speak different "languages" all day long. They come together at the end of the day and have to try to meld their different lives back into one before separating them again the next morning.

This is not noted as a negative or positive thing, merely a reality. The less overlap there is between two people's lives the more difficult it may be for them to find common ground—especially emotional ground—between them.

8. Conflict Differences

Conflicts are emotional events. How two people handle conflict is a reflection of many of the factors already cited: maturity, spiritual orientation, background, and others. The wise individual or couple is the one that steps back and says: "I'm making a mountain out of a molehill" (maturity), or "I swore I'd never act toward you the way my dad acted toward my mom" (background), or "You're right. I apologize. Would you forgive me for what I did?" (spiritual).

9. Knowledge Differences

Men and women who expand their understanding of communication—by reading books, going to seminars, getting counseling—will become better at it. Remember Ronald Reagan and Demosthenes. It is possible to learn to communicate and have such education bear fruit in our relationships. Every person is increasing his or her knowledge base in some area of life all the time: sports statistics, cooking skills, computer skills, home repairs. All of those skill sets require an investment of time, talent, and/or treasure. Those who invest time in increasing their communication skills will lower their frustrations levels markedly.

NEW DIRECTIONS

In the early 1990s, Dr. Barbara De Angelis wrote a *New York Times* bestseller for women about men. Her three secrets for communicating with us guys aren't just helpful tips for the women in our lives, they also remind us of truths we may already know but rarely consider or, more likely, express to those same women (I've added my thoughts following her main points):

1. Men communicate best when they have a focus for the conversation.

Most guys feel at ease in conversation when there's a clear reason or context for the dialogue. At work, we converse to get a project done. At home, we talk with our children to help them out with a situation. Obviously, this doesn't mean we need a clear-cut purpose every time we speak with others—that's both unhealthy and absurd. Communicating is one of the fundamental elements of being human, and that connection with others includes simply shooting the breeze or hanging out. Yet De Angelis' point suggests that, within the context of relating to women, we are often at our best when the point of conversation has been clearly defined. If that's something you struggle with in your relationships with women, let them know that you may work best given a spoken agenda.

2. Men internalize their thinking process and only communicate the end result.

Women tend to think out loud by talking; men tend to think silently by considering. Problems arise when both sides forget this mode of operation and expect the other to work on their terms. To avoid broken communication lines with certain women, talk with them about your needs in verbally sorting through a matter. Let them know that you'd prefer a time gap between the presentation of a subject and the conclusion they may be seeking. If they haven't already discovered it, help them know that you may need time to think before diving into a discussion with them.

3. Men don't have access to their emotions as easily as women do.[9]

It's not that we aren't emotional. We just don't wear our hearts on our sleeves the way most women do. Because we're generally more logic based, we're often slower to react with emotion. But don't buy into the belief that you don't truly feel something unless you express it outwardly. If the women in your life often thrust this expectation upon you, carefully and tactfully convey to them before deep conversations that just because you may not show your emotions the same way they do doesn't mean you don't care or are unimpassioned.

Sometimes it really does seem that, as Gray puts it, men and women are from different planets—at least when it comes to communicating. Still, it's possible for us to break through the "foreign language problems" we frequently encounter with women by remembering to stop and think before reacting and speaking. Just as we would consider our words carefully when speaking to someone from another country, we may need to use the same deliberation when discussing heart matters with our beloved female counterparts.

NEW CONNECTIONS

"Every living person, man or woman, is good at communicating about what's interesting to them," writes Patrick Morley.[10] I've never met a man yet who couldn't communicate articulately, thoroughly, and for extended periods of time about that for which he possessed a passion. Same for women. Men and women both like to talk about what they like to talk about. If those don't happen to be the same things at the same time (what are the odds?), then someone has to yield.

Maybe men and women need to make each other the focus of their interests. If both sexes like to talk about their interests and passions, then maybe they'd spend more time talking and listening if they were more interested and passionate about one another. When a wife says, "We never talk," and her husband replies, "What do you want to talk about?" the focus is on the wrong objective. Communication is a by-product of passion, something that happens without effort.

When husbands and wives purpose to become more passionate about one another, communication will take care of itself.

Chapter 16

PRAISE THE PERFORMANCE, LOVE THE MAN

I grew up in a home where performance brought praise and attention. Early on I realized it is what you do that really matters. When I entered my adult years, "doing" was far more important than "being."

As a result of being praised early on for my accomplishments, I learned to get things done and be successful. I felt good about myself when I accomplished a goal and felt bad when I failed. If I received negative feedback from or was disappointed by someone close to me, I took it as a judgment on my self-worth. I would revert back to my childhood and the absence of praise that followed failure. As an adult, if I gave all I had to a person or project and it still was not enough, I felt unloved, unappreciated, and taken for granted.

Over time I came to understand that I had codependent issues; I depended on others' praise of my performance in order to feel good about myself. I lived at the extremes: ecstasy when I succeeded or was approved, despondency when I failed or was taken for granted. As my career took me further into the realm of human behavior and psychology, I learned I was not the only man who felt this way. I knew brilliant therapists who lived under a standard by which the more they succeeded, the more they questioned what people really thought of them apart from their accomplishments.

When a man is only appreciated for what he does and not who he is, he begins to think of himself as a paycheck or meal ticket for others instead of a person.

WHAT WE KNOW ABOUT MEN'S FEELINGS OF BEING TAKEN FOR GRANTED

Mark Twain once said, "I can live for two months on a good compliment." As Dr. Gary Chapman points out, about six compliments a year would have gotten Twain through the average year in good shape.[1] And, believe it or not, that's probably true for most men. My impression of men through the years has been that they don't need daily "attaboys" for their existence to be validated or to feel appreciated for their contribution. But they do need *something*, some evidence that what they are doing and who they are is recognized and appreciated. And they need it consistently (which is different from frequently). Specifically, they need for their wives to communicate to them something that lets them know they are not being taken for granted.

When I began working on this chapter, I queried my own mental database—that reservoir of miscellaneous data about men, women, marriage, Christianity, and so on, that has been collected over years of reading, writing, and counseling. When I searched for the idea of being "taken for granted," the first and only thing my database returned was "women are often taken for granted by their husbands." This hit me as clearly as if it had popped up on my computer screen right in front of me.

And I couldn't argue. It's true that men sometimes take their wives for granted. But the more I thought about the concept, the more I wondered why I didn't get another mental return: "Husbands are often taken for granted by their wives." After all, a marriage is just two people. Isn't it equally likely that each would take the other for granted? And yet, upon reflection, I had to admit that being taken for granted—that is, not being cherished, adored, appreciated, and the like—was a pretty one-sided discussion from the perspective of my experience.

To see if it was my experience that was lopsided or whether I was, in fact, onto something, I turned to the final arbiter of all things data-worthy: not the Library of Congress, not the Bodleian Library at Oxford, not the Smithsonian Institute, but Google. I submitted several general searches looking for variations of "taken for granted" and was surprised when I scrolled through the results. The ones that had to do with relationships, or with men and women, all seemed to deal with the wife or woman being taken for granted; nothing about men being taken for granted.

So I dug deeper. I queried the exact phrase "taking husbands for granted" and got one return. *One!* Are you kidding me—there is but a single document on the entire Internet that contains the phrase "taking husbands for granted"? I then tried searching under "taking her husband for granted" and did a little better. There were a total of six documents returned, only one of which had anything to do with a devotional or practical approach to marriage. (With Google as my witness I immediately, as an act of solidarity with my underappreciated brethren of the world, began to feel taken for granted.)

At this point I concluded that my personal mental database had not been far off: most of what we think about when it comes to marriage is husbands taking wives for granted. But that is not an accurate reflection of what husbands are thinking about. When we conducted our own survey of 3,600 men, the fact that husbands don't feel "adored and cherished by their wives" returned the ninth-most positive responses out of the twenty-five survey questions. To this statement—"Men need to feel more intensely adored and cherished by their wives"—6 percent of the men said "always," and 29 percent said "often." Add in the 53 percent who said "sometimes" and that makes more than three-quarters of all the respondents.

Now, there is obviously more on the Internet about wives *cherishing* their husbands than what I implied above. But I hope you get my drift: we just don't tend to think of men needing to be appreciated as much as we do women.

WHAT BEING TAKEN FOR GRANTED MEANS TO MEN

There is a perception in life, especially in the Christian community, that men are strong and women are weak. The famous phrase that has become standardized in Christendom from the old King James Version of the Bible is that, of the two, the woman is the "weaker vessel" (1 Peter 3:7). This is obviously not a reference to any moral, spiritual, or intellectual standing given other Bible verses that place men and women on an equal plane (Galatians 3:28). It is a reference to physical stature alone. And in that sense, men are stronger and have therefore been seen as the protectors of women through the ages (except for those in the modern women's movement, of course).

Couple the characterization of weakness with the notion of the wife being responsible for submitting to the husband (Ephesians 5:22) and you have a combination ripe for misinterpretation and misapplication: weakness and servitude. Who is more likely to be taken for granted and taken advantage of than a servant who is too weak to fight back or demand her rights? Of course, that is a complete misappropriation of biblical truth. Neither women in general nor wives in particular are said in Scripture to be the servants of men or husbands. And I don't know any man who considers women weak in spirit. While their bodies may not have as many fleshly muscle fibers as a man, they bear the same image of God that men do and are therefore just as formidable in their own right.

But trends and characterizations happen over time. And over time the idea has developed that men are more likely to take women for granted than vice versa. I may not be able to prove that belief untrue. Yet even if it is, it doesn't negate the idea that men need and long for the same kind of affirmation, encouragement, cherishing, and appreciation from their wives or significant others as women do.

In fact, I think this is one of the most deeply hidden of men's secrets. I would imagine there are very few wives whose husbands have said to them, "Babe, I really need to know that you appreciate what I do for our family. I know I'm not perfect, but I'm home every night instead of out on the town; I don't gamble away the rent money; I'm at work every morning to provide for you and the kids; and I'm working on getting my cholesterol down so I don't keel over from a heart attack. Those things are worth something, right?"

If a wife does hear those kinds of appeals from her husband, it's more likely in an explosive retaliation after being reminded that he still hasn't learned to take out the garbage without being asked. When a volcano erupts, it's an obvious sign that something's been cooking beneath the surface for a long time. And I think what's brewing, in many cases, is this tri-une secret: men sometimes feel they're taken for granted; men sometimes feel they get little or no recognition for the good choices they make and the good work they do; and men sometimes feel that they are viewed as wallets, as vending machines, to which their wives and children come to get the provisions they need on their way out the door to their own happy life.

Dr. Emerson Eggerichs, in his excellent book *Love & Respect*, says this about men:

> Wives must grasp that their husbands aren't half as big and strong and impervious to being hurt as they might seem. A woman may envision herself as a sweet little dewdrop and her man as a big, strong bear who should be able to absorb any kind of punishment. One huge fellow was stunned by his beloved's attack and said to her, "You hate me."
>
> Frustrated, she replied, "When I scream 'I hate you,' you should know I don't mean it. You are 6'9" and weigh 260 pounds, for goodness' sake. I do that because you can take it." The truth is, however, a lot of men can't take it. No matter how big they may be physically, emotionally they are vulnerable to what sounds like contempt.[2]

There it is—a perfect example of the misconception that because men are "big" and "strong," they have their own self-appreciation system going, a built-in reservoir of pats-on-the-back that makes them automatic when it comes to performing life's duties. Women sometimes forget that life is a series of choices for men, just as it is for women. They don't *have* to choose to do the right things for their families. When they do choose correctly, it's because their internal value system has assigned worth to preserving their relationships with their wives and children, a choice for which they deserve to be commended. The whole concept of "well done, good and faithful servant" (Matthew 25:21, 23) is an indication that God appreciates good choices and rewards them with commendation—given out to women *and* men. If God commends both, it's likely a good sign that commendation is needed by both.

Patrick Morley reprinted a letter sent to him by a man whose wife got this notion. Having been married for thirteen years, this particular man was leaving for a weeklong business trip. When he arrived at his motel and began unpacking his suitcase, he found the following note from his wife:

"I love you, honey! Thank you for being such a special husband. Someone who cares about his family enough to get up at early hours and go to work to support them. A man who spends much of his time and energy with his son and his friends, teaching them. A man who spends time with the Lord each day to lead us in Christ.

How wonderful that the Lord led me to you! I pray for you daily, my love. I thank him for you, that he gave you to me to spend my life with. I pray that he will give you strength and peace and joy. I hope this week goes quickly for all of us. I pray God keeps you safe. I love you more now, honey, than the day I said "till death do us part."[3]

The man said he kept that note tucked in his Bible to pull out and read whenever he needed encouragement and affirmation. What man wouldn't? That wife understood the reality of road trips for the husband who travels. Many wives think these trips consist of expense accounts, great food, and high times—a vacation from work that they don't get. In fact, men who travel frequently will say just the opposite. For the most part, they'd rather be at home sleeping in their own beds than schlepping in and out of generic hotels in unfamiliar cities, battling loneliness and the temptations that come with it. The wife who commends her husband for paying that price goes a long way toward letting him know his faithfulness isn't taken for granted.

A man that Dr. Gary Rosberg and his wife knew at their church was going through a rough period at his job. Indeed, his job and career were on the line. When a man's job is threatened or terminated, for whatever reason, it can be terribly emasculating. It's like telling a warrior to go fight a battle and defeat the enemy without giving him a sword. Because so much of a man's identity and self-confidence comes from his work, when that work is taken away, a man's self-image is devastated. And it's just as hard for the wife. Not only does she see the man she loves suffering, but she silently worries about financial security and the future. It's a tough situation when both husband and wife are weak, vulnerable, and worried. For that reason Dr. Rosberg and his wife came alongside this couple in a supportive way.

But what they saw was a wife who rallied in support of her man. She decided to focus on affirming her husband despite the difficult season he was in. She stepped outside the self-fueling downward cycle and began injecting encouragement into him. Here's Dr. Rosberg's description of what he observed over the following weeks:

As we've kept in contact with this couple, we have seen Jody responding just the way she needs to:

- She is reminding her husband of God's grace.
- She is drawing the kids close to Todd in the midst of this struggle.
- She is calling Todd's buddies to tell them that they need to be
- present in Todd's life.
- She is on her knees praying.
- She is right beside him, as close as she can be, encouraging him.

That's what an encouraging wife does, in the tough times and the good times. This is what those wedding vows are all about—to love, honor, and cherish.[4]

And it's amazing what that kind of affirmation does to a man. Many women have learned that, while one way to a man's heart may be through his stomach, another way is definitely through his shoulders—that is, with a loving arm draped over them and an affirming word whispered in his ear.

Chapman relates how a woman poked her head in his office one day and asked for a minute of his time. She was at her wit's end with her husband. For nine months she had been after him to paint a bedroom in their home, and it still wasn't done. Anytime he had free time, she would interrupt whatever he was doing and remind him that he could be painting the bedroom. Chapman asked, "Are you certain that your husband knows that you want the bedroom painted?" Since it was obvious the husband knew after nine months of reminders, Chapman urged her to drop the subject: "You don't have to tell him anymore. He already knows."

Instead of reminding her husband of the unpainted bedroom, the woman was told to begin a gradual process of thanking her husband for the good things he did for their family. Whether it was taking out the garbage, paying the bills—whatever. "Every time he does anything good, give him a verbal compliment," she was advised. With a marked lack of enthusiasm for this plan, she agreed.

Three weeks later, she stopped by Chapman's office to report that the bedroom—after nine months of nagging and three weeks of complimenting—was painted.[5]

Affirmation is the key to a man's heart. When a man thinks he is being taken for granted and not appreciated, he develops a "why bother?" perspective. It's not that he stops doing what all men do best—working, conquering, achieving, driving forward—*it's that he stops doing them for the benefit of those for whom he wants to do them, those he loves.* All too often something terrible happens: a man discovers someone else who affirms and appreciates what he does—someone who (it appears) doesn't take him for granted—and begins directing his efforts to that person. We all know the terrible results that follow.

Working backward, is an unappreciative wife responsible for her husband's infidelity? Absolutely not! But the tapestry of life is sewn with a thousand threads, any one of which have the capacity to alter the final appearance a little or a lot. Looking back, one never knows what might have been if . . .

NEW DIRECTIONS

As task- and goal-oriented beings, men like to be rewarded. We thrive upon working for a defined prize, even when that reward is simply a kind word of praise from our wives. Again, this isn't necessary every time we set out to complete an assignment (if so, we've got some performance issues); but it is needed every once in a while to keep us motivated and to remind us why we work in the first place.

I've seen men who suffered from a lack of appreciation from their wives. And I've watched other guys who were flat-out taken for granted. They amounted to little more than cash cows—and their marriages showed it. After years of working hard with no pats on the back, many of them wore away with bitterness and, eventually, hatred toward their wives—even their own children.

So what can you do if you fear your relationship with your wife is headed in this direction? Worse yet, what if your wife already seems to be silent when it comes to expressing her thanks for your hard work?

First, it's important to remember you can never force anyone to offer a true compliment. Thanksgiving and appreciation stems from the heart. We all know the difference between a heartfelt thank-you and a hollow one. Because of this, vow not to attempt to manipulate your wife into praising your actions.

Second, check your own heart. Have you become bitter over your wife's apparent attitude of ungratefulness? Has it begun to taint why you serve your family? If you find yourself grumbling as you wake up and head off to work *every day* or every time you're forced to sacrifice something for the sake of providing for them, it's definitely time for change. Talk to your wife about this. Open up about how you feel. You can't expect her to read your mind; in fact, she may not even be aware that she hasn't complimented you in a long time.

Along the same lines, make sure you're giving out free praise as well. It's foolish to expect verbal accolades from your wife if she hasn't received one from you all month or, in the worst case, all year. Appreciation flourishes when it's reciprocal, so shower her with kind words. Remember the woman who visited Dr. Chapman's office? Her husband didn't move an inch toward painting their bedroom until she began making an effort to commend him for his daily work. It may be the same case with your wife. Are you man enough to be the first one to offer unconditional, unprovoked words of kindness?

NEW CONNECTIONS

"To admire a man is to regard him with wonder, delight, and pleased approval," writes best-selling author Dr. John Gray in his classic book, *Men Are from Mars, Women Are from Venus*. "A man feels admired when [his wife] is happily amazed by his unique characteristics or talents, which may include humor, strength, persistence, integrity, honesty, romance, kindness, love, understanding, and other so-called old-fashioned virtues. When a man feels admired, he feels secure enough to devote himself to his woman and adore her."[6]

Allow me to direct the next few paragraphs specifically to wives. If you are already in the habit of affirming your husband, you need do nothing but continue your good work. Most likely your husband is already confident and feeling anything but taken for granted. Yet two considerations remain for those wives who, for whatever reason, are not in the habit of affirming their husbands.

First, you may be at a place where you can't see your husband's good points and good works. You may think there's little to affirm—but there is. Any wife can take paper and pencil and quickly make a list of a dozen or more of her husband's characteristics or behaviors for which he can be commended: he works, he repairs things around the house, he washes the dishes, he reads or plays with your children. . . . If that list is difficult to write, think of the things you're happy he *doesn't* do. The opposite of every one of those things is an admirable trait.

Second, once you have made that list, you can begin to work on *slowly* (emphasis on slowly) integrating your appreciation into your relationship with your husband. If he isn't used to receiving compliments from you, will he be suspicious? Probably. But, over time, when he sees your appreciation is genuine and there to stay, will he appreciate it? Absolutely.

Any wife who chooses to encourage her husband through affirmation and appreciation will soon discover that she will reap what she has sown. Which brings me to a closing point: why all the emphasis on showing appreciation to men? Don't women need to be shown that they are not taken for granted as well? Of course. But this is a book on secrets men keep. And a deep secret men keep is that they often feel taken for granted.

The law of reciprocity that God has built into His creation says, "Give, and it will be given unto you." When someone—husband or wife—decides to put that law to the test with a pure heart, it will set in motion a self perpetuating cycle of blessing. Husbands and wives can feed off each other's appreciation for the rest of their lives together if one will have the courage to begin by faith. The connection that results will be unbreakable.

Chapter 17

A MATTER OF RESPECT

Mark appeared to have it all together. He had done a lot in his life and was admired by many. He was one of those men who could light up a room when he walked in. He had a confidence and a presence that exuded self-assurance. On the outside he looked like the least likely guy to struggle with low self-esteem, yet he did.

I asked Mark who he talked to the most and his answer was both surprising and creative. He said he talked the most to himself. He admitted that all his life there had been a running dialogue in the back of his head questioning every move, commenting on every relationship, and evaluating all that he did or did not do. The internal dialogue was torture to him; it shaded all that he did. The air of confidence he projected was manufactured to act as a muffle to suppress the noise in his head.

Mark had been raised in a Christian home, or at least a churchgoing home. But Mark's mother wasn't exactly the greatest model of how to have a biblical relationship between husband and wife. She was obsessed with herself and her needs and gave very little to Mark's dad. If there was an ounce of respect for him, she never showed it. Mark listened through thin walls as she lectured his father. His father never argued with her because she would not allow it. She would shut him down and demand that he just listen to her. She also openly criticized and tried to control him in front of others. His mother's controlling comments and biting criticisms became scripts for Mark's internal dialogues. It was virtually impossible for him to *not* hear them.

Mark's goal in finding a marriage partner was to avoid anyone who was like his mother. But as often happens, he could not help himself and ended up in a relationship much like his parents'. Before he and his wife married he felt like a king, but afterward her criticism and anger roared and raged. It was so devastating to him that he considered suicide. He could not imagine spending the rest of his life in the "hell" he was in.

When men with a measure of character are trapped in a relationship in which there is no respect from a wife, they usually don't retaliate with an affair or kill their pain with booze or drugs. Instead, they simply absorb the disrespect and live in despair, often wanting to end it all but never justifying violating their marriage vows.

After meeting Mark and getting to know him, I wondered what kind of "hell" his wife was raised in where a woman learns that a man is to be used rather than respected, where a woman learns to take what she can rather than honor what a man can provide. It must have been a pretty sad existence, maybe even worse than Mark's.

When a man lives without respect from a woman, he lives without the fourth-most important thing to him as a human being—the first three being oxygen, water, and food. Yes, for men respect is that important.

WHAT WE KNOW ABOUT MEN AND RESPECT

Everybody knows that Rodney Dangerfield "got no respect." He said that his twin brother forgot his birthday . . . that when he called the suicide prevention hotline they tried to talk him into it . . . that his bank offered him a free gift if he'd close his account . . . that his doctor told him, "With a face like yours you don't need a vasectomy" . . . that when he was drowning and screaming for help the lifeguard told him to hold it down.

We can all identify with Rodney at some level. But there is a large category of the population that would say "Amen!" to his laments: men—and especially married men. They feel like their need for respect has gotten lost amidst the world's predominant interest in love. Not that men are against love. Whereas for women love is spelled l-o-v-e, for men love is spelled r-e-s-p-e-c-t. Women get love directly, but for men there's a detour involved; love is only received via respect. And most men feel that women miss that detour altogether.

In our survey of 3,600 men we made this statement: "Men need to be more greatly respected by women." Twenty-five percent of the men surveyed said they feel that way "often," while 8 percent said they feel that way "always." Another 52 percent felt disrespected "sometimes." I found it interesting that Christian men felt more disrespected (34.3 percent) than non-Christian men (28.7 percent).

There's a subtle secret going on here. If we were to substitute the word *love* in our original survey statement—"Men need to be more greatly *loved* by women"—women viewing the results (85 percent responding positively to some degree) would likely say, "So? I feel the same way. I need to feel more loved too." In other words, because love is a woman's greatest need, she might view men as simply responding likewise and say, "Okay, we're even. We both need the same thing."

What is surprising to women—and this is the secret men carry—is that love and respect aren't the same things (more on this later). In fact, women are very surprised, if not shocked, to learn that men feel such a deep need to be respected. This is something they don't always comprehend: "Love I get; respect I don't."

Author Shaunti Feldhahn describes going to a retreat shortly after graduating from college. The speaker divided the attendees into two groups: men on one side of the room, women on the other. He asked both groups which of two bad situations they would choose if they had to make a choice: one, to feel alone and unloved, or, two, to feel inadequate and disrespected. She remembers thinking what a simple choice that was—who would ever want to feel unloved?

But when the leader asked the men how many of them would choose to feel unloved over feeling disrespected, the women in the room let out an audible gasp. The majority of the men's hands were raised. Only a few men said they'd rather be disrespected than unloved. When the leader turned to the women, the results were exactly the opposite: the majority of women said they'd rather be disrespected than unloved.

When Feldhahn commissioned her own surveys on men for her book, she included this question, and the results were similar to the unofficial survey at the retreat she had attended. Seventy-four percent of the men said they would choose being alone and unloved over inadequate and disrespected. Twenty-six percent chose the opposite.

When she was beta testing the survey questions, she received unusual comments about this particular survey question. Some men didn't think there was a difference in the two choices. Since the difference between love and respect was totally clear to her, she wrestled with this problem—until the light bulb went on: For a man, love and respect are one and the same. That is, "If a man feels disrespected, he is going to feel unloved."[1]

Emerson Eggerichs, who has written the bible on the difference between love and respect in marriage, contributed the following question to the survey Feldhahn used with men:

Even the best relationships sometimes have conflicts on day-to-day issues. In the middle of a conflict with my wife/significant other, I am more likely to be feeling . . .

a. That my wife/significant other doesn't respect me right now.

b. That my wife/significant other doesn't love me right now.

Eighty-one percent of the men chose "a" and 19 percent chose "b."[2]

This chapter is about why men want respect need respect—and how it makes them feel loved when they get it. The secret for women to discover is that when they love men the way they (women) want to be loved, it leaves men with a deficit that only one thing can fill: respect.

WHAT RESPECT MEANS TO MEN

I said above that our culture is more about love than respect. Actually, a lot more. Don't write me about the validity of this research method, but for the sake of discovering more about these subjects I put each of those two words into Google to see what would happen. There were 1.78 billion returns for *love* and 756 million returns for *respect*. What does that mean? Nothing definitive, of course. But at the very least it means that in our world love gets discussed (the word gets used) more than twice as often as respect.

I wasn't surprised by the results of that simple piece of research.

Somehow love gets more press, especially in the Christian community. The word *love* appears 551 times in the NIV Bible, while *respect* appears thirty-two times. In the Bible we're told that God is love, not *respect* (1 John 4:8); we have a whole chapter devoted to love (1 Corinthians 13) and none devoted to respect; we are told to love God and our neighbors, not respect them (Matthew 22:37–40).

But when it comes to the most extensive passage in the Bible on husbands and wives we find something interesting. Nowhere in Ephesians 5:22–33 are wives told to love their husbands.[3] Husbands are told to love their wives, but wives are told to respect their husbands: "However, each one of you also must love his wife as he loves himself, and the wife must respect her husband" (v. 33). To get the full contrast between those two responsibilities, read the verse in the Amplified Bible, a translation that offers an expanded version in English of the Bible's meaning in its original languages:

"However, let each man of you [without exception] love his wife as [being in a sense] his very own self; and let the wife see that she respects and reverences her husband [that she notices him, regards him, honors him, prefers him, venerates, and esteems him; and that she defers to him, praises him, and loves and admires him exceedingly]."

In 1984, Tina Turner asked in song, "What's Love Got to Do with It?" There are probably many women who'd like to ask, "What's respect got to do with it?" We've seen a lot of prominent men do little to earn respect in recent years. Beginning with our forty-second president's sexual trysts in the Oval Office to the failure of some of America's largest corporations due to accounting scandals—corporations run by men, and, in at least three cases, men who were outspoken Christians—women are heard to say, "Puh-lease. I'll show some respect when men do something respectful."

When wives find themselves married to someone they profess to love but not to like, the respect factor falls away. In other words, women view respect as something to be earned, while they don't feel that way about love. Love is to be unconditional; respect is to be earned. But for a man, respect should be as unconditional as is love.

Emerson Eggerichs has often asked men, "Does your wife love you?" and they say, "Of course."

"Does she like you?"

"Nope."

When he counsels women who say, "I love my husband but don't respect him," Eggerichs asks, "What if your husband said, 'I respect you but don't love you'?" Women are horrified at this turn of the tables. Yet they feel it is completely acceptable to tell their husbands that they love them but don't respect them.[4]

He goes on to say, "In many cases, the wife's dislike is interpreted by the husband as disrespect and even contempt. In his opinion, she has changed from being the admiring, ever-approving woman she was when they courted. Now she doesn't approve, and she's letting him know it. So the husband decides he will motivate his wife to become more respectful by acting in an unloving way. This usually proves about as successful as trying to sell a pickup to an Amish farmer."

At that point something begins that Eggerichs calls the "Crazy Cycle": The man doesn't feel respected, so he tries to motivate his wife by withholding love. She feels unloved and tries to motivate her husband by withholding respect. And so the downward cycle begins.[5] For many couples this power struggle has gone on for decades; their marriage has become characterized by it. All because they don't understand that the cycle can become self-perpetuating in a positive direction if they will only reverse the trend. Love can stimulate respect, which stimulates more love, which stimulates more respect, and so on.

Marriage researcher Dr. John Gottman describes it this way: "Such interactions can produce a vicious cycle, especially in marriages with high levels of conflict. The more wives complain and criticize, the more husbands withdraw and stonewall; the more husbands withdraw and stonewall, the more wives complain and criticize."[6]

Often the result of such bitter tit-for-tat living is divorce.

The story of the Roman centurion who sought Jesus' healing for his servant is a good paradigm to understand how men think about respect (Luke 7:1–10). Jesus was going to go to the soldier's home when the centurion sent word to Jesus that it wasn't necessary for Him to be there personally. The soldier understood the nature of authority—that if Jesus just gave the "order," the servant would be healed. Jesus and the centurion thought alike about authority—different domains, but the same principle.

Men think about respect for themselves the same way they think about respect in the military. (Which is why so many men identify with the military, no doubt.) In the armed forces, respect is given to the uniform and what it stands for: the frozen Delaware winter of the American Revolution, mustard gas and trench warfare in World War I, Normandy in World War II, and Hamburger Hill in Vietnam. It stands for men who, while maybe not liking each other personally in camp, would risk their lives for each other in combat. It stands for a given, an unconditional principle upon which the safety of the nation depends.

Men think of respect in marriage the same way, as an unconditional principle upon which the safety of the marital union depends. Husbands see themselves as wearers of the uniform of manhood, a uniform that deserves unconditional respect even if the person wearing it may not. (To keep the scales balanced here, women see themselves as wearers of the uniform of womanhood, a uniform that deserves unconditional love even if the person wearing it may not.)

When wives fail to respect their husbands, they do a disservice to something far bigger than the "carbon-based life-form" with whom they exchanged wedding vows. They do a disservice to an institution God designed to run on the fuel of respect. (Again, the same is true for men who fail to love their wives.) When men don't get the fuel they need from their wives they do what any fuel-based system does: they lose power and eventually quit. And if the fuel of respect is provided from an alternate source, it's often enough to jump-start them into action.

Author and marriage guru Dr. Willard F. Harley Jr. counseled a couple where respect was in short supply for the husband, a commercial artist. Before their marriage, the wife had heaped praise upon her future husband's artistic talents—and continued to do so after they were married, urging him to pursue a career as an artist and develop his potential. The husband interpreted her urgings as dissatisfaction with who he was at present and began to resent her efforts. As the years went by, he found himself paired at work with a female graphic designer who showered praise and respect upon him for his hard work and his skills as a commercial artist. Finally someone respected him for who he was, not who he might be.[7]

You can guess the sad ending to this story. It illustrates the power of respect in a man's life. Respect is the fuel his engine runs on, and if he is not careful about the source he can end up in serious trouble.

NEW DIRECTIONS

Early in this chapter we distinguished between the two ways men and women define love: for women, it's love; for men, it's respect. Most of our discussion centered on men not being respected enough and therefore not feeling loved. Often, however, we men are guilty of forgetting the flip side of this coin. We prefer to mope around with Rodney Dangerfield attitudes, taking solace only in our equally disrespected brethren. But the truth is, there may be a logical reason why we're missing out on respect from our wives: we're not loving!

The apostle Paul's words in Ephesians 5:22–33 aren't just a primer for wives. Within a handful of verses, he states no less than four times, "Husbands, love your wives." This isn't rocket science. To get love (which, in our case, is respect) requires giving love. And whether you're single, a newlywed, or have been married for forty years, loving that special someone involves a universal yet entirely unique ingredient: loving her the way *she* wants to be loved.

Just as each woman was created to look different, each was made to be loved in her own special way. Don't do the typical "man" thing and toss out generic signs of affection. Show your woman that she matters simply because she is who she is. Discover (or in the case of relationship veterans, remind yourselves) what things matter the most to her, what she appreciates receiving from you the most. And remember, this has little, if anything, to do with your preferences. Often men will hold back on what they give because they're uncomfortable with how women want to be loved. Allow me to offer a reminder: true love is, by its very nature, selfless. Aspiring to that kind of love in both words and actions could transform you from a Dangerfield impersonator to a general among your own troops.

NEW CONNECTIONS

We have already discussed in this book the concept of languages and cultures. When it comes to respect women must take this as a language and culture to be learned, one that is not native to them. (Just as husbands must do with the language and culture of love.) A natural question to ask, then, is this: why did God create men and women with these different languages and culture? Wouldn't it have been easier if both husbands and wives fed off the same value or need?

The reason men and women need different fuels is so they feed one another as a perpetual motion machine. When each gives what the other needs, a mysterious, contrapuntal dance begins—two distinctly melodic lines that play off one another to create a beautiful harmony.

If this is not happening now in your marriage, then ask yourself, Who will begin the dance? Who will put his or her foot forward first?

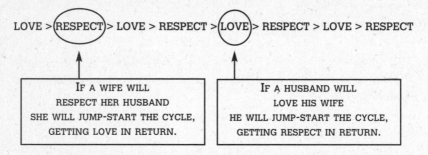

LOVE > RESPECT > LOVE > RESPECT > LOVE > RESPECT > LOVE > RESPECT

IF A WIFE WILL
RESPECT HER HUSBAND
SHE WILL JUMP-START THE CYCLE,
GETTING LOVE IN RETURN.

IF A HUSBAND WILL
LOVE HIS WIFE
HE WILL JUMP-START THE CYCLE,
GETTING RESPECT IN RETURN.

Whether you are a husband or wife reading these words, they are for you. Truth is no respecter of gender or persons.

Chapter 18

MEETING HER NEEDS

David was married to Sharon for five years when he uncovered her affair with an old acquaintance. David had spent those five years trying to give his wife what she wanted and needed. He was involved in every way he knew how, but nothing he did seemed to meet her needs. She wanted to control his words, his actions, and where he went. So he gave her that control. He stopped saying things that upset her. He stopped doing things that she did not like. He reported in no matter where he went. He gave her the control she wanted and said she needed in order to feel attached and secure in their love. Then, after he had given it to her, she walked outside the marriage and attached herself to a person from her past.

When David went into counseling he was told that he had contributed to the affair. His counselor said that if he had tried to connect with his wife, she would not have strayed. This was hard for him to hear, given all he had done to try to please her. It wasn't like he had ignored her; he gave her everything. So he switched counselors.

The second counselor told him something that made more sense. He said he had not contributed to the affair—she was the only one responsible for the affair—but he had contributed to the problems in the marriage. He could accept that and began to grow comfortable with the counselor.

The toughest thing the counselor told him was that it was his responsibility to forgive her for what she had done, knowing full well that it might happen again, because his wife was so ambivalently attached to him that it would be hard for him to ever meet her real needs.

Sharon's father had abandoned her at age fourteen. One day he was home and the next day he was gone, never to come back again. She felt abandoned, isolated, out of control, and alone. She also felt shame for anything she had ever done that would make her father unhappy enough to leave. To make amends, she took it all on herself and began to take control of everything she could. Because she never healed from her father-wound, David took the impact full-force when she married.

Meanwhile, David was not the most secure man in the world. He wondered how he measured up against other men. He doubted his sexual competency. He longed to make a woman happy because when he did, he felt adequate. But he picked a woman who would not be made happy. She was only content when she was in total control. She was only secure when the whole world was responding to her as predicted. She was an empty chasm of needs that was so large no man could meet them completely. And as she found out, not even two men could help her.

David accepted the reality of who she was and why he had been attracted to her. He came to realize that he had been feeding into her need for control and in the process had lost himself. He had also become a "role player" rather than a man. She had watched him go from a man with stature to a wimp who allowed himself to be ordered around. In trying to meet her needs, he had made their marriage worse. While attempting to please her, he had destroyed her respect for him. And in the process, he never fully understood what it was that she really needed.

WHAT WE KNOW ABOUT MEN MEETING WOMEN'S NEEDS

The men at Gordon MacDonald's church were gathering for their monthly First Monday (night) meeting—a talk by Gordon followed by food and the Monday night football game. As the men were talking and drinking coffee before the meeting began, a man approached Gordon and handed him a book-sized gift in wrapping paper. "A woman at the door gave me this and asked me to give it to you," he said. Gordon took the wrapping paper off to find a book titled *Everything Men Know About Women*. Opening it he found exactly one hundred blank pages containing not a single word.

Later, as Gordon was introducing his talk, he showed the gift to the large crowd of men. Some laughed—but some didn't. He writes, "Is the woman's 'gift' a practical joke or a serious message? None of us know. But it does concentrate the male mind."[1]

After thirty years of research into the feminine soul, renowned psychoanalyst Sigmund Freud is reputed to have said that he was still unable to answer one great question: what does a woman want?[2]

One of the largest efforts to gather data that might have helped Dr. Freud was *A National Survey of Families and Households*. The NSFH surveyed five thousand married couples in various years from 1987 to 2003 to gather a broad range of information on family life from which researchers in various disciplines might draw conclusions and make applications.[3] In March, 2006, two University of Virginia sociologists, W. Bradford Wilcox and Steven L. Nock, published a NSFH-based report regarding the key factors leading to wives' happiness in marriage. Here are some of the findings they reported:

- The single most important factor in a wife's marital happiness is her husband's emotional engagement—how affectionate and understanding he is and how much quality time they spend as a couple.
- "I was very surprised to find that even egalitarian-minded women are happier when their marriages are organized along more gendered lines" (Wilcox).
- Contrary to academic conventional wisdom, wives are happiest in their marriages when husbands earn 68 percent or more of the couple's income (provided the husbands are also emotionally engaged).
- Wives who don't work outside the home are happier than wives who do.
- Wives who share a strong commitment to lifelong marriage with the same man (marriage is a "lifetime relationship and should never be ended except under extreme circumstances") are happier than wives whose commitment is weaker. Shared commitment leads to

mutual trust and higher emotional investment from husbands, both factors that lead to wives' happiness.

• Wives who think the division of housework in their marriage is fair are happier than wives who think their husbands don't do their fair share. It should be noted that this doesn't necessarily mean a fifty-fifty division of housework. Because the happiest wives view their husbands as working hard to earn the family's finances, they are happy with doing more than half the housework and consider that to be "fair."

• Wives with more traditional views on marriage (e.g., women should take the lead in caring for home and children, and husbands should take the lead in earning) are happier.

• "Conventional and academic wisdom now suggests that the 'best' marriages are unions of equals. Our work suggests that the reality is more complicated. . . . We interpret our results to suggest that part-ners need to pay more attention to how their partners feel about their relationship and about marriage generally because equality does not necessarily produce equity" (Nock).[4]

The above information is obviously helpful in assessing the big picture of what women want and need (that is, what makes wives happy). It's all too easy to grab a sound bite from the media and draw the conclusion that women are following the instructions of broadcaster Howard Beale in the 1976 movie *Network*: "So I want you to get up now. I want all of you to get up out of your chairs. I want you to get up right now and go to the window. Open it, and stick your head out, and yell, '*I'm as mad as h—, and I'm not going to take this anymore!*'"[5]

Based on the NSFH study there are apparently a good many wives who are happy in their marriages. But there are also many men who would agree with Dr. Freud—they're not sure what women want, and they're equally uncertain with what to do to meet their wives' needs. When we proposed to the 3,600 men in our study that "men feel inadequate in meeting women's needs (emotional, spiritual, or sexual), a mere 2 percent said "always," 21 percent said "often," and 60 percent said "sometimes." That's a total of 83 percent who are confused, at least part of the time, about how to make the contributions to their wives' lives that they feel they should make.

WHAT MEETING WOMEN'S NEEDS MEANS TO MEN

I'm going to make this chapter as simple as I can by saying that no one really knows what women need. Conversely, no one knows what men need. If I knew the answer to those questions I'd write one short book on each and then retire to a tropical island with my gazillions of dollars in book royalties. Unless something happens to men like what happened to Mel Gibson in the 2000 movie *What Women Want*—where as a result of an electric shock he suddenly had the ability to "hear" what women were thinking—we are going to remain clueless. Clueless, that is, except for one strategy: asking.

I don't know what kind of woman Eve was in the Garden of Eden. Did she have a multifaceted personality that Adam had to figure out, or was a woman a woman, like Gertrude Stein's "a rose is a rose is a rose"? While we're not likely to know the answer to that question, this we do know: there is no such thing as "woman"—a generic biped, a clone of which becomes the wife of every man who marries. We can generalize certain things about women as a gender: they are emotional, they like to communicate verbally and intimately, and they like to be cherished and honored.

Someone who just read those words is right now either disagreeing with me ("My wife is nothing like that!") or calling me a chauvinist ("That is so last century!"). See? As soon as you lay down even a few principles for what women (or men) are like, someone will rise up and disagree.

General principles obtained from years of surveys and observations are a safe place to start. But men who want to decrease their frustration level and move themselves from the "always," "often," or "sometimes" categories on the next survey to the "rarely" or "never" categories need to begin an intensive process of discovery. To be honest, it doesn't matter what it takes to meet the needs of women. It only matters what it takes to meet the needs of the woman in your life.

Every married man is joined to a person who is more complex than a NASA space shuttle—by a mile. Besides the fact that the human brain is infinitely more complex than anything else known to man, it has had several decades of outside influences by the time a woman is settled into marriage. Think of all the things that could have influenced a wife in her developmental years (some of which a husband may not even know about):

praise vs. criticism, wealth vs. poverty, health vs. sickness, large family vs. small family, school experiences, sexual experiences (voluntary and forced), intelligence, self-image, role models (of womanhood, manhood, and marriage), emotional comfort vs. pain, abuse of various kinds, and on and on.

Every woman's life map is different, and as a result, no two women are alike. That means that every man's wife is like a delicate flower that spends years unfolding, revealing the beauty and grace—and perhaps scars and developmental wounds—within. Wouldn't it be nice if husbands and wives, on their wedding day, in addition to exchanging rings and vows, could hand each other a book titled *My Life So Far*? In it would be everything—including a chapter titled "How to Meet My Needs"—each person knew to reveal to his or her spouse about themselves, making the "getting to know you" process that much easier.

Alas, that doesn't happen. So couples end up in a dance (or a joust) for years trying to understand the "real" person they married. Every woman has experienced the post-courtship dismay that comes when the guy that smelled like Ralph Lauren before the wedding smells like a gym bag after. And the man discovers that the woman who had a face as smooth as a baby's only got it that way with a half hour of work every morning. And those surprises are the easy ones. The hard ones are the deep ones—the emotional ones that only become visible as the petals of the flower slowly open over the years, revealing sometimes long-held secrets.

There are two parts to the flower-opening revelation: the opening itself and the observing of what is revealed. Flowers have to open up; wives don't. Even when they do open up, husbands aren't always sensitive enough to see what is revealed and take it to heart. I have a feeling that the secret men harbor—that they don't know how to meet their wives' needs—is due more to the latter than the former. I think men often miss out on the fact that their wives are revealing who they are all the time—even in the so-called negative moments. We simply aren't studious enough to conclude, "That word met a need, but that action definitely didn't. Being a smart guy, I'm writing that down in my book for future reference."

If men seriously want to learn how to meet their wives' needs, they can. And the best place to start is by asking. That suggests, of course, that wives are open to having the conversation, that they will take their husbands seriously (despite any prior track record of insensitivity) and participate in the dialog. Yet all a man has to do is recall the initial process of getting to know his wife when they were courting. It wasn't rocket science, and still isn't: They spent hours and hours together talking and exploring one another's personalities. And the most important thing they did was *act on what they learned*. If a guy discovered his girl liked this music or that food or those flowers, he hopped to. There was nothing he wouldn't do to show the object of his affections that he was serious about the relationship.

It's at this point that a time-tested principle comes into play: courtship for men is a conquest. Once they leave the wedding reception, the get-to-know-you graph takes a dive like a dot-com stock in early 2000. Okay, not that fast. But it begins to fall nonetheless. Despite a guy's best intentions to think otherwise, there is something in him that says, "I know my wife. I wouldn't have married her if I didn't." The truth is, he only thinks he knows her. He only knows as much as x number of months of courtship can reveal, and more importantly, he only knows what she has disclosed. What he doesn't know is what will be revealed as the flower continues to unfold and the pressures of life change: merging their money, balancing time, respecting preferences, having and raising children, adjusting to personal styles of living (cleanliness, bathroom habits, eating habits, personal routines). And then there are the families. It's true that when you marry, you don't marry a person—you marry a family. A wife's sensitivity to her immediate and extended family throws a huge set of variables into the mix.

My encouragement to every man who wants to know how to meet his wife's needs is to begin, for the second time, to court his wife. If a man will devote the same intensity and interest to his wife after marriage that he did before—and maintain that interest level throughout his marriage—he will learn his wife's needs and how to meet them.

NEW DIRECTIONS

For the man who thinks systematically (as most men do), it helps to have a plan. I would encourage you to create a journal of sorts—a word processing document on the computer works better than hard copy since it can be expanded infinitely without getting to the bottom of a "page." In this document, begin to paint a verbal picture of the woman to whom you are married. In it, you'll be describing to yourself everything you know about your wife, particularly her needs. Obviously, this doesn't mean your wife is a "needy" person. Instead, think of her needs as being similar to her needs for oxygen, food, and water. I don't recall anyone being criticized for needing those three essentials, so think of your wife the same way.

You may need to think of these needs in terms of categories to help you, in time, realize that you know more or less about different areas of her life:

- **Emotional:** How would you describe your wife as an emotional being? How are her emotions affected by your presence in her life as the person who loves her?
- **Spiritual:** Where is she spiritually? Are you keeping up? Behind? Right alongside? What could you do to relieve her spiritual tension?
- **Physical:** How is your wife changing physically? How are you—and how is she—reacting to those changes? What does she need from you depending on who she sees in the mirror?
- **Sexual:** Your wife is a sexual being. Looking at her sexual needs rather than yours, what can you do to give her freedom to be who she is and become who she wants to be in this area?
- **Financial:** What does money represent to your wife? How does that differ from what it means to you? How can you communicate to your wife that she is more important to you than money?
- **Friendship:** Who is your wife's best friend? Where do you stand on the good/better/best scale? If you're not her best friend, do you know why? What does her best friend do that you could begin doing?
- **Intimacy:** To what degree does your wife seek intimacy through time together and conversation? How willing are you to make a greater investment in her by adjusting your schedule and comfort zone?
- **Domesticity:** Are you a help or hindrance to your wife's domestic desires to have a home that reflects who she is as a woman? Do you know what she would like your home to be but can't achieve—and why?

After reading that list, you may be asking, "Hey, is this all about me changing?!" In fact, yes, it is. This book is about men and their secrets. And a big one is that men don't understand how to meet women's needs. So unless you are in the 2 percent of the population of men (in our survey) who said this is "never" an issue, then yes, this is about you.

But take heart—Dr. John Gray lists six reciprocal things that happen when a man begins meeting his wife's needs:

1. He gives caring, she returns trust.
2. He gives understanding, she returns acceptance.
3. He gives respect, she returns appreciation.
4. He gives devotion, she returns admiration.
5. He gives validation, she returns approval.
6. He gives reassurance, she returns encouragement.[6]

Get Gray's book, *Men Are from Mars, Women Are from Venus,* and read the details. It's another example of the reciprocity God has built into the giving process: we reap what we sow (Galatians 6:7). When men begin meeting their wives' needs, they suddenly begin to discover that more of their own needs are being met as well. When the joust turns into a dance, both partners begin to appreciate and enjoy the process. (If you go to the bookstore to buy Gray's book, I also encourage you to get Gordon MacDonald's *When Men Think Private Thoughts.* Chapter 9, "What a Wife Really Wants," is probably the most insightful discussion of ten things a wife wants that you will find in print. While no list is perfect, his is well worth considering.)

NEW CONNECTIONS

Years ago, Dr. Bruce Wilkinson offered a new paradigm for education in his book called *The Seven Laws of the Learner.* In his book he said it was the teacher's job to cause the student to learn. Instead of making class exams a mystery in which the student tried to figure out what the teacher thought was important and would thereby be on the test, Wilkinson suggested three steps: tell the student what is important; cause the student to master that material; then build the student's confidence by allowing a display of his or her newfound mastery on a test.

By working together, couples can take the mystery out of meeting one another's needs by talking. Instead of husbands trying to guess what their wives' needs are, wives should tell them. It's not true that, "If I have to tell you, it destroys the romance." Does asking where someone would like to go for dinner destroy the meal? Of course not! The one asking is simply yielding his preferences to another's in hopes that she will enjoy the evening even more. Telling your husband your needs is the way you allow him to demonstrate his "mastery" of you by doing what pleases you.

So husband, talk to your wife. And wife, take the mystery out of the dance by helping your husband know you better. Remember, how and when the flower unfolds is up to you.

Chapter 19

SUCCESS:
THE INTIMIDATION FACTOR

When Tim was single he met a woman he was really attracted to. Lots of girls had been attracted to him, but this girl was the first one that grabbed a piece of his heart and wouldn't let go. She was tall, beautiful, successful—and from a wealthy family. As soon as Tim got to know her and discovered the background of success and achievement she came from, he began to pull away. Whenever he was around her family he felt intimidated by them all. He clearly was a fish out of water—or at least that's how he felt. He loved everything about this girl as a person. What he didn't love was the way he felt when he contemplated never being able to live up to the expectations he knew she must have. Even the cushion of financial comfort her resources might bring to their marriage didn't help. He withdrew from the relationship on the basis of an invisible perception—that he could never compete with this woman and her success.

So when Tim met a woman who was from a lower middle-class background without particularly high expectations for herself or who she married, he latched onto her. She worshiped him, which he loved, and they married. Unfortunately, her perspective on life went from grateful to entitled. She saw in Tim the opportunity to enjoy a larger piece of the pie than she had been used to and insisted that he provide more and more. It turned into an unhappy marriage.

Tim realized that he would have been much better off marrying the well-to-do woman he had been crazy about. He lay awake at night wondering why he had been afraid to walk through that open door.

WHAT WE KNOW ABOUT MEN AND SUCCESSFUL WOMEN

On April 10, 2002, the well-known and widely read editorial columnist at the *New York Times*, Maureen Dowd, set off a firestorm among bloggers and other columnists. Her 755 words that day were titled "The Baby Bust," motivated by the 2001 publication of *Creating a Life: Professional Women and the Quest for Children*, by economist Sylvia Ann Hewlett.

Hewlett surveyed women and found that 55 percent of thirty-five-year-old career women are childless; between one-third and one-half of forty-year-old professional women have no children; the number of childless women age forty to forty-four has doubled in the past twenty years; and among all corporate executives earning $100,000 or more, 49 percent of the women are childless, compared with only 10 percent of men. Dowd quotes Hewlett's conclusion: "Nowadays the rule of thumb seems to be that the more successful the woman, the less likely it is she will find a husband or bear a child. For men, the reverse is true."

Dowd cited part of a CBS *60 Minutes* segment profiling Ms. Hewlett's book in which two women enrolled at Harvard's Business School were interviewed. They both said that when they met men they might be interested in they hid the fact that they go to Harvard, calling it the kiss of death—"the H-bomb." "As soon as you say Harvard Business School . . . that's the end of the conversation," one of the women said. They also noted the opposite is true: "As soon as the guys say, 'Oh, I go to Harvard Business School,' all the girls start falling into them."

Ms. Dowd (mid-fifties and single) is not known as a friend of men. She started her column by noting how a man she ran into at a Broadway play took her aside to talk. He said he had wanted to invite her out but had been afraid to because her job made her too intimidating: "Men, he told me, prefer women who seem malleable and overawed. He said I would never find a mate, because if there's one thing men fear, it's a woman who uses her critical faculties."

Summarizing the points in her column, here are Dowd's conclusions:

- "Men, apparently, learn early to protect their eggshell egos from high-achieving women."
- "The more women accomplish, the more they have to sacrifice."
- "Men veer away from 'challenging' women because they have an atavistic desire to be the superior force in a relationship."
- "If men would only give up their silly desire for world dominance, the world would be a much finer place."[1]

Ms. Dowd seems to interpret economist Hewlett's findings to mean that the reason successful career women are going childless is because men are too intimidated by them to take them as marriage partners. (The Pulitzer Prize-winning Dowd followed up in 2005 with *Are Men Necessary: When Sexes Collide*. Given the book's mediocre reviews, one wonders if women like herself are middle-aged and childless because of men's intimidation of their success or dislike of their tone. But I digress.)

Whether Dowd has interpreted Hewlett's data correctly or not, she has definitely touched on something that is supported by a substantial amount of research, both empirical and anecdotal: some men are intimidated by successful women. We probed that issue in our own survey and found that just over 21 percent of men said they were either always (2 percent) or often (19 percent) "intimidated by successful women." Another 54 percent said they were sometimes intimidated, boosting the total to 75 percent of 3,600 men who are "made timid" (intimidated) by successful women.

Women must be feeling this discomfort. A survey of 234 women in upper management positions found that 80 percent believe that men are uncomfortable working with them. They also said not enough money is invested in corporate training to prepare men for the reality of women entering upper-level executive positions.[2]

Four British universities pooled resources in a thirty-year study to measure the impact of intelligence on success. They began by measuring the IQ of nine hundred eleven-year-olds and examining them again at age forty. The brightest women were less likely to find a man who wanted to marry them; for each sixteen-point rise in their IQ their chances of getting married decreased by 40 percent. By contrast, for each sixteen-point rise in the boys' IQ their chances of marriage increased by 35 percent.[3]

A study at the University of Michigan found that men are more likely to want to marry someone ranked under them at work than a peer or superior. Stephanie Brown, a psychologist at the university's Institute for Social Research and the lead researcher on the study, said, "These findings provide empirical support for the widespread belief that powerful women are at a disadvantage in the marriage market because men may prefer to marry less accomplished women. . . . Our results demonstrate that male preference for subordinate women increases as the investment in the relationship increases. . . . Our results also provide further explanation for why . . . adult males typically prefer partners who are younger and make less money."[4]

After looking at this kind of evidence, the question practically asks itself: short of looking down the barrel of a gun, why would any man be intimidated by a successful woman?

WHAT SUCCESSFUL WOMEN MEAN TO MEN

It's helpful to start by defining success. In general, success is achievement—reaching some kind of goal, attaining some kind of status. In the culture we live in, success is often measured by dollars and cents, the number of windows in one's office, or other markers such as house, car, and other possessions. Are these the things that intimidate men? Probably yes, in some cases.

But women can succeed in other ways that are just as threatening to men. Perhaps they are not rich or famous, but they have displayed the same kind of drive and tenacity in reaching their own goals as some in the corporate world. Perhaps they started a nonprofit agency working with inner-city families and refused to take no from bankers, politicians, and social service people until they got the help they needed. Are these women just as successful, and therefore just as intimidating to some men? More than likely.

And what about a woman who is successful in an even smaller venue: her own family and close circle of acquaintances? The woman in Proverbs 31 comes to mind, one who displays the same two characteristics as any other successful woman: confidence and competence. Is this kind of woman intimidating to her husband? If he is intimidated by successful women, he is probably intimidated by her. And if he is intimidated, then his marriage is probably one of those about which his male friends whisper opinions concerning who actually wears the pants. Not because she is purposefully intimidating but because he is needlessly intimidated.

What is it exactly that intimidates men about successful women? First of all, we must keep in mind that intimidation of any sort is not from God. It is a carnal experience. Intimidation itself is the act of using fear to coerce another person into compliance. The Bible says clearly that "God did not give us a spirit of timidity, but a spirit of power, of love and of self-discipline" (2 Timothy 1:7). Timidity is the result of intimidation. And if God does not intimidate us (make us timid through fear), we can assume that intimidation is not an appropriate response of men to successful women.

Still, intimidation can happen two ways: a woman can purposefully use her success to threaten or coerce a man into compliance. Or a man can wrongly respond to a woman's success and *feel* intimidated. In the former instance, the fault lies with the woman; in the latter it lies with the man. And while there are probably some women in this world who use their power or position to intimidate men, I'm going to suggest that they are in the vast minority. That leaves this conclusion: for the most part, men who are intimidated by successful women are acting out of their own immaturity. They, not the successful women, are at fault.

Gail Dean is a successful thirty-eight-year-old black woman, a college-educated social worker. She has never married and doubts she will. In a series of interviews conducted by the *Washington Post*, the Henry J. Kaiser Family Foundation, and Harvard University, she said, "What strikes me the most is how black men are intimidated by successful women. I own my own home, I'm independent, and I meet guys who are intimidated by that—they feel they're not the man if the woman has more than they have."[5]

Assuming Ms. Dean is not leveraging her success inappropriately in relationships with men, this would be an example of a man bearing the responsibility for his own intimidation. What legitimate reason could there be for being intimidated by a woman who has a career and owns her own home?

If men are being intimidated by women like this, they need to repent of such feelings and the behaviors that accompany them. Instead of being intimidated, they need to rejoice in the success of another human being who is making her way in this world, realizing her potential and achieving good goals. Jealousy, pride, insecurity, embarrassment over one's own position or level of accomplishment, envy, greed, resentment—these attitudes simply have no place in the heart of a man who wants to be mature and have a profitable relationship with women. Whether the woman is a wife, a possible life-partner one is dating, or a co-worker, all those relationships can be sabotaged by a man's self-induced perception that a woman is seeking to intimidate him into compliance or submission.

It's easy to identify inappropriate intimidation based on pride, jealousy, and the like. And once acknowledged, sins and failings such as those can be dealt with. But there is another aspect of how a man looks at a successful woman that is not nearly so easy to explain, diagnose, or correct. It is part of the murkiness of our existence, the place where who we were created to be meets the realities of the world we live in.

I'm going to let John Eldredge set the stage with a story about himself from *Wild at Heart*:

> My wife and I were driving home the other day from an afternoon out and running a bit late to get to our son's last soccer game of the season. I was in the driver's seat and we were enjoying a lingering conversation about some dreams we have for the future. After several minutes we realized that we were caught in a traffic jam that was going nowhere. Precious moments slipped by as tension mounted in the car. In an effort to be helpful, Stasi suggested an alternate route: "If you take a right here and go up to First Street, we can cut over and take about five minutes off the drive." I was ready to divorce her. I'm serious. In about twenty seconds I was ready for separation. If the judge had been in the car, I'd have signed the papers right there. Good grief—over a comment about my driving? Is that all that was going on in that moment?
>
> I sat at the wheel silent and steaming. On the outside, I looked cool; inside, here is what was happening: *Geez, doesn't she think I know how to get there? I hate it when she does that.* Then another voice says, *She always does that.* And I say (internally—the whole dialogue took place internally, in the blink of an eye), *Yea, she does . . . she's always saying stuff like that. I hate that about her.* A feeling of accusation and anger and

self-righteousness sweeps over me. Then the voice says, *John, this is never going to change*, and I say, *This is never going to change*, and the voice says, *You know, John, there are a lot of women out there who would be deeply grateful to have you as their man*, and I think, *Yeah—there are a lot of women out there....* You get the picture. Change the characters and the setting and the very same thing has happened to you.[6]

To be fair to Eldredge, he is not talking about intimidation in this passage. He is talking about how the enemy of a man, the devil, can stir up a man's soul in an instant and cause him to blame someone else for his own rage.

But I think his story is a good illustration of what happens when a man comes up against confidence and competence *in a woman*—even the woman he loves. I would be so bold as to suggest that if one of John's male friends had been in the car instead of his wife and made the exact same suggestion, his reaction would have been totally different. In that case, it would have been two amigos, two compadres, two alpha males standing on the bank of a raging stream and figuring out a way to get across: "We can do this . . . and use that . . . and tie here . . . leap there . . . swing out and *boom!*—we're on the other side. Let's do it!"

There is something inherent in a man that wants to say, "I know the way!" And I'm not just talking about driving directions. I'm talking about the way through life. When a man hears another man say it, he hears it in a totally different language than when a woman says it. Translation: When a man encounters a woman who seems to know the way all by herself (is successful), it literally can scare him (intimidate him). It can tempt him to pull back and say, "Whoa—who, or what, is this?" When in the presence of a woman who already knows the way in life (is successful), a man *can be tempted* to feel like he has no place there, like he's simply not needed.

There's another aspect of men and women that comes into play here, and it's a point that I also take from *Wild at Heart*. Eldredge says that besides needing a battle to fight and an adventure to live, every man needs a beauty to rescue. As hard as it may be for women to understand, men are hardwired to be rescuers of damsels in distress. In this day of women's independence, it's not PC for women to say they'd like to be swept off their feet by a man. And probably not all women feel that way. But many do—it's how they're hardwired.

So when a man meets, lives, or works with a woman who doesn't seem to need his strength, protection, or provision (i.e., is successful), he *can be tempted* to feel as useless as in the former example (intimidated). He looks at this woman like she's Wonder Woman—a woman who definitely doesn't need a man.

Recall Eldredge's thoughts from the story above: *You know, John, there are a lot of women out there who would be deeply grateful to have you as their man.* It's at that point, if men yield to what they're feeling in the presence of a competent and confident woman, that they'll start looking down the pecking order, down the food chain, for a woman who doesn't know the way and needs rescuing. The feeling Eldredge articulated is completely consistent with some men's tendencies to leave the presence of successful women and look for another.

Where do these feelings come from? Man was created to live in a perfect world, to know the way through life and provide strength for the woman that was his co-partner in life. Reciprocally, there would be things the woman would do for him that she was created to do. Together, they would complement one another; they would both be successful without a trace of intimidation.

But we don't live in a perfect world. We have men and women walking through life with no attachment whatever to "the ideal." And yet they still "feel" those hardwired preferences and inclinations. The challenge, therefore, is to learn to manage themselves appropriately in an imperfect world.

Eldredge, after telling the story above, went on to say that his response was inappropriate. Nor would the response of any man be appropriate in the presence of a woman who already knows the way she is going and doesn't need a man to "rescue" her. It becomes a man's responsibility to guard these feelings and not allow them to completely disrupt appropriate relationships.

NEW DIRECTIONS

It's important for us men to examine every situation in which we feel intimidation, fear, or uselessness in the presence of a woman. If our drive to lead and provide is inappropriate in that setting, it is our job to keep those feelings in check. (If a woman is purposefully attempting to intimidate, that's another story. But that rare occurrence is not the situation we're addressing here.)

If we have been negative, critical, withdrawn, judgmental, self-pitying, angry, or anything less than supportive and appreciative when in the presence of a successful woman, we need to completely change our attitude. It is clear that God has gifted women with incredible talents and abilities, and if we are not mature enough to recognize and celebrate those gifts, then we're the ones at fault.

At the same time, we must recognize and celebrate our own instincts to lead and protect a woman in the appropriate setting—*which includes submitting to her leadership and protection when offered and needed.* It is for such reasons that the apostle Paul exhorts Christians, especially husbands and wives, to "submit to one another out of reverence for Christ" (Ephesians 5:21).

NEW CONNECTIONS

It's rare when a man can fully explain why he feels what he feels in the presence of a woman, regardless of whether she is strong or weak, successful or not. Men often know what they feel even when they don't exactly know *why*. But together, couples can provide safe harbor for one another as they listen to things that a spouse needs unconditional acceptance—and an ironclad commitment to privacy—to share.

Husbands and wives can explore together the mysteries of their innate desires and tendencies. Along the way they may rise and fall like the peaks and valleys in a mountain range as they interpret their "innateness" unlike any other couple. And they will need to "take by faith," without judgment, the explanations of each other's feelings on matters that are so sensitive and deep.

But therein lies the mystery of the union—diverse, yet unified; different in gender, the same in humanity; weak in failure, strong in confession; more confident and competent together than apart.

Chapter 20

DID I MARRY THE WRONG WOMAN?

When asked to reveal his secret for staying married for (at that time) fifty-four years to the same person, Billy Graham replied, "Ruth and I are happily incompatible."

That's a great answer to a question every man and woman asks at some point during his or her marriage: how can I stay married to this person? Eventually, the root of this line of questioning is revealed through a single question: did I marry the wrong person? Unfortunately, the notion that incompatibility is a sign that one has married the wrong person is epidemic in our culture today. Divorce rates among Christians and non-Christians alike have hovered around the 50 percent mark for years. And though I don't have statistics to back this up, I'm guessing that the primary reason given for divorces is "incompatibility," or in legalese, "irreconcilable differences."

WHAT WE KNOW ABOUT MEN AND THEIR MARITAL REGRETS

At some point everyone feels incompatible with the person he or she married. Most of the men we surveyed responded positively to the statement,

"Men wish they had married someone other than their wife." One percent said "always," 13 percent said "often," and 59 percent said "sometimes." Together that represents nearly three-fourths of the respondents in our survey. Include those who said "rarely" and we're at 94 percent. Again, at some point in life nearly everyone wishes he or she had married someone else.

While most men harbor that secret like they're the only person in the world who has ever thought that way, I've just revealed an even bigger secret: *everybody* thinks that thought. And any time everyone is doing something, is it really a secret? The news is not that people wish they had married someone different, it's that they're calling what they're feeling by the wrong name. *Everybody* goes through difficult periods in marriage, and *everybody* feels like throwing in the towel. And if you want to know the truth, everybody did marry the wrong person. That's according to Stanley Hauerwas, esteemed professor at Duke Divinity School at Duke University. In fact, his view on our choice in marriage has come to be called "Hauerwas' Law":

> In a marriage course I used to teach at the University of Notre Dame, I always gave the students one absolute they could write down and put in their pockets; when times got tough they could pull it out and say, "God, it's great to have an absolute to guide my life." My absolute was that you always marry the wrong person. It's a reversible absolute, though: You also always marry the right person. The point is we don't know who we are marrying.
>
> That absolute is meant to challenge the presumption that a person's life is fundamentally a matter of choice. It's a matter of choice, but often one doesn't know what one is choosing. That's where fidelity comes in. A couple marrying must be willing to make a promise although neither person knows exactly what kind of promise is being made.[1]

In his book, *Community of Character*, Hauerwas added this thought: "The primary problem morally is learning how to love and care for this stranger to whom you find yourself married."[2] In America we have not done so well at this loving and caring after marriage.

Mike McManus, president of Marriage Savers, the leading organization in America working to preserve and strengthen marriages, cites the following benchmarks:

- The marriage rate has plunged 48 percent since 1970. If the same percentage of couples were marrying now as in 1970, there would be a million more marriages a year—3.3 million marriages, not 2.2 million. The percentage of never-married thirty- to forty-four-year-olds tripled from 14 percent to 44 percent.
- Half of all new marriages end in divorce. There have been 38 million divorces since 1970, hurting 35 million children. One quarter of all adults ages eighteen to thirty-five have grown up in divorced families.
- The number of unmarried couples living together has soared twelvefold from 430,000 in 1960 to 5 million now. As stated earlier, there are only 2.2 million marriages a year. This means that *cohabitation has become the dominant way male-female unions are formed.* Those who marry after living together are 50 percent more likely to divorce than those who did not.
- Out-of-wedlock births jumped from 5.3 percent to 34.6 percent, or from 224,000 to 1.4 million children from 1960 to 2003. Cohabiting couples are as likely to have a child under eighteen as married couples (42 percent vs. 45 percent).

As to the effects of divorce, McManus notes that divorced men are twice as likely to die in any given year as married men of heart disease, stroke, hypertension, or cancer, four times as apt to die in accidents, seven times higher by cirrhosis of the liver and pneumonia, eight-fold greater by murder. Married men live *ten years* longer than divorced men. Divorced women also live shorter lives.[3]

Those men who wonder if they married the wrong person will find some comfort in the Marriage Savers ministry. This group takes as much satisfaction in seeing ill-fated couples not marry as seeing couples who are married stay together. That is, they work hard at helping couples, through premarital counseling lasting four to six months, determine whether they should, in fact, get married. In their own church, McManus and his wife worked with 302 couples in premarital counseling from 1992 to 2000. Of that number, twenty-one broke up and dropped out before the course was over, and another thirty-four couples completed the course but decided not to marry. That's 18 percent who would have married but decided they shouldn't after counseling. (In other words, had they married, they would have married either the wrong person or the right person at the wrong time.) Out of the remaining 247 couples, only seven divorced—a 3 percent failure rate (or 97 percent success rate) over a decade. Compared to the national marriage failure rate of 50 percent, these are enviable results.[4]

Marriage Savers has found that, on average, 10 percent of the couples who take their premarital inventory decide not to marry. *Those who break up have the same scores on their inventory as those who marry but later divorce*, providing more evidence that it is possible to avoid a bad marriage.[5]

Many "what have I done?" feelings surface soon after marriage. A study of several hundred newlywed couples found that . . .

- sixty-three percent had serious problems related to their finances.
- fifty-one percent had serious doubts about their marriage lasting.
- forty-nine percent had significant marital problems.
- forty-five percent were not satisfied with their sexual relationship.
- forty-one percent found marriage harder than they had expected.
- thirty-five percent stated their partner was often critical of them.

A large number of newlyweds at the crossroads evidently choose to terminate their marriage since divorce most often occurs during the second and third years of marriage. Half of all first marriages that end in divorce end within the first seven years.[6]

Marriage is indeed a culture shock, and it's no surprise that so many divorces happen early on. But what about those who remain married but are still plagued with doubts about their decision?

WHAT MARITAL REGRETS MEAN TO MEN

If a person lives life from a purely humanistic viewpoint, without a relationship with God, then the choice of a marriage partner is like any other choice: "You pays your money and takes your chances" as the saying goes. But if one spouse is a Christian, a different mystique has developed: finding God's will. A school of thought exists in some spiritual camps that

God has one and only one person for you to marry. Those approaching marriage do their due diligence—prayer, counsel, Bible study, more prayer—and make their choice. Then, once into the marriage, when things begin to go wrong (not "if" they go wrong, but "when"), their first thought is, "I made a mistake! I missed God's perfect will for who I should marry. I tried hard to find His will, but it's obvious I missed it!" And to correct that mistake, they divorce.

Besides this "bull's-eye" mentality, there exists what I call the "moral corral" view of choosing a mate. That is, a Christian man could "herd" all of those women who meet basic moral and spiritual standards—love for God, biblical lifestyle, commended by those who know her—into a "corral" and then choose the one for whom he develops a special love and commitment. In other words, God's will in marriage has to do with the broad scope of moral and spiritual acceptability, not the specific choice of an individual.

Those who follow the bull's-eye philosophy can torment themselves both before and after marriage as to whether they made the correct choice. Those who arrived at matrimony with the broader view may be less tormented about the choice but equally tormented about the result; they may wish they had married someone else.

In typical style, Zig Ziglar cuts through the fog and focuses on the real issue once a person is married:

Several years ago while coming in on a plane (which is generally the way I fly), I noticed that the fellow seated next to me had his wedding band on the index finger of his right hand. I couldn't resist the temptation so I commented, "Friend, you've got your wedding band on the wrong finger." He responded, "Yeah, I married the wrong woman."

I have no way of knowing whether or not he married the wrong person, but I do know that many people have a lot of wrong ideas about marriage and what it takes to make that marriage happy and successful. I'll be the first to admit that it's possible that you did marry the wrong person. However, if you treat the wrong person like the right person, you could well end up having married the right person after all. On the other hand, if you marry the right person, and treat that person wrong, you certainly will have ended up marrying the wrong person. I also know that it is far more important to be the right kind of person than it is to marry the right person. In short, whether you married the right or wrong person is primarily up to you.7

That puts the ball squarely back in the camp of the person who wonders if he married the right person or not. There is a significant amount of research that should help anyone contemplating divorce rethink that option. Here's a summary of some of the findings in a 2002 report by the Institute for American Values:

- On average, adults who divorced because of unhappiness were no happier five years after the divorce than were equally unhappy adults who stayed married (based on twelve measures of psychological well-being).
- Two-thirds of unhappily married people who stayed married reported their marriages were happier five years later.
- Even among couples who said their marriages were "very unhappy," 80 percent were happily married five years later.
- The data suggests that if a couple is unhappy they have a 64 percent chance of being happy and married five years later, but only a 19 percent chance if they divorce and remarry.
- The study found three ways by which unhappy couples became happy while staying married:

1. Endurance—sticking it out through hard times with the expectation that good times will come.
2. Seeking help—rather than being passive, many partners and couples seek help from others.
3. Diversification—spouses were found to seek happiness in other ways while continuing to seek happiness in marriage (rather than divorcing).

- Divorce did not reduce depression or raise self-esteem compared to unhappy spouses who stayed married.
- The majority of divorces (74 percent) happened to adults who had been happily married five years previously (the "short memory" syndrome).
- Unhappy marriages were less common than unhappy spouses.8

Operating under the theory that people perish for lack of knowledge (Hosea 4:6), here are more reasons why divorce is not a panacea for those unhappy in marriage:

• A married man at age forty-eight has an 88 percent chance of living till age sixty-five, but a divorced man has only a 65 percent chance. This is because married men settle down and participate in fewer life-threatening activities. When men lose their wives to divorce or death, they resume bachelor habits and are four times as likely to be in car crashes or to commit suicide.

• Married people are twice as likely as those who are single for whatever reason to say they are "very happy." Some 40 percent of married couples say they are very happy, compared to 15 percent of those separated and 18 percent of divorced couples. What's surprising is that only 22 percent of the never-married and cohabitants are very happy—the same percentage as widows.

• A married couple in their fifties in 1994 had net assets averaging $66,000 per person, compared to a divorced person's average assets of $33,600. A never-married person age fifty-five averages $35,000 in net worth, a separated person $7,600. A married man earns 30 percent more than a single man with the same education; the happier his marriage, the larger the wage gap. If his marriage breaks down, the wage premium erodes due to the effects of a more erratic (bachelor) lifestyle. Wives act as excellent career counselors and help men live healthier lives.

• Married sex is better. Some 43 percent of married men had sex at least twice a week, versus only 26 percent of single men. Both sexes enjoy married sex better than their unmarried counterparts because of the added secret emotional ingredient: commitment.[9]

Even in the face of an overwhelming barrage of statistics about the wisdom of working through difficult seasons of marriage, there is still the emotional part: being unhappy in marriage just *feels* bad. Unfortunately, we live in a culture that has as one of its many mantras, "If it feels good, do it!" The converse of that philosophy is obviously, "If it doesn't feel good, don't do it!" We have put such a premium on feeling good that we have neglected the time-tested truth that, in the long term, *feeling* good is always a result of *doing* good. And doing good involves the will, that steady sentry that stands silent guard over a man's moral matrix. *The Lord of the Rings* author J. R. R. Tolkien wrote about this to his own son in 1941:

> No man, however truly he loved his betrothed and bride as a young man, has lived faithful to her as a wife in mind and body without deliberate conscious exercise of the *will*, without self-denial. Too few are told that—even those brought up "in the Church." Those outside seem seldom to have heard it. When the glamour wears off, or merely works a bit thin, they think they have made a mistake, and that the real soul-mate is still to find. The real soul-mate too often proves to be the next sexually attractive person that comes along. Someone whom they might indeed very profitably have married, if only—. Hence divorce, to provide the "if only." And of course they are as a rule quite right: they did make a mistake. Only a very wise man at the end of his life could make a sound judgment concerning whom, amongst the total possible chances, he ought most profitably to have married! Nearly all marriages, even happy ones, are mistakes: in the sense that almost certainly (in a more perfect world, or even with a little more care in this very imperfect one) both partners might have found more suitable mates. But the "real soul-mate" is the one you are actually married to. You really do very little choosing: life and circumstances do most of it (though if there is a God these must be His instruments, or His appearances).[10]

NEW DIRECTIONS

Tolkien is no doubt right: what more perfect specimen of anything in life—house, car, appliance, investment, spouse—might not be found with just a bit more looking? But at some point each of us makes an imperfect choice from the imperfect options (the lesser of evils) and gets on with living, driving, cooking, making money, and marrying. It is the *living* that is important, not the *choosing*.

Choosing a wife, however, for a practical man, must be seen as different from any other choice. No other purchase or decision in life is made the way the choice and consummation of a wife is made: with a vow to remain faithful until death takes you. A wise man, the ancient king of Israel, had strong words for any who made vows before God and man:

It is better not to vow than to make a vow and not fulfill it. Do not let your mouth lead you into sin. And do not protest to the temple messenger, 'My vow was a mistake.' Why should God be angry at what you say and destroy the work of your hands? (Ecclesiastes 5:5–6)

Marriage vows are vows not to be broken lightly. Yes, there are some circumstances under which marriages are better dissolved, where moral failure, abuse, drugs, and other exigencies may put a spouse or children in danger or take the offending party beyond the point of short-term help or rehabilitation. To return to our own survey, it is not likely that 73 percent of the men we surveyed are in such a difficult situation. Rather, they are in the situation that every married man has been in to a greater or lesser degree in his life, wondering if he married the right person, or even wishing he had married someone else.

Such feelings are part of the vicissitudes of life—to be expected. A new rattle in the undercarriage after two years does not warrant returning the car. Instead, you remember the joy it has brought you and get it fixed. Complications don't negate commitments.

Having grown up with their music, the lyrics of Crosby, Stills, Nash, and Young's "Love the One You're With" comes to mind. Of course, their original lyrics reflected the "free love" mentality of their age. Their song encouraged their audience, in the absence of a true love, to "love the one you're with." That's really bad advice in a moral sense. But it is also profoundly good advice in a marital sense. If you are married, the most profound, noble, and morally meaningful thing you can do is to "love the one you're with"—the person to whom you committed yourself until death separates you.

A social worker named Rose Starks penned a verse in the early twentieth century that reflects that sentiment:

Some pray to marry the man they love,
My prayer will somewhat vary;
I humbly pray to Heaven above
That I love the man I marry.

Another author wrote these simple words: "Choose your love, then love your choice."[11] And another, "Happy marriages begin when we marry the ones we love, and they blossom when we love the ones we marry."[12]

NEW CONNECTIONS

Our survey question and men's responses to it can put wives in an uncomfortable position: "Is my husband one of the 73 percent who said, at least sometimes, that he wishes he had married someone else?" Well, statistically, there's a 73 percent chance he is. But so what? Can you say that you are a wife who has *never* thought the same thing? Remember, we're talking about nothing being new under the sun. We're talking about feelings common to every marriage. We're talking about a more dignified version of buyer's remorse that afflicts everyone in a dark hour.

The point is not to keep score but to come together and admit the reality that marriage has its hard spots. It is also to agree that marriage holds potential the depths of which no couple can plumb completely. It is to think like this, as stated on one Web site:

In fact, successful couples have the same number of disagreements as the couples who divorce. Even more interesting, all couples disagree about all the same basic issues—money, kids, sex, housework, in-laws, and time. The difference between successful and unsuccessful couples is how they handle their differences. Successful couples disagree in a way that makes their relationship stronger. They also have other skills and attitudes which help them build long-term happiness and satisfaction. The good news is that anyone can learn to do it better and smarter. Couples can unlearn the behaviors that destroy love and . . . replace them with behaviors that keep love alive. Learning the skills also gives couples a new can-do attitude. We all need the same basic skills. We can use the tools to build a good relationship from the ground up, and keep a good relationship healthy—or to rebuild one that's seriously in need of repair. It turns out you *can* get the feelings back—and keep love alive.[13]

In Thornton Wilder's play, *The Skin of Our Teeth*, the character Maggie says to her husband, "I didn't marry you because you were perfect. I didn't even marry you because I loved you. I married you because you gave me a promise. That promise made up for your faults. And the promise I gave you made up for mine. Two imperfect people got married and it was the promise that made the marriage. And when our children were growing up, it wasn't a house that protected them; and it wasn't our love that protected them—it was that promise."[14]

The power of a promise to protect has never been equaled. It can save a marriage when all else has failed.

SECTION 5

SECRETS ABOUT
SEXUALITY

Chapter 21

THERE'S AN EGO IN MY BED!

A friend of mine has four fabulous, fun-filled boys that keep her going all day. She is a traditional mom, and a terrific one at that. She's organized like a CEO, treats injuries like a nurse, does homework like a teacher, cooks like a master chef, and drives her brood around like a highly paid chauffer. She also meets their emotional needs like a master psychologist. It seems that every day her boys exercise their developing egos in some new way. *Am I powerful enough? Am I strong enough? Am I smart enough? Am I adequate, capable, and competent enough?* Every day she tends to their ego development, ever sensitive to the fact that how she feels about them and who they are will impact them for the rest of their lives.

One day my friend's hardworking husband came home with a bad case of the "I dunnos." From the moment he walked through the door he began muttering the mantra: *I dunno if I can take this job much longer. I dunno if I have what it takes. I dunno if it's all worth it* . . . and on and on. She got the picture of where he was mentally and emotionally, walked over to him, looked into his eyes, and said, "Honey, I've been doing 'young male ego' all day for the boys and just don't think I have what it takes to do 'middle-aged man ego' all evening." Fortunately, they both burst out laughing, simultaneously realizing that her comment was both right on target and hilarious.

It doesn't surprise most women that males have egos that need to be tended to. It might come as a surprise, however, that one of the places where male egos are most fragile is in the bedroom.

WHAT WE KNOW ABOUT THE MALE EGO
IN THE BEDROOM

For all their bluster and bravado, men have a reputation for being turned into quivering Jello-like masses in certain situations. Or at least that's what modern media would have us believe.

There was a time in our culture when men were pictured as secure (I'll use the word *insecure* to refer to the fragile male ego throughout this chapter). Two well-known examples come to mind. First, there was Jim Anderson, manager of the General Insurance Company, who resided on Maple Street in Springfield with his brood: wife Margaret and children Betty ("Princess"), Bud, and Kathy ("Kitten"). Every night on this 1950s sitcom, Jim would arrive home from work and prove that *Father Knows Best*. It wasn't that he was perfect. In fact, Margaret stood her ground and at times proved Jim wrong. But that was okay because Jim's ego wasn't fragile. He was a secure man, able to lead his family with confidence. He always seemed comfortable with himself and competent, no matter what the situation or challenge.

Another good example was Ward Cleaver, husband to June and father of Wally and Theodore ("Beaver"). On *Leave It to Beaver*, Ward and June ran a stable 1950s household. We never learned for certain what Ward did for a living, but it involved wearing a suit and things such as "sales," "reports," "the home office," and the occasional business trip. Ward was always there for his two boys, the youngest of whose escapades dominated the show. Like Jim Anderson, Ward wasn't perfect, but was generally unflappable and secure in his post-War version of maleness.

There were other admirable men on the small screen as well: Ozzie Nelson (*Ozzie and Harriet*), Steve Douglas (*My Three Sons*), Ben Cartwright (*Bonanza*), and Dr. Alex Stone (*The Donna Reed Show*). All of these men were secure—their egos were anything but fragile.

Try as I might, I can't think of their equal in today's prime-time line-up. In the early 1980s we had Charles Ingalls on *Little House on the Prairie*. The mid-'80s and early '90s gave us *The Cosby Show*'s Dr. Cliff Huxtable. And in recent years there's been Rev. Eric Camden on *7th Heaven*. But for the most part, men, and especially husbands, are portrayed as insecure, bumbling boobs who leave the intelligent, secure side of life to their wives and kids.

That's just on sitcoms. The TV commercials are worse. In modern-day advertisements it's always a calm, poised, well-informed wife who comes to the aid of her doofus husband to resolve the thirty-second crisis du jour.

There is a chicken-and-egg puzzle here. Is the media simply mirroring a trend it sees in society? In other words, are today's TV sitcoms an accurate portrayal of modern men? Or is Hollywood driving the boat, with its writers and producers attempting to emasculate America—a scripted effort to feminize the culture? Or, as a third possibility, could this be a downward, self-perpetuating cycle of male insecurity that feeds off itself: culture—media—culture—media—culture . . . ad infinitum?

I suspect the question can't be answered definitively, but I do know this: if we combined all modern American males into a composite "Man," I believe his ego would be much more fragile than it was fifty years ago. Political correctness, tolerance, the need for approval, the women's movement, homosexuality, metrosexuality—all these movements have contributed to (or mirror) a current generation of men who are less sexually secure than they need to be and want to be.

Perhaps nowhere is this insecurity most consistently seen and felt than in the bedroom. For whatever reason, a large number of husbands in our culture confess to having "a fragile ego in the bedroom" (33.1 percent in our survey of 3,600 men; Christians and non-Christians were within less than one percentage point of each other in their positive response).

Though I'm generalizing here, this means that a third of the men surveyed enter the sexual domain of their relationships with their wives with some measure of fear and trembling. That obviously cannot be a comfortable situation for those men, nor can it result in a fulfilling sexual relationship for a couple. The reasons men feel insecure in the bedroom are as many as the number of men polled—and then some. On a good day, the mysteries of sexual satisfaction between a man and woman are infinitely complex. Gratifying sex is more art than science, more felt than explained. Yet despite all the variables and unknowns, we can identify some of the things that create insecurity for a man as he seeks the pleasure of his wife's company.

WHAT A MAN'S EGO MEANS TO HIM IN THE BEDROOM

Picture, if you will, what it means for the modern American male to enter into a sexual encounter with his wife. It doesn't happen like this, but humor me for a moment. The man's wife is already in bed awaiting his arrival. He enters the room and stands stark naked before her, waiting for permission to approach. She eyes him from top to bottom (he detects a smirk when her eyes pause momentarily at the midpoint) as if he is a rump roast in the cooler at the grocery store. After what seems like an eternity, with what sounds like a sigh of resignation at best and condescension at worst, she motions him forward. Feeling like he should prostrate himself in thanksgiving, he wipes the sweat from his brow and meekly approaches the bed, still unsure what his fate will be once he is tucked in. (Think of the *Seinfeld* episode in which Elaine questioned her suitor about his "sponge-worthiness.")

I have used absurdity (at least I hope it's more absurd than reality) to illustrate the stereotype of married sex in our culture. In marriage, the impression is that sex is something men want—a must-have that they are required to *get* from their wives. And because they want it frequently, men soon begin to feel bad for asking. Think of how you feel if you have to ask to borrow something from a neighbor over and over. After a while, you begin to approach sheepishly, then apologetically, then ashamedly. The obvious question you read in your neighbor's eyes is, "When are you going to get your own hedge trimmer/bicycle pump/stepladder?"

Over time, men begin to feel sheepish, apologetic, and even ashamed about approaching their wives for sex. For the most part, this is the only area of their lives in which this is true. At work, they wear their pinstripe suit and power tie, or their rugged tool belt, or police or military uniform, or some other suit of armor that gives them credibility on the street. They are *somebody*!

But when it comes to sex, the body armor comes off and they are forced to stand buck naked, devoid of anything to commend them to their wives. When it comes to sex, every crummy thing they've ever done hangs on them like medals on the chest of a Red Army general. No one else knows a man like his wife, and yet he still has the gall to ask her for sex despite his lower-than-scum status.

If you're a man reading this, I know you can identify. You may be married to a wonderful woman who loves sex as much as you do and makes you feel like you're doing her a favor every time you come to bed. But what I've just described lurks down in your gut. I don't know how it gets there, but it's there.

And if you're a woman reading this, you could be either shocked (not likely) or unnerved that the curtain has been pulled back on the boudoir. You may be that wonderful woman I just described who welcomes her husband to bed at all times. If so, may your tribe increase! But even if so, you know the tension I'm referring to.

When it comes down to it, men sometimes approach sex as if they were five-year-olds asking their mommies for a treat. It is the rare marriage in which a man and woman share an equal and communicative relationship . . . where sex is viewed as a gift from God to promote pleasure and build intimacy . . . where the bed is not a chessboard . . . where lovemaking is not a reward for good behavior to be withheld in the case of unatoned-for transgressions.

I am not suggesting that the opposite of the above describes your marriage or even most marriages. But I am saying that it is consistent with a stereotype that exists about sex in modern marriages.

The emasculation many men experience when approaching sex in marriage (obviously, the above scenario is not true of singles who hook up for a one-nighter) is reminiscent of the male insecurities described by psychologist Alon Gratch:

[Robert] Stoller, together with anthropologist Gilbert Herdt, has found and described a remote tribe from New Guinea whose entire social structure is based on the explicit and conscious notion that women are dangerous. According to Stoller, men in that Sambian tribe believe that women's menstrual and vaginal fluids are contaminating. They believe that through sexual intercourse women empty men of their male substance, semen, the essence of vitality and masculinity. Naturally enough, in order to protect themselves from these female dangers Sambian men impose a strict separation between the sexes. Even in the family hut, where married men live with their spouses and young children, there are separate female and male spaces and paths. And all contacts with women, most particularly sexual intercourse, are scrutinized and regulated.[1]

There it is: *women are dangerous*. That's what makes men insecure, at least in the bedroom. That's what makes their male egos so fragile. Though for different reasons, the feeling of danger is just the same among modern Western men as it is for males in the Sambian tribe. Women have the potential, whether through their actions, words, or mere presence, to crush a man's self-esteem.

How can women hold such sway over their men? Here are six reasons why men are insecure about sex in marriage.

1. Inability to Perform

We live in the Viagra generation, and for men who want to have sex but can't, it's a devastating experience. To a man, nothing says "over the hill" like losing the ability to perform sexually. The *New York Times* says that as many as half of all men over the age of forty experience mild or occasional impotence. Yet sales of erectile dysfunction (ED) drugs began falling in 2005, and overall they have not reached the sales level expected since Viagra was introduced in 1998. Many experts believe the reason is, in part, due to men's hesitancy to admit they have a problem with impotency.[2] If that doesn't say "fragile male ego," nothing does.

2. Feelings of Inadequacy

The older men get, the more they can look in the mirror and recognize that it isn't Casanova staring back at them. At the end of the day, a balding, overweight, or obese man who needs a shave and hasn't had a shower since he got home looks in the mirror and sighs. He knows it will take more than a dash of cologne to transform him into something appealing. He knows that what he is offering to his wife is not what it should be. And all it takes is a comment from his wife about his weight, breath, smell, favorite raggedy pajamas, long hair—whatever—and the edge is gone.

3. "Headaches"

The stereotypical excuse for the wife who doesn't want to participate in sex with her husband is, "Not tonight, dear. I have a terrible headache." Whatever the reason (and, granted, who wants to do anything except sleep when they have a headache?), getting "No" as the answer to a verbal or non-verbal request for sex is a bummer for the average man, especially if he thinks the "headache" is just an excuse. Being denied for sex is like being turned down for a raise from your boss. It takes all week to work up the nerve to ask, only to be told there's a wage freeze in place, your last year's performance was subpar, the whole company is in a revenue crunch, and/or the generic "Let me see what I can do." In short, you feel stupid for asking when the answer is "No."

4. Lack of Attraction

It's possible that the tables are reversed in some situations: the wife wants to have sex but the husband, for reasons mentioned above or others, is not interested. Perhaps he's not attracted to his wife physically because of her failure to keep herself attractive over the years. Or he may not be attracted to her emotionally; maybe she has been so critical or unsupportive over time that he doesn't want to risk getting another bucket of harsh words poured over him. Whatever the reason he is not attracted to her, he will feel guilty about it. And guilt is a guaranteed destroyer of a person's self-image and ego. Normally when our image or ego suffers a blow, we'll justify or rationalize it away, and a husband may do that. But it will not work in the long run. Guilt will simply become another reason for fearing the bedroom.

5. Lack of Know-How

Hard as it may be to believe, a significant percentage of men are deficient in their sex skill set. They're still operating out of what they learned in high school or college. Yes, they know how parts A and B fit together. But the subtle nuances of sexual relationships, in particular their wives' stimulation and response networks, have escaped them. Most men have never read a book, listened to tapes, attended a class, or talked to a counselor about sex. They've invested about as much time in learning how to pleasure their wives as they have in discovering how to change their car's oil—and they do them both with about the same degree of grace and sensitivity. It's no wonder, then, that their wives may be less than enthusiastic when they see them revving up for some bedroom action.

6. Betrayal

Nothing sends the fragile male ego crashing into pieces like the betrayal of a wife. Most men already struggle to feel adequate; discovering that your wife has either been flirting with the idea of an affair or has already been unfaithful can be devastating. The mere possibility of such unfaithfulness wreaks havoc at the core of your manhood. Yet the reality is that female adultery is on the rise inside and outside the church, and it's a threat that hangs over the head of every man: "Either I perform or she goes looking somewhere else." When she actually does and he finds out, the pain is usually beyond description. It is tough for a woman to recover when her husband has an affair. Yet in my experience, it is almost impossible for a man to do so when his wife is unfaithful. I wonder if as many women would have affairs if they knew the level of devastation it would cause their men. Women tend to think a man can shake it off and move on, but that's usually not the case.

NEW DIRECTIONS

As with most things marital, the porcelain-like male ego in the bedroom is not a binary problem that can be simplified into an "either/or" situation. It's not a case of the wife at fault or the husband at fault. It's a gray area, as is most of life, that will require communication and understanding to resolve.

When it comes to improving the sexual relationship in marriage, we husbands need to be willing to assess the status of our own ego, self-image, or level of security. As difficult as it may be, opening up to our wives about our bedroom fears and anxieties can often lead to nothing but positive changes. As always, communication can be the most powerful solution.

Yet it's important for us to also own the weaknesses we find. If we discover we are unappealing physically or emotionally, we need to put forth the effort to improve those areas. It's unrealistic to expect our wives to look like knockouts at all times when we can't even discipline ourselves at the dinner table or with regular trips to the gym (we'll discuss this more in Chapter 25). Likewise, it's important to remember that, for women, emotional attractiveness is often just as important in a man as physical appearance.

Finally, if we don't know how to make love to our wives with sensitivity and patience, it's time for us to learn. The sanctuary of the bedroom provides a safe place where we can set aside the cultural baggage of "what sex is supposed to be like" and instead concentrate on the ultimate pleasure of selflessly meeting our wives' sexual needs. (If your bedroom is a case of "all giving, and no taking" on your part, we'll talk about what to do in Chapter 24.) It's also a safe haven in which we can discover exactly what pleases our wives. Yes, we should be reading books to increase our knowledge of how to satisfy our wives; but ultimately, book smarts only go so far when it comes to the bedroom. There's no substitution for talking things out with our mates and discovering together why sex is truly one of God's greatest gifts to marriages.

NEW CONNECTIONS

Like the brain creating new nerve endings when it experiences or learns something for the first time, husbands and wives can establish new connections in the realm of sex. The greater the perceived threat—"I don't know if we could ever have this conversation"—the greater the actual reward.

Within the safe boundaries of marriage, sex is as close as modern-day men and women will come to replicating the purity and transparency that Adam and Eve experienced in the Garden of Eden: "The man and his wife were both naked, and they felt no shame" (Genesis 2:25). When a husband and wife can stand on even ground in the sanctity of their bedroom, wearing nothing except their respect and honor for one another, they will experience a level of intimacy and affirmation that God designed for no other setting in this life.

But physical transparency requires spiritual and emotional transparency as well. Men know they have failed their wives. What they need to know is that they are forgiven and loved anyway. They need to feel accepted despite their faults and failures—and the same is true for women. When sex is shared as a manifestation of love instead of a reward for perfection, there will be no fragile egos, male or female, in the bedroom.

There is an irony in all of this. The male ego can be destroyed by a woman who has an affair, but it cannot be repaired by a woman. Men with security issues often seek out a woman to tell them that they are okay, that they're adequate and manly. Some men, feeling inadequate or unlovable, turn to a woman to shore up their ego—even to pornographic pictures of women. The woman in the picture makes him feel good about himself as he fantasizes about her loving him.

That reassurance is fleeting, however. It fixes nothing because men become men only in the presence of other men. Iron really does sharpen iron, and the man who struggles with ego issues needs the company of other men to become and feel like an adequate man—all the more so if his wife becomes an adulterer and turns her back on him. He may look to her or another woman to help him heal, but it won't work. The adulterer cannot play the healer. Only the affirmation of other men can help to restore his soul and rebuild the manhood that has been taken from him.

Chapter 22

MEN HAVE SEXUAL FANTASIES— SO WHAT'S NEW?

A pastor came to me one day and told me that he had a serious problem that was impeding his ability to preach. Whenever he approached the pulpit to preach, his eyes, like a radar, would find an attractive woman and lock onto her. All the while he was preaching to his congregation of a thousand people he was fantasizing about this woman and what it would be like to have sexual relations with her. On a recent Sunday morning it got so bad that he completely lost his train of thought and said aloud, "Where was I?"—then waited until someone reminded him of what he had just said.

As we talked, I asked him to tell me about his early memories of puberty and his first realizations of excitement about the opposite sex. He recalled constantly feeling inadequate and insecure. His three older brothers all had girlfriends and seemed competent around girls. His father died when he was six, leaving him with no one to guide him through the maze of hormones, desires, and sexual fantasies. As he matured, his feelings of inadequacy and insecurity stayed with him, and he retreated into a world of fantasy, fearful of being rejected if he tried to initiate a relationship with a girl his age.

He thought marrying his wife would solve everything sexually. They had met when he was in seminary, and she was everything he wanted in a wife. She even wanted to marry a pastor and was excited about serving alongside him. While they were dating, his fantasy life was focused on her as he anticipated their union. Unfortunately, married sex turned out to be fulfilling for her but disappointing for him. She simply couldn't measure up to his prior fantasy life, into which he gradually drifted again. Over time, it became impossible for her to compete with the sexual life he lived in his mind. The result was a disconnected couple that was not enjoying marriage or their sexual relationship.

Fantasy is a part of most every male's life. But before a man can center his fantasies on a single legitimate person—his wife—the couple must be connected. There has to be a true, thriving relationship between the two before a man can stop the obsession. In time, my pastor friend began to recognize that his fantasy life was rooted in his feelings of inadequacy, his low sense of his own manhood, and his disconnect with his wife. Real victory began when he opened up to his wife about his problem. As usually happens, bringing his dark secret into the light took a lot of the power out of it. With his wife's help, he was eventually able to refocus his sexual desires on her and regain control of his thought life.

WHAT WE KNOW ABOUT MEN'S SEXUAL FANTASIES

First of all, let's establish a fact: almost every man who has ever breathed has fantasized about a woman. If you have an imagination or have ever had a creative thought (about anything) not based in reality, you have fantasized. Given that all-inclusive qualifier, the subject of this chapter—men's frequent and intense sexual fantasies—isn't exactly a big secret. It's not a giant leap to go from "everybody fantasizes about something" to "most men fantasize about sex—a lot."

An ABC News *Primetime Live* poll found that 70 percent of men "think about sex every day," while 43 percent "think about sex several times a day" (the numbers for women were 34 and 13 percent, respectively). It doesn't take George Gallup to discern that "How often do men think about sex?" is not a very helpful question for getting beneath the surface of men's sexual fantasies. When men think about sex they could be thinking about sex with their wives—or not; sex in God-honoring settings—or not; sex in conscience-preserving ways—or not.

In the same survey, 16 percent of the total respondents (not just men) had been unfaithful, but 30 percent had "fantasized about it." Fourteen percent had participated in another nontraditional sexual activity (I'll spare you the details), while 21 percent had "fantasized about it."[1] Obviously, the fantasy realm is a buffer zone between what is permissible and what is not.

In our own survey of 3,600 men nearly 57 percent admitted to having "frequent and intense sexual fantasies" (of the Christian respondents, 54 percent responded positively; of the non-Christian respondents, 64 percent responded positively). My hunch is that the phrase "frequent and intense" probably colored the responses to the low side. I would guess that way more than 57 percent of men—probably 90 to 100 percent—have sexual fantasies. Perhaps some men don't have what they consider to be "frequent" or "intense" fantasies, but they fantasize to one degree or another.

The secret, therefore, is not that men have sexual fantasies; this is old news (see Matthew 5:27–28). Rather, what is revealing is that more than half of all men have them *frequently* and *intensely*. Those words change this discussion from one of "weather" (something that happens every day) to "storms" (something that can alter the course of life in a dangerous way) "Frequently and intensely" may border on "obsessively" for some men—something that influences, perhaps even dominates, their lives.

WHAT SEXUAL FANTASIES MEAN TO MEN

As noted, fantasies are omnipresent. Like money, they are amoral, neither good nor bad. Yet mention fantasies to most people and you'll get a negative response that implies these thoughts are inherently evil.

Proverbs 28:19 says, "He who works his land will have abundant food, but the one who chases fantasies will have his fill of poverty." We think of fantasies as being the food of dreamers, people whose lives are not grounded in reality. They're for those who would rather while away the day on their back picking shapes out of the clouds than putting their hands to the plow. And there is something to be said for that perception.

Fantasies have probably fueled far more personal *de*struction in this world than *con*struction.

But if that's true, it's not the fault of a fantasy; it's the fault of the one who lacks self-control over that fantasy. The person who fantasizes (dreams) about finding a cure for a disease and spends thirty years laboring until he succeeds is a person whose fantasy was controlled by discipline and values. But the person who fantasizes about an immoral or unfaithful sexual encounter is a person who has failed to establish parameters around his or her thought life. Fantasies are available twenty-four-seven, 365 days a year. The human mind knows no limit as to what it can conceive. It is up to individuals to establish guidelines for the kinds of fantasies—and the intensity of those fantasies—that they will allow their mind to conceive, conceptualize, and consummate. As the saying goes, "You can't prevent birds from flying overhead, but you can prevent them from building a nest in your hair."

Our English word *fantasy* derives from a Greek work meaning "to show" or "to make visible." From it morphed nouns and adjectives meaning "imagination" and "able to make visible."[2] It's easy to see the connection between these roots and our modern understanding of fantasy, in which we try to make visible or visualize something in our minds. Based on the evolution of the word in English, *The Oxford English Dictionary* says *fantasy* is "the process or faculty of forming mental representations of things not actually present."[3]

Those definitions address the "what" but don't explain the "why." *The American Heritage Dictionary* lends a hand at this point: a fantasy is "an imagined event or sequence of mental images, such as a daydream, *usually fulfilling a wish or psychological need*" (italics mine).[4]

That's helpful. Take fantasy sports leagues, for instance, in which more than thirty million Americans (80 percent of which are men) spend $100 million a year.[5] These leagues are a way for people to own their own sports teams and compete against others by creating fantasy teams with players chosen from actual professional team rosters. Wins and losses are calculated on the basis of the actual players' statistics in a given week.

Fantasy sports is *serious* fantasy in terms of numbers, but also in terms of fulfilling a "wish or psychological need" of the participants—namely, to be involved, even remotely, in pro athletics. Think of the millions of student athletes who invest themselves in sports in city leagues, then high school, then college, only to never make it to the pros. Does the longing to be involved in sports die just because they couldn't earn a living at it? Of course not. They, and millions of others who love sports, competition, gambling, and the entrepreneurial thrill of building a winning team, get their needs fulfilled through fantasy sports leagues.

But what need is being fulfilled for men when they engage in "frequent and intense" sexual fantasies? Remember, sexual fantasies are not like fantasy sports leagues. In the latter, there is a host of activities involved: choosing players, recording statistics, scouring Web sites for leads and information on players, wagering, and others. It's also done via actual interaction with other people. Sexual fantasies, on the other hand, involve an individual playing a mind-only game. Granted, many men stimulate their fantasies through visiting Web sites, watching pornographic movies, visiting adult bookstores, and the like. Yet the fantasies themselves are made up of nothing but electrons firing by the billions between brain cells. What wish or need does this satisfy?

Based on my past and present work among men with sexual addictions and problems, I believe that the desire men are seeking to fulfill boils down to one thing: total intimacy.[6]

I'm not talking about complete intimacy within marriage, as if to say that a husband's sexual fantasies are his wife's fault. A man's current level of intimacy with his wife is certainly a contributor to the mind games he chooses to play. Ultimately, however, this desire for real intimacy goes much deeper and further back in a man's life.

The Hebrew word for "fantasies" is *reyq*, as used in Proverbs 12:11 and 28:19. At its core, the word signifies something that is empty.[7]

Thus, a fantasy is something that is devoid of substance or reality, an empty imagination unconnected to reality. But the concept of emptiness can be extended. I believe the degree to which men engage in frequent and intense sexual fantasies correlates with their feelings and experience of intimacy with others in the real world. That means the emptier a man's reservoir of intimacy, the more he engages in sexual fantasies. The fuller his reservoir of intimacy, the less he engages in sexual fantasies. In other words, the more complete and satisfied he is in the realm of real-world intimacy, the less need he has to seek intimacy in the world of fantasy. The more connected he is with the reality of the woman he has chosen for a wife, the less connection there will be to the fantasy world of women who should be physically and emotionally off-limits.

The discouraging aspect of our search for intimacy is that it will never be over. We live in a fallen world in which every human relationship is scarred by the wounds of weakness, conflict, inadequacy, and responses to fear. The first people from whom we were to gain security, love, wholeness, and intimacy—those whom we needed to tell us who we are in this world—were our parents. Unfortunately, they were not whole people themselves. Perhaps we didn't even have both parents in our home. Or if they were both there, perhaps there was a distinct lack of love, affection, and intimacy between them. They were unable to pass on to us what they did not possess.

At an early age, children learn to compensate by seeking out the intimacy they instinctively know should be there. Imagination and fantasy substitute for the real world, and imaginary friends become close companions. Sadly, as children grow older, they retreat into practices such as masturbation as a temporary release from the feelings of distance and separation. Or they acquiesce to the sexual advances of an older "friend" who recognizes their emotional vulnerability.

More often than not, however, by the time young adults mature into adults, the natural process of separation from their parents leaves behind many loose, dangling threads. Like swallows who have heard of Capistrano but whose deformed wings will not take them there, these young adults live in the imaginary world of wholeness and intimacy that has its ultimate roots in the physical closeness of their birth experience.

In his book *When Men Think Private Thoughts*, Gordon MacDonald beautifully outlines the rationale for connecting a man's sexual insecurity with the breakdowns of intimacy in his growing-up years.[8] More than young girls, young boys have a significant break to make as they leave the warmth and comfort of their mothers' breast. When it begins to dawn on them that they are more like the father in the house than the mother, they turn their backs on what God intended to be the most secure place they've ever known: the womb, then the loving arms, eyes, heartbeat, and breast of their mothers. The conclusion, MacDonald writes, is that "a man is likely to live his entire life with these sensitivities and these issues emblazoned in the deepest recess of his mind."[9]

If a boy's father is there with warmth, hugs, kisses, and affirmation (that is, intimacy) to receive the boy as he leaves his mother, all is well. But that rarely, if ever, happens perfectly, which echoes my earlier sentiment that the search for human intimacy is never completed in this life. Some fathers don't have the capacity to welcome their sons with love and affirmation. Some fathers are away at war during this crucial crossroads, some are deceased, some are workaholics and missing from the home, some are physically present but emotionally absent, some have left the home to pursue their own search for intimacy and affirmation. There are as many reasons why intimacy is not found as there are men who seek it.

To summarize how this imperfect cycle leads to fantasy, MacDonald suggests that "what nature or custom or circumstance denies or forbids, the imagination is likely to create."[10] Because every man (and every woman, for that matter) has been denied the experience of complete intimacy at the human level, every man will allow his imagination to suggest to him ways in which it may be found. If the fantasies are strong enough, he may act them out—a capitulation that may lead to adultery or other immoral acts, as well as the breakup of a marriage. If his self-restraint is strong enough, he may limit his search for intimacy to the realm of his mind alone (as the results from the surveys mentioned earlier suggest).

There are other factors that contribute to the draw toward sexual fantasy: the desire to have total control over a woman, to completely satisfy a woman, to alter a mood, to soothe past hurts, to feel like a "real" man, etc. Yet the truth is, a real man does not live in a fantasy world controlled by subconscious desire and driving lust. A real man is able to control himself—what he does and what he thinks about doing. He is not a common animal with base urges and desires that rule over him, nor is he a victim chained to old ways of coping with pain and feeling manly. He can either choose to live out his desires in a fantasy world, or he can tackle the realities of who he is, what he really fears, and how he compensates for his inadequate feelings.

It is crucial for every man to deal intently with his thought life because, from God's perspective, that which is forbidden in practice is also forbidden in thought: "You have heard that it was said, 'Do not commit adultery.' But I tell you that anyone who looks at a woman lustfully has already committed adultery with her in his heart" (Matthew 5:27–28). Therefore, the realm of sexual fantasy violates standards of purity as well as mental health. What is needed is a way for husbands to explore *in the real world, not the fantasy world*, the intimacy they missed and still seek.

NEW DIRECTIONS

The ABC News *Primetime Live* survey revealed another response that I am reluctant to mention but feel the need to address. Fifty-one percent of the respondents in the poll said that they discuss their sexual fantasies with their spouses. Given the tenor of the survey in general, what is implied is that half the people surveyed discuss their fantasies as a way of spicing up their sex life, much as a couple might watch a pornographic movie together to stimulate their arousal. Indeed, discussing sexual fantasies is the same thing; it's downloading a mental movie off the mind's screen and relaying the details to a spouse.

I don't believe discussing sexual fantasies for that reason is a healthy practice. But I do believe that conversations between a husband and wife about the frequency and intensity of sexual fantasies can be helpful. Few couples probably share a level of intimacy that would allow for such discussions from a therapeutic point of view. But they could. There is no reason for couples not to discuss and pray together about that which is *real*. And the reality is that many men commit a portion of their daily mental cycles to vain imaginations of a sexual nature.

I have spoken with innumerable men who would like nothing better than to be free of the never-ending barrage of sexual fantasies they entertain. They can be when they connect the lost intimacy of their growing-up years with the search for intimacy-via-fantasy of their adult years.

Exposing and sharing this secret may require a new direction for husbands and wives. It will involve intimacy, honesty, sacrifice, compassion, grace, and mercy. These are the very things that lead to lasting, deep, and rich relationships. They can be found in a connected couple. Whatever the problem that destroyed these things in the first place, keep in mind, they can be developed and restored. In fact, the source of destruction can become the very excuse to build these positive relational traits to new and more intense levels.

NEW CONNECTIONS

The search for intimacy isn't a straight and narrow path. At times, seeking this treasured destination will take you along a bumpy road. The challenge is committing—*fully* committing—to the journey. Sexual fantasies can be addictive, and if we have encouraged them willingly for years, they may not cease easily. But I believe as our reservoir of intimacy is filled with love, acceptance, forgiveness, and grace—the elements couples should offer each other because Christ offers it to them (Ephesians 4:32)—the fantasy world will lose its sustaining fuel.

Sexual fantasies are driven by hunger. Not a hunger for sex, but a hunger for that which sex affirms: worth, desirability, importance, and esteem—in short, intimacy. When the appetite for intimacy is satisfied, sexual fantasies will become less intense and less frequent. Obviously, it's impossible to go back and become a child again. But by renewing our minds with Scripture (Romans 12:2), growing in affirmation from our Father God (Romans 8:14–17), and sharing our deepest longings for wholeness with our wives, we can become better, *real* men—men who replace the world of fantasy with the world of reality and a satisfying connection with a woman.

Chapter 23

PORNOGRAPHY:
A COMMUNITY STANDARD

I host a daily one-hour, call-in radio show called *New Life Live!* in which we try to help callers with any kind of emotional, relational, or spiritual problem that might concern them. Every day we answer an array of questions. Yet without exaggerating, we could likely fill each show exclusively with the calls we receive about men and pornography. It has saturated our society, including the Christian community.

Recently a woman called to tell us she had caught her husband viewing pornography on the Internet. She wanted to know what she should do. I told her she should tell him to either attend the Every Man's Battle Workshop (a three-day intensive program for men struggling with sexual integrity) . . . or move out. Though this was likely more drastic a measure than she'd anticipated, I explained to her that the least he could do was to get help for his problem. Then I asked her how she felt when she discovered the Web sites.

Her answer, as expected, was multilayered. She felt like a piece of meat that had been used in the same way he was using the women on the Web. She felt hopeless, knowing she could never measure up to all the images in his head of perfect bodies and their respective parts. She felt as betrayed as if he had been with a woman in person—though in that case, at least she could compete with a live woman rather than the virtual goddesses he was worshiping. She felt that their whole marriage was a fraud—meaningless and dead. She felt totally neglected, ignored, worthless, and sick.

I don't think most men understand how a woman feels when she discovers her husband is viewing pornography.

WHAT WE KNOW ABOUT MEN AND PORNOGRAPHY

While this is a book about secrets, pornography is no secret to anyone. Nor is the fact that men are its primary consumers. The degree to which pornography has become an open aspect of modern American culture is expressed by *Time* magazine columnist Richard Corliss:

> Pornography is big business: an industry that earns an estimated $57 billion worldwide annually—$20 billion just for adult movies in the U.S., where some 800 million videos are rented each year, according to Paul Fishbein, the founding president of Adult Video News. "And I don't think that it's 800 guys renting a million tapes each," he told CBS News. Fishbein means that the phenomenon can't be simply a big-city, left-wing perversion; a good many of those renters, those consumers of hotel porn, have to be red-staters. Which is why, among all the cries in favor of traditional values and against naughty TV, you haven't seen many county sheriffs or G-men forcing the old smut peddler to do a perp walk. Porn doesn't affront contemporary community standards. It *is* a contemporary community standard.[1]

That says it about as well as it could be said: pornography is no longer an affront to community standards—it *is* a community standard. It is especially the community standard in the online world. The millions of pornographic Web sites that are available at the click of a mouse have made a small problem in the 1950s become one of the greatest, if not *the* greatest, threats to sexual integrity and fidelity among men.

Our communities, which together comprise our culture, allow pornography to exist. You can go to your neighborhood movie rental store and find pornographic movies just a couple of shelves over from *The Passion of the*

Christ or *The Ten Commandments.* You can drive to certain parts of town and find an adult bookstore just down the block from the convenience store. And if all you're looking for is a couple of girly magazines, you can pick those up in the convenience store along with milk and bread. Of course, for hard-core fare, you'll still have to make a trip to the adult peep show down the street. (There are still a few community standards in place regarding pornography—for the time being.)

The online world, on the other hand, creates a limitless scope of pornography. There the standard is maximum availability to as many perversions that exist or can be created. And as we've seen within the past few years, what happens online will almost immediately seep into other areas of modern technology. As of this writing, pornography has already been made downloadable for iPods, MP3 players, cell phones, and an assortment of other on-the-go gadgetry.

At the same time, the widespread cultural acceptance of pornography is blatantly displayed on almost every college and university campus across America. Undergrads at the State University of New York at Buffalo can take a course titled "Cyberporn and Society." If you're enrolled in "Anthropology of the Unconscious" at New York University you'll be required to read and discuss X-rated Japanese comic books. And at the University of California at Berkeley, undergrads enrolled in "Cinema and the Sex Act" are required to view clips from Hollywood NC-17 releases.[2]

To be fair, these schools aren't necessarily promoting pornography in their courses. Yet that's exactly the point: they're treating pornography academically (free from moral judgment), just as you would any other societal reality such as racism, politics, war, poverty, or the GNP. Whereas a couple of decades ago there might have been an outcry against such courses in the curriculum, today they hardly register a blip on the radar because pornography has become such a part of the mainstream culture.

That's some of what we know about pornography in general. Because we know the majority of pornography consumers are men, it's fair to extrapolate these findings, then, to the broader scope of men and pornography. For instance, if we know that a certain number of pickup trucks are sold in the United States each year, it's not a stretch to assume that most of those are being bought and driven by men (90 percent in 1995).[3]

The same relationship between "product" and "product consumer" exists in the world of pornography. In fact, pornography generates far more revenue in America than automobile sales, and all the statistics coming out of the industry cite men as the primary purchasers and "users."[4]

And it's not just the Average Joes who indulge in and struggle with pornography. In a *Christianity Today* magazine survey released in December 2001, 51 percent of pastors said that cyberporn represents a real and ongoing temptation, while 37 percent said it was currently a struggle in their life.[5]

In our own survey, 40.1 percent of men said they are "drawn to pornography in movies, magazines, or on the Web." The overall percentage was lowered because the majority of men taking the survey were Christian, 39 percent of whom answered the question positively. (As opposed to the 53.4 percent of non-Christian men who answered in the same fashion.) Regardless, those are huge numbers creating huge problems for the development of intimacy between men and women.

Once again, the vagaries of surveying likely influenced the answers we collected. Specifically, how do we define *pornography*? Admittedly, it means different things to different men, especially with its expansion into various mediums. One man, Supreme Court Justice Potter Stewart, probably spoke for all men in 1964 when writing an opinion on a case dealing with obscenity: "I shall not today attempt further to define the kinds of material I understand to be embraced . . . [b]ut I know it when I see it."[6]

Does that still ring true today? Do we really know anymore when we've seen pornography?

WHAT PORNOGRAPHY MEANS TO MEN

Pornography is best defined in terms of what it means to a man. And therein lies the secret behind this overwhelmingly destructive force: men—at least most men—*hate* their involvement with pornography.

That fact will sound strange and contradictory to women, most of whom are not attracted to pornography. When women discover that the men in their lives are involved with pornography, they are disgusted and angry. What they don't know, however, is that the men themselves are usually just as disgusted and angry at their own involvement.

At the core, being involved with pornography is the same as taking part in any other sin. And those who have a commitment to doing right instead of wrong obviously get angry at themselves when they cave in and commit a sin. It's no different with men and pornography. Like dogs that are drawn to their own vomit (Proverbs 26:11), men are disgusted when they return to pornography.

The Bible doesn't talk about pornography in the modern sense of the word. It mentions *porneia*, defined as "sexual immorality," as a practice (Mark 7:21; Acts 15:29; 1 Corinthians 5:1), but it doesn't distinguish this specifically as written or illustrated sexual images for purposes of sexual stimulation. (The word *pornography* actually comes from combining two Greek words: *porneia* and *grapho*, which means "to write.") However, the Bible does talk in length about that which pornography stimulates and encourages: lust (Proverbs 6:25; Matthew 5:28; Colossians 3:5).

To ask why men are drawn to lust is to ask a question that was first raised in the Garden of Eden. The first man and his wife enjoyed complete intimacy and openness with one another—physically, intellectually, spiritually, and emotionally. Not only did they enjoy that state with each other, but they enjoyed it with God as well. They lived unclothed before each other and before God: "The man and his wife were both naked, and they felt no shame" (Genesis 25). After they disobeyed God and sinned, however, their intimacy was interrupted. Their nakedness became apparent to one another, and they were ashamed, as evidenced by their hiding from their Creator (Genesis 3:10–11). When that happened, not only were the man and his wife split off from God, they were split off from each other.

When God created mankind, He created him "male and female" (Genesis 1:27). When the first man and first woman were joined in marriage, they became one flesh—a complete human. The marriage ceremony in the Judeo-Christian tradition is, in part, a picture of the uniting of the two parts of the constitutionally "bipolar" nature of man—male and female.[7] Thus, since his separation from both God and woman, man has been in a continual state of longing for wholeness. That search to be united with a woman is, in a basic sense, a search for himself (as is his search for communion with God).

When a man seeks to disrobe a woman, either physically or, in the case of pornography, with his eyes, it is almost a primal longing for the days of Eden in which nakedness was "the community standard"—in the healthiest sense. Ever since God clothed our naked ancestors with animal skins (Genesis 3:21), the man, who was the visually oriented of the pair, has been seeking to remove the woman's coverings. Obviously, that doesn't justify the thought of doing so. Rather, it proves that, once outside the garden, our desire for intimacy and wholeness became tainted by a selfish sense of self-gratification that is now ever-present. Man has to constantly walk the tightrope that exists between looking and lusting. And because of the sense God left intact from the garden, man instinctively knows the difference between the two, though pornography gradually erodes such discernment. For that reason, the question surrounding Justice Stewart's opinion—Do we know when we see pornography?—can be answered with a resounding "Yes!" By his core nature, every man knows pornography when he sees it.

The Bible clearly states that "it is not good for the man to be alone" (Genesis 2:18). In other words, it is natural for a man to seek out a woman. However, since the earliest of post-garden days, men have been deceived into thinking that they establish their manhood by conquering a woman sexually either physically through rape or mentally in the act of masturbation facilitated by pornographic images. Consider the wisdom of author Gordon Dalbey on this deception:

> The so-called "Playboy philosophy," for example, focuses on the enticing Playmate. The good news of the Playboy gospel is that the woman confers masculinity upon the reader by sexually arousing him with her "come-on" posture. In reality, however, the reader has simply yielded his manly initiative to the woman and her desires. He has given his masculine spirit over to the goddess and thus lost it.
>
> The Good News of Jesus Christ, on the other hand, proclaims that Father God confers masculinity upon the man who humbles himself in response to Jesus' posture on the cross. By yielding his natural desires to Father God, the believer gives his masculine spirit over to Him and thus gains it, that is, *it becomes subject to him, rather than he to it* [italics mine].
>
> We men today must be weaned away from the popular notion, ranging in expression from pornographic magazines to cheerleaders, that a woman can confer manhood upon us. The woman's admiration and desire are a *consequence* of our authentic manhood—not the source of it. Like the black widow spider who

lures the male to copulate only to kill him afterward, the woman who discovers she can manipulate a man through her sexual charms will disrespect and eventually destroy his manhood.[8]

It is through an earthly father that the heavenly Father's voice should be heard calling a young man out of childhood into manhood. But, as mentioned in the previous chapter, rarely does that happen in today's fatherless, gender-confused culture. As a result, we have a world full of men seeking their manhood by trying to conquer women, physically or mentally, who become pornographic objects of desire.

Dalbey summarizes this point: "Without the earthly father to call the son out into manhood, the boy grows up seeking manly identity in women—whose voices seem to call him to manhood through sexual conquest. But this deception has been recognized by men for thousands of years, as in the ancient myth of the siren women, who cried out for sailors only to dash their ship upon the rocks as the men responded. Masculinity grows not out of conquering the woman, but only out of conquering the man—and not another man, as in war, but oneself."[9]

The obvious response to Dalbey's insight is to ask how—how does a man conquer himself and prevent himself from dying while trying to conquer a pornographic image? The apostle Paul faced the same dilemma: "I found that the very commandment [e.g., do not lust after women] that was intended to bring life actually brought death. . . . I do not understand what I do. For what I want to do I do not do, but what I hate I do" (Romans 7:10, 15 addition mine). After further explanation of his inability to master himself, he exclaims, "What a wretched man I am! Who will rescue me from this body of death? Thanks be to God—through Jesus Christ our Lord!" (vv. 24–25).

The only way for us to regain our Eden-lost manhood—to stop the idiocy of trying to find wholeness in something that can only bring deeper fracturing and separation—is by dying to who we are and receiving new life back from the heavenly Father.

Paul put into words the secret men carry about pornography: "What I hate I do." Women think men love pornography and pursue it out of selfish pleasure. They don't. They pursue it out of a sense of the deepest pain and longing for wholeness. In marriage, the anger that erupts when pornography is discovered serves only to further alienate a man from the one person to whom he joined himself in hopes of finding his other half—that part of himself from which he became separated in Eden.

NEW DIRECTIONS

In the same *Time* magazine column referred to earlier, Richard Corliss cites an interesting fact:

> In hotel rooms where pornography is available, two-thirds of all movie purchases are for pornos; and the average time they are watched is twelve minutes. The image instantly summoned is of the traveling businessman who wants a smidge of sexual exercise before retiring, but who is too tired, timid or cheap to summon a call girl. He cares little about whatever niceties of dialogue or mise-en-scène the movie may contain. He seeks only [momentary gratification], then clicks off the TV, and so to bed.[10]

He's probably right. Those statistics reflect the nightly occupation of America's hotel rooms by her corporate road warriors. Their aloneness in those dark quarters is a perfect picture of man's post-sin solitude in Eden, then in the world at large. Cut off from God and from woman, and thus from his whole self, man searches in this world for a moment of gratification before closing his eyes on another lonely day.

As men, we must begin to see pornography (and all sexual immorality, real or imagined) for the destructive mirage it is: an illusion, a counterfeit, a make-believe siren luring us to a false port in an emotional storm. If we don't, here is what we can expect to find, based on current research:

1. Marital distress, separation, and divorce
2. Decreased sexual satisfaction
3. Decreased sexual intimacy
4. A form of infidelity in the eyes of women
5. Overspending and debt
6. Decreased job security[11]

The new direction we must take is toward God, as did the apostle Paul. It is too late for most men to be called into manhood by their own fathers, though hopefully that will happen where possible (in the form of repentance and by establishing new bonds of love that serve to undergird and support a man's truthful perception of himself as a man). Absent the healing of the father-son relationship, the establishing and deepening of the heavenly Father-earthly son relationship is the only recourse.

Pornography can be addictive and destructive. Any man who is in danger of succumbing to its downward spiral must reach out for help.

NEW CONNECTIONS

Though pornography is perhaps the most difficult of topics for a husband and wife to discuss—after all, the husband is admitting that he has been mentally sleeping with and ravishing women other than his wife—such mutual efforts can lead to the deepest kinds of renewed love. The deeper the sin that is confessed, it seems, the deeper the love that springs from the wounds where the sin has left its mark.

If you are a woman and your man has, is, or might be struggling with pornography, I urge you to view him not as a vow breaker but as someone who is living with a kind of pain you probably cannot feel. Remember, his secret is not that he succumbs to pornography but that he hates himself for doing so. You are God's gift to him, and you possess the power to assure him that love can cover a multitude of sins. Within your God-ordained love, his search for human wholeness can begin and end.

Chapter 24

MUST I TAKE THE LEAD . . . AGAIN?

There aren't that many nice ways to describe Lisa, but I'll do my best to, as the apostle Paul says, "speak the truth in love." She was a nagging, self-obsessed woman who thought she deserved everything while giving barely anything back. She wanted attention and made it clear that her husband owed it to her to serve, care for, and pamper her. He, meanwhile, was an all-around decent man who wasn't keeping any dark secrets from her— except, perhaps, how frustrated he was with the woman he realized he was going to spend the rest of his life with. She wasn't satisfied with the money he made, the clothes he wore, or the house they lived in, and he was growing more and more depressed. He was giving and giving and giving . . . and getting nothing in return except ten minutes' worth of compliant sex every Saturday night.

"Compliant" may be a generous way to describe their sex life. The only thing Lisa did at that weekly meeting was show up. She didn't initiate or respond to anything. She was completely passive in their lovemaking and showed no signs of enjoyment. Even when her husband tried to arouse her or please her, his efforts were met with nothing but criticism.

By the third year of their marriage Lisa's passive sexual demeanor and active criticism finally became too much for her husband. One day he simply didn't come home from work. He rented an apartment and filed for divorce. Her passivity in the bedroom wasn't the main problem, but it was definitely symptomatic. "I gave and gave and gave until I had nothing left," he said. "For all of what she got from me, if she couldn't try to reciprocate with just ten minutes a week of trying to please me, then I was done. She couldn't get out of her own world long enough to participate in what should have been a pleasurable time for both of us. When I didn't come back she acted like she didn't even care."

WHAT WE KNOW ABOUT MEN'S FRUSTRATION WITH WOMEN'S SEXUAL PASSIVITY

Unlike Lisa's husband, most men's number one concern is not passive sex, but it is a big one. Contrary to popular opinion (at least among women), the number one thing most men want in a woman is not sex. A poll of 1,052 men and women conducted by Leger Marketing-Canadian Press in January 2004 proves this and more. Participants were asked to choose the three attributes they valued most in a potential mate (therefore the numbers add up to more than 100 percent), and this is how they responded:

What Women Want Most in a Man:
- Faithful partner: 54 percent
- Respect for each other's independence: 40 percent
- Ability to listen: 35 percent
- Physical attraction: 13 percent
- Being good in bed: 6 percent

What Men Want Most in a Woman:
- Faithful partner: 47 percent
- Respect the other person's independence: 36 percent
- Intelligence: 35 percent
- Physical attraction: 26 percent
- Being good in bed: 13 percent

(An incidental yet encouraging note from the above survey: 90 percent of those polled believe it's possible to be happy with one person for a lifetime.)[1]

These survey results should surprise no one: faithfulness and loyalty are the most desirable traits when seeking and keeping a life partner. But for the purpose of this chapter, it is interesting that "being good in bed" was twice as important to men as to women. As with all surveys, there are likely as many definitions of "being good in bed" as there are respondents to the question. Yet when poll after poll points in the same general direction regarding an issue, it's safe to say a trend has been established. And there's no question that men appreciate it when their wives are "good in bed." To some this might sound crass and carnal, but to others it will simply ring true. No matter how you view it, the reality is in the statistics: performance in the bedroom counts.

Author and speaker Patrick Morley asked the 150 or so men in a weekly class he teaches to tell him how important sex was to them. "Sex is *no* issue to you, a *medium* issue, or a *major* issue," he offered as options. This was a non-scientific, raised-hands poll. Not a single man indicated that sex was "no issue," and a handful raised their hands for "medium issue." But when Morley asked about "major issue," the hands that shot up looked like amber waves of grain swaying in the wind. No less than 95 percent of the men said sex was a "major issue."[2]

Women reading those results will say, "So? Where's the news?" That response is indicative of a (true) stereotype: sex is important to men. Yet despite being true, there's a serious problem with that belief, one that was evidenced by the initial survey I cited. Yes, sex is important to men. But it is not the *most important* thing to men. In addition, the stereotype suggests that the physical act of sex is what men are most interested in—"Wham, bam, thank-you, ma'am," as the locker room saying goes.

But there is more to a man's feelings about sex than just the desire to "do it" as often as possible. In our research, we found that 38.9 percent of the 3,600 men surveyed "are frustrated that women are not more aggressive sexually." (Interestingly, the responses by Christian and non-Christian men varied by less than 2 percent.) This means more than a third of men are less than satisfied ("frustrated") about the *kind* of sex they have rather than the amount. Wives would likely associate the word *frustrated* with the assumption that their husbands are not getting enough sex, making this a quantitative issue. In their eyes, they're walking around like boilers about to blow. What may surprise these women is that their husbands are concerned about the quality of sex, not just the *quantity*. And that's the secret we'll talk about in this chapter: just because a husband is having sex doesn't mean he's satisfied.

WHAT WOMEN'S SEXUAL PASSIVITY MEANS TO MEN

To be more specific, many men are frustrated by their wives' passivity when it comes to lovemaking. The stereotype—what might immediately pop into a wife's mind—is that her husband expects her to dress and act like a *Playboy* centerfold after an exhausting day working and/or managing the home and children. That may be true for some husbands, but it's not the expectation of most. There's something deeper going on with the passivity issue.

When it comes to being proactive, women often have other things in mind, as illustrated by the following joke:

A woman was sitting at a bar enjoying an after-work cocktail with her girlfriends when an exceptionally tall, handsome, extremely sexy young man entered. He was so striking that the woman could not take her eyes off him. The young man noticed her overly-attentive stare and walked directly toward her.

Before she could offer her apologies for being so rude for staring, the young man said to her, "I'll do anything, absolutely anything, that you want me to do, for $100, on one condition."

Flabbergasted, the woman asked what the condition was. The young man replied, "You have to tell me what you want me to do in just three words."

The woman considered his proposition only for a moment before withdrawing from her purse five twenty-dollar bills, which she slowly counted out on the table. She then picked them up and, along with a scrap of paper with her address, pressed them into the young man's hand. She then looked deeply into his eyes and slowly said, "Clean my house."[3]

For a split second, that young man thought he had met a proactive woman, someone who was able and willing to take the initiative when it came to sex. She was proactive alright—she just had different priorities at that moment!

So what are a man's priorities when it comes to making love to his wife? What does a man mean when he says he is frustrated that his wife is passive in bed?

In 1981, Dr. Kevin Leman wrote a book called *Sex Begins in the Kitchen: Renewing Emotional and Physical Intimacy in Marriage*. The point of the title was directed primarily toward a wife's need to have sex be the consummation of a process that begins long beforehand. "The kitchen" represents the part of a wife's life where she needs her husband's support and involvement, the kind of day-long, domestic foreplay by which a husband says to his wife, "I enjoy being with you all the time, not just in the bedroom. I appreciate and value all you do to make our home and family a wonderful environment."

I believe there is a corollary book waiting to be written about sex from a man's perspective—*Sex Ends in the Office: How to Make Your Husband Feel Indispensable*. When a wife *responds* sexually, she shows her love for her husband. But when she *initiates* sexually, she shows her *need* for her husband. And if there is *one thing*—I repeat, one thing—a man needs above all else, it is to be needed by his wife. Think about it: there is only one area of life in which a husband is the only person who can meet his wife's needs, and that is sex. For everything else, she can turn to the Yellow Pages: plumbers, carpenters, carpet cleaners, landscapers. But when it comes to sex, a husband is all a wife has—and he knows it.

When a wife is passive in the bedroom, she says two things to her husband:

1. I don't need sex.
2. Because I don't need sex, I don't need you.

Back to *Sex Ends in the Office*. For a wife, sex is about what's happened beforehand: the kind of mood she's in, the kind of day it's been, how her husband has treated her, the number of things percolating on her mental back burner, the status of the children, and more. Most, if not all, of those items are irrelevant to a husband when it comes to sex. For him, sex is about the emotional feeling he has afterward. When he knows his wife really needs to have sex with him (as demonstrated by her proactive posture in the bedroom), he gets up in the morning with a new shine on his masculine armor. He goes into work with a glow that is inexplicable.

Shaunti Feldhahn, in her book *For Women Only*, reminds us of the Viagra commercial that aired on television. As a man walks through the halls of his office his colleagues notice that something is different: New suit? *Nope.* Been working out? *I wish.* Promotion? *Someday.* What only he and we know is that he had a great night of sex the night before, thanks to Viagra.[4] Product spotlighting aside, the commercial comes pretty close to being on-target. The biggest impact of sex on men is the way it makes them feel afterward—either on top of the world or under it.

When a wife is proactive in lovemaking, it gives a husband the sense that he's needed and desired. It makes him feel good about who he is, because he's proven his ability to meet a need for his wife that only he can meet.

If you haven't noticed, we're now talking about the emotional part of a man's life instead of the physical. Men and women are alike in that they have a physical side and an emotional side. Unfortunately, we tend to think of women as being the emotional ones and men leaning purely toward the physical aspects. And in the aggregate, that's probably true. But that doesn't mean that women don't have a physical side (a need for the physical release brought about by sexual consummation), nor men an emotional side (a need to be needed by their wives). In other words, both have physical and emotional needs that are satisfied by lovemaking. The emotional needs between the two, however, are different. Women need to be appreciated for who they are, while men need to be needed for what only they can do.

Dr. John Gray, author of the classic *Men Are from Mars, Women Are from Venus*, puts it this way: "Men are motivated and empowered when they feel needed. When a man does not feel needed in a relationship, he gradually becomes passive and less energized; with each passing day he has less to give the relationship. On the other hand, when he feels trusted to do his best to fulfill her needs and appreciated for his efforts, he is empowered and has more to give."[5] A wife's proactivity in sexual matters is her way of saying, "I need you to make love to me."

When a husband doesn't feel needed, Gray continues, "He withdraws from relationships or intimacy and remains stuck in his cave. He asks himself what it is all for, and why he should bother. He doesn't know that he has stopped caring because he doesn't feel needed. He does not realize that by finding someone who needs him, he can shake off his depression and be motivated again."[6]

How many men have struck up a relationship with a younger woman because she "needed" him? Obviously, that does not justify such behavior, but it does often explain it.

Gray adds insight to this idea: "A man's deepest fear is that he is not good enough or that he is incompetent. He compensates for this fear by focusing on increasing his power and competence."[7] How many men have become insensitive, even demanding, toward their wives when it comes to sex in an attempt to reestablish their competence? That aptitude deteriorates as a wife communicates over time that her husband is completely inept at meeting her needs. She fails to communicate that she has sexual needs or that she desires for him to meet those needs. She is passive in lovemaking, which is a nonverbal way of saying, "I have no needs that you can meet in our bedroom. I'll participate for your physical need to be met, but that's all."

Think about marriage vows: husbands and wives commit to limit their sexual activity to one person for the rest of their lives! That's a commitment that is easy to make at a time when hormones are as active as salmon in an Alaskan river. It's a vow that means, "I commit to give myself to you, and I commit to receive only from you, 'til death do us part."

But what happens if that giving and receiving wanes over time? Dr. Willard F. Harley Jr., author of *His Needs, Her Needs*, describes the case for the husband:

> If his religious or moral convictions are strong, he may try to make the best of it. Some husbands tough it out, but many cannot. They find sex elsewhere. . . . A man cannot achieve sexual fulfillment in his marriage unless his wife is sexually fulfilled as well. While I have maintained that men need sex more than women, unless a woman joins her husband in the sexual experience, his need for sex remains unmet. Therefore a woman does her husband no favors by sacrificing her body to his sexual advances. He can feel sexually satisfied only when she joins him in the experience of lovemaking.[8]

This area of truly needing meaningful sex is tricky, especially for men. It's easy for men to cross a thin line when talking about their wives being proactive in lovemaking. Their expectations can be both healthy and unrealistic. On the one hand, they can have the desires I've been discussing: a legitimate need to be needed by a wife. On the other hand, if a Victoria's Secret catalog has arrived in the mail that day, they can cross that line and begin coveting something that isn't real: an airbrushed, pouty, over-endowed, perfectly coiffed, and made-up fantasy image that will slink into the bedroom and take them on a two-hour roller-coaster ride. Not only is that a joke, it's incredibly disrespectful and damaging to a man's wife.

To be honest, most men don't want to seek out that kind of woman any more than they want to indulge in pornography. They don't want "hot sex" if it means they're left with a guilty conscience. And if and when a man ever pays a woman for sex, it's not about the sex; it's about needing to be needed. So strong and deep is a man's need to be needed by his wife that he will stoop to paying someone to fulfill that role in her stead.

If you're a wife reading this, don't misinterpret that last statement. I'm not saying that passive wives are the reason husbands are unfaithful. Far from it. However, there is more to the equation of affairs than the stereotypical scenario of a husband who's sexually bored with his wife. The truth is, when men *are* unfaithful it's not always about hotter, greater, wilder, or sexier sex. It's about the need men have to be needed by their wives. And that need can be filled by a thirty-, fifty-, or seventy-year-old wife who carries the sags and scars from years of hard work, childbearing, and loyal love. When it comes to satisfying sex, a husband's dream wife is one who is proactive in letting her husband know that she needs him to make love to her.

NEW DIRECTIONS

It's frustrating when a wife refuses to take the lead in the bedroom and expects her man to initiate sex on his terms. For us guys, we interpret that to mean sex isn't a big deal to our wives—which, given the fact that *it is* a big deal to us, can make for some highly unsatisfying encounters. We must understand there's more to this situation than what is on the surface.

We've already talked about the different needs women and men have when relating to sex. Any man who hopes to up his wife's passion in bed must realize he has to approach sex with consideration to her desires, not his—which often means paying close attention to matters most men consider *anything but* sexual. As Dr. Leman suggests, it's crucial that we make sure we're catering to our wives' needs throughout the day, regardless of how small those seem.

Yet there is another issue that often lies beneath the surface of a woman's passivity in the bedroom. Dr. David Schnarch, writing from a decidedly secular and clinical perspective, has observed that women may often hold back when it comes to lovemaking because of traditional or religious norms or out of a fear of making their husbands feel inadequate. They feel sex should be gentle, not aggressive.[9] I believe this might especially be true for committed Christian wives who have inherited a Puritanical, even Victorian, attitude toward sex.

Hebrews 13:4 does say that the marriage bed should be kept "pure," an injunction easy enough to misinterpret. Couple that with Paul's instructions for wives to be submissive to their husbands (Ephesians 5:22) and you have wives who bring a meek and mild persona with them to bed. They believe their role is to respond, not initiate, to please rather than be pleased.

The problem with that view is that it starkly contrasts with what we see in the Song of Solomon, that energetic Old Testament love story in which both bride and groom are proactive in their love for one another. In that beautiful portrait of marital passion, the wife speaks boldly about her love for her husband, even his ripped anatomy (5:10–16), as does the husband about his wife (4:1–7; 6:4–9; 7:1–9). That book alone is adequate justification for the biblically guided woman to initiate a proactive posture toward sex in her marriage. It also may be the "evidence" she needs her husband to show her, proof that could lead to a release of passion previously suppressed under a guise of being spiritually pure.

For Christian couples, the Bible does not say what is allowed or not allowed in the marriage bed. The apostle Paul does say that husbands' and wives' bodies belong not to themselves but to their spouses, particularly in terms of being a vehicle for sexual satisfaction (1 Corinthians 7:3–4). In all things sexual, the principles of honor and servanthood prevail. Or, as Harley puts it, "Meet your spouse's needs as you would want your spouse to meet yours."[10]

NEW CONNECTIONS

As in all matters marital, communication is critical when it comes to sexual satisfaction. Heart-to-heart talks can break new ground and open new vistas of pleasure—and not just sexual pleasure, which pales in comparison to the gratification of being affirmed and told that all your spouse's needs are being fulfilled in you. The day a man hears his wife say, "I need for you to make love to me" is a day that will be indelibly marked in his memory. He will view that statement not as an invitation to "let the games begin," but as an affirmation of his role and a fulfillment of his vows to be his wife's sole source of sexual satisfaction 'til death do them part.

Obviously, that parting by death will eventually come. Yet research now proves that even sex can be a contributing factor to staving off that imminent time for men. When wives become more proactive about sex, the number of sexual encounters for their husbands will likely increase. And according to a study by researchers from the University of Bristol and Queen's University of Belfast, men who have three or more orgasms a week are 50 percent less likely to die from coronary heart disease.[11] Though the coauthor of the study cautioned that "further research is necessary," the preliminary findings give just cause for a wife who wants to do the best for her man!

For women, the bottom line on this secret is that if you want to win the heart of a man, being the seducer, aggressor, or temptress in the bedroom is a near-certain way to accomplish it. Because of past hurts and present dysfunctions, it is difficult for a wife to jump into this role. But it is a goal to work toward.

Perhaps you or your spouse have issues to work through. Remember, take your time. Being aware of this secret can encourage wives to work through any insecurities while becoming sexually competent and active with their spouses. And for husbands, knowing that your wife is now aware of your desire for her to be more assertive can change the entire atmosphere in the bedroom. In the process, both of you can learn the deeper lesson that makes the experience gratifying on multiple levels. Sex is a great gift from God, one that's worth the work to switch from a passive to an active role—and one that's certainly worth the time to learn how to serve and please each other.

Chapter 25

WHY APPEARANCE MATTERS

The first time I saw my wife I thought she was the most beautiful woman I had ever seen. I was helplessly drawn to the perfect beauty of her face, her deep, ocean-blue eyes, and brilliant white teeth. Misty was so stunning that when I finally contacted her several months later I was amazed to find her receptive to my initiative. I could not imagine someone as gorgeous as she was being interested in me.

When she became pregnant with our little boy, Solomon, she took on another kind of beauty—different, but with the same radiance. On the occasions I had to be out of town, when I returned home I was amazed at how much more dazzling she looked than how I remembered her from a few days prior.

I began to wonder if other men felt the same way about their wives as I did about Misty. Did they find the outer appearance of a woman as important in their ongoing relationship as they did in the initial stages of courtship? The survey we conducted provided the answer, which to many will be a no-brainer: men are definitely attentive to the physical attractiveness of their wives.

WHAT WE KNOW ABOUT MEN AND WOMEN'S APPEARANCE

Author Shaunti Feldhahn has compiled some of the most recent information about how men feel about their wives' appearance. In her research, she asked a large group of men whether the following statement was true or false: "I want my wife/significant other to look good and feel energetic. It is not as important that she look just like she did the day we met. It is more important that she make the effort to take care of herself for me now."

If you're a woman reading this, what percentage of the men would you guess responded "true," and what percentage said "false"?

If you're a man reading this, how would you have responded?

In Feldhahn's survey, the response was what pollsters would call overwhelming: 83 percent answered "true," while 17 percent answered "false." Granted, binary (either/or) survey questions don't allow for the expression of any gray-area responses such as, "I love my wife regardless of her appearance." On the other hand, they are valuable because they force respondents to make a choice despite any mediating circumstances. And when forced to choose, 83 percent of the men in the survey essentially said, "Yes, I definitely want my wife to look good and make an effort to present her best self for me and for our marriage."

In their response to a hypothetical scenario Feldhahn presented, 70 percent of the male respondents said it would bother them *emotionally* if their wives let themselves go and stopped devoting energy to looking good and staying fit.[1] Don't overlook the word *emotionally* in this scenario. This isn't just a matter of husbands being frustrated if their wives don't look hot or sexy. Apparently, the men responding to this survey would be wounded at some deep level by their wives' failure to take care of themselves and their appearance.

In our own survey, the question was broader but to the same point: "Men place a high level of value on the physical appearance of women." Out of 3,600 respondents, 64 percent answered affirmatively (52 percent said "often," while 12 percent said "always").

From both polls, we can safely gather this: the physical appearance of a wife or female partner is a significant issue to the vast majority of men. What we also know is that men might express these feelings in an anonymous survey, but they rarely are willing to express them to their wives. Most men would rather ride a pogo stick through an abandoned minefield than bring up the subject of their wives' appearance to their face.

WHAT WOMEN'S APPEARANCE MEANS TO MEN

Seinfeld was known throughout its nine-year run as "a show about nothing," but anyone who watched it knows it was anything but that. The show's writers, Jerry Seinfeld and Larry David, had their fingers directly on the pulse of American culture, especially when it came to relationships. For instance, two episodes dealt candidly with the subject of "dress codes" for men and women.

The first one was called "The Engagement." Shortly after George impulsively asked Susan to marry him, they moved in together. Though not yet married, George immediately began suffocating from the presence of another person—a woman—and her efforts to change him. One evening, as they prepared to go out, Susan looked at George and, without a moment's hesitation, said, "You wearing *that* shirt?" You could hear guys all over America groaning in empathy with George. Been there, heard that.

The second episode involved Jerry and his new girlfriend, Christie, who piqued his interest by always wearing the same dress every time they went out. He began to obsess over this, expressing his curiosity to everyone but Christie. "What in God's name is going on here?" he wondered. "Is she wearing the same thing over and over again? Or does she have a closet full of these [dresses], like Superman? I've got to unlock this mystery." When he finally got up the nerve to ask, she hung up the phone on him and the mystery went unsolved.[2]

Though the two episodes were completely unrelated, the point was crystal clear: even though both men and women care about their significant others' appearance, women are the only ones who have "permission" to bring it up. And if we use *Seinfeld* as an accurate barometer of cultural norms, men are intimidated about commenting on a woman's appearance in any manner other than an overt compliment.

As a result, men who are frustrated with their wives' appearance find themselves on the horns of a dilemma: they aren't happy, but they don't feel the freedom to address the source of their unhappiness. A husband may not be talking about his wife's appearance, but he is thinking about it (this probably comes as a surprise to most women). If a woman wants to know what he is thinking, or if she cares about what he is feeling, she needs to make it safe for him to share. In particular, she must not allow a less-than-complimentary comment to escalate into a major blowup.

There is a cultural conclusion that says women are the experts on beauty, attractiveness, and appearance. Men may have GQ and *Esquire*, but women have dozens of glossy magazines devoted to making their lives attractive with clothes, makeup, relationship skills, assertiveness, physical conditioning, diet, and a myriad of other self-improvement methods. The cultural stereotype says that men are dolts when it comes to appearance—their idea of cleaning up is to change T-shirts. Wives and girlfriends replace men's mothers, assuming the role of keeping them from being an embarrassment in public.

While that may be the stereotype, it does not hold true in most cases. Just because every other guy on TV is an Al Bundy-ish oaf who equates being fashionable with a lack of manliness doesn't mean that's how it is in real life. In fact, more men than given credit for know what looks acceptable or good and want to meet that standard. The metrosexual male takes it further and attempts to look as chic and cool as possible. Truth be told, it's getting harder to find men who embarrass their women as walking fashion faux pas.

Having said that, allow me to throw in a case study that gives credence to the stereotype. My assistant is a single, attractive young woman who is available to date respectable young men. At a conference for singles where I was speaking she met a young man who appeared to have a lot going for him. I met him and found him to be a great guy, as far as I could determine in a five-minute conversation. When Julie told me he had asked her out I was excited for her. She was looking forward to their time together.

A few days later they had their date and I asked Julie how it went. She had a pleasant time but was a little curious about the guy's fashion sense. The date was for dinner and Julie dressed nicely for the restaurant they would visit. But for some reason her date picked her up wearing a T-shirt and jeans—the T-shirt bearing the imprint "Git-r-done!" We all know that you only get one chance to make a first impression . . . and his certainly could've been better.

While there are some men still stuck in the "git-r-done" mode, many have moved on and know how to present themselves in the sharpest manner possible. On the flip side, they also hope their wives will take the effort to maintain the standards that initially sparked their attraction. Yet what happens when they don't? What happens when a woman becomes a source of embarrassment to her man—either publicly by becoming overweight, even obese, and out of shape; or privately by padding around the house, sans makeup, in slippers and sweats with a carton of Ben & Jerry's idling on the kitchen counter?

The problem is that men are afraid to broach the topic. "Who am I to raise the issue of her appearance?" they think. "I've done it before and have a stump now where once I had a hand. I think I'll keep my dog out of that fight."

Even if men muster up the courage to raise the question of their wives' appearance *sensitively* (not a given, by any means), they often get one or more of these responses:

- "Your priorities are out of order. Isn't who I am on the inside more important than my outward appearance?"
- "I think you should love me for who I am, not for who you want me to be."
- "You're making judgments about me by criticizing my appearance, and I don't appreciate it."
- "When you lose your extra weight and clean up your own act, then you can come and talk to me about my appearance."

Ouch! Once bitten, twice shy. Sometimes men earn these defensive responses by the way they broach the subject, or by not taking the log out of their own eye before attempting to remove the speck from their wives'. But sometimes they do it right, bringing up the issue of appearance with proper motives and loving methods, yet still get burned. As a result, they pull back and begin to stoke the fires of resentment, or at least double up on their prayer time in asking God for wisdom and grace to know how to handle the situation.

For men, the bottom line is this: as far as appearance goes, many would not have proposed to the woman they find themselves married to five, ten, or fifteen years into the marriage. And this creates an obvious and serious problem in any relationship.

There are two kinds of beauty by which a man is attracted to a woman during courtship: physical and non-physical (spiritual and emotional). Obviously, there is no way to assign percentages to these two areas, but for the sake of discussion, let's say each area represents 50 percent of the reason a man is attracted to a woman. She presents herself as beautifully as possible in her search for a mate, and he responds positively to her efforts. Likewise, she is on her best behavior personality-wise, which causes him to respond in the same manner as well.

So what happens when, years into the marriage, half the reason he married her is gone? Granted, there is nothing in the marriage vows about "keeping up appearances." But for a man it's an implied part of the deal since it represents a major part of the reason he entered into the marriage in the first place. (Note: I could make the same argument on behalf of the wife who finds herself married to someone who bears little external resemblance to the dashing knight who captivated her years before—"Who are *you* and what have you done with my husband?!" Nevertheless, this is a book about the secrets *men* keep, so the discussion is obviously one-sided.)

Men aren't lying when they respond positively in surveys to questions about their wives' appearance. They're saying something on paper that they often don't feel the freedom to say in person. It's a secret they keep, and a serious one at that. Men wish their wives would give adequate attention to their physical appearance: diet, weight, clothes, makeup, exercise—the whole thing. They're not saying this is the most important thing, but *most* of them are saying it *is* important.

In working with women and their weight issues through the Lose It for Life project, I found an interesting justification some women use to keep the pounds on. Many times I have heard women express the need to be loved by their husband "for who they are" and not what they look like. They hang onto their overweight condition as a test of their husband's love. I find this reasoning fascinating—hearing a woman say she is deliberately making herself unattractive to test her husband's love.

There are two problems with this. First, a husband wants to be seduced by his wife. He wants to see the goddess come out of her as she shows her desire for him, over and over again. Whether fair or not, a woman who is extremely overweight and unkempt will likely struggle to do that in this culture. Second, the reality is that these women would not be the same if they lost the extra weight. With fifty pounds shed they would do different things, think different thoughts, respond differently to comments, and be treated differently. Ultimately, turning yourself into something other than the best you can be is a poor way to test the love of your mate. It's also a poor excuse for putting your health and future in jeopardy.

NEW DIRECTIONS

It's no secret: we men are visual creatures. We wash and wax our cars and manicure our lawns and organize our tools because appearance matters to us. And the appearance of wives matters in the same way. It's not for prideful or possessive reasons, but for organic reasons: We don't get it when someone willingly allows their appearance to deteriorate. (Again, there are many men who are exceptions to that rule, letting their own physique and looks deteriorate over time. This doesn't negate the "appearance" rule; it just means those men are living with guilty consciences over who they've allowed themselves to become.)

We must realize, however, that women often have different standards and reasons for looking good, especially in the context of marriage. Author and businessman Patrick Morley has noted five different motivations that a woman draws from when determining what level of commitment to make to her appearance:

1. Her husband
2. Her peers
3. Other men (work, church, civic settings, sports)
4. Herself
5. No one (she doesn't invest any effort in her appearance for anyone)[3]

For a wife, the primary source of motivation (in the human realm) for looking good should be her husband since she spends more time with him than with anyone else. If she maintains a committed investment in appearing good for him, she will look good everywhere else as well.

But it's possible for us to unknowingly smother that motivation with something that all men are naturally prone to do: *compare*. In the Song of

Solomon, the man says about his betrothed, "Yes, compared to other women, my beloved is like a lily among thorns" (2:2, NLT). Carnal as it may sound, we men are comparison shoppers. In fact, we can't *not* compare. We visually survey everything, subconsciously comparing and ranking—houses, boats, cars, jobs, watches, tools, education, income. That's not wrong or sinful; it's just what men do.

It can become sinful, however, if envy, jealousy, or vain ambition take over. And regarding the issue of our wives' appearance, it can become an instant whopper of a problem if we allow ourselves to openly compare our wives' looks to other women. Obviously, we can flatter our mates by reminding them how outstanding they are in contrast to other women. But as a motivational tool for a wife who is lagging in this department, comparison is incredibly detrimental and hurtful and should be completely off-limits. (Put yourself in her shoes for just a moment and you'll understand why.)

So what can you do if your wife has abandoned any semblance of concern for her appearance? Or what are you supposed to do when the motivators Morley pointed out are rearranged and you've suddenly been demoted to number two, three, or four on the list? In other words, what happens when a working wife invests lots of energy in her appearance for her job, but then lives like a sad sack at home? Even when she and her husband are running errands on Saturday, it's sloppy sweats, no makeup, and fallen hair. But come Monday morning, she's a fashion plate as she heads out the door.

This may be the situation you face at home. Maybe you've tried dropping hint after hint to inspire your wife toward caring more about her appearance not just at the office but also at home—for you. And it's possible you've dealt with feelings of demotion. Knowing that everyone puts his or her best foot forward for that which is most important, maybe you've concluded that there may be something, or perhaps someone, at work that's become more important than you. Before you go any further down that trail of thought, however, make sure you and your wife have completely connected on this issue. Talk to her—directly. No more subtle hints, no more ambiguous statements. Since it is a topic rarely broached, it will likely be difficult, for reasons we've already discussed. But as with virtually every marital issue covered in this book, open communication can eventually transform a dark situation into one of light.

Be forewarned, however: if we hope to express a desire for our wives to appear better, we can expect the tables to be turned—and rightly so. We harbor a double standard if we expect our wives to look their best yet have allowed our own physiques and appearances to fall by the wayside. Author and rabbi Shmuley Boteach goes so far as to suggest that husbands bear some of the blame for their wives losing interest in their appearance:

"First, there is something just a little hypocritical in the contemporary contention of husbands that only their wives need appear sexy while they can have endless folds of whale blubber hanging down their stomachs. Sorry guys, but just as you don't want to be married to Aunt Jemima, she doesn't want to be married to the Pillsbury Doughboy. You complain that it is challenging making love to the Goodyear Blimp, but having the Michelin Man climb on top of you might not be the most pleasurable experience either."[4]

If we husbands want to talk about appearance, we have to allow ourselves to be fair game.

NEW CONNECTIONS

A key insight for any woman is the disconnect I cited earlier in this chapter: men care deeply about their wives' appearance but are hesitant to bring up the subject not knowing how their wives will respond. The solution? Let your husband know that the discussion of appearance is safe ground, that you're willing to be part of the conversation and the solution, if needed.

Wives will be interested to know that when Feldhahn asked four hundred men how many of them would be willing to invest effort, money, or time to help their wives improve their appearance, a whopping 97 percent said they were willing to make a "reasonable" (31 percent) or significant (66 percent) effort.[5] Part and parcel with that endeavor are things such as coming up with more money for clothes or gym memberships or spending time taking care of the children so the wife can invest time in her appearance and physical well-being. And yet once again, these numbers speak for themselves in terms of men's seriousness about this subject.

Another way to connect on the subject of appearance is for a wife to ask her husband to talk about what drew him to her when they were dating. What was it about her clothes, her hair, her style, or her physical appearance that appealed to him? No one is suggesting that a forty-five-year-old woman could, or even should, try to look like she did when she was twenty. That's not the goal. Instead, the objective is to regain a sense of care and commitment. It's not that women's bodies shouldn't change after bearing children, or that their hair should never begin showing flecks of gray. Obviously, those are unhealthy, unrealistic expectations. The problem is that those life stages often cause women to stop caring about how they look.

Most mature men are far more excited about a committed, caring, attractive, disciplined, energetic, and wise-from-experience forty-five-year-old wife than they are about a twenty-year-old airbrushed model in a magazine. The sense of self-care and self-respect that a woman exercised when she was trying to capture her husband's heart at age twenty is what will capture his heart again at age forty-five and beyond.

Men care about appearance and for reasons that are different than most women think. It's not all about sex. It's about self-respect, commitment, and being a good steward of a life that is a gift from God.

Lest a woman leave this chapter feeling hopeless and helpless, there is one thing that seems to override a man's focus on a woman's appearance: a deep, rich, and intimate spiritual and emotional connection between the two of them. I witnessed this firsthand just last year. Misty and I attended what could be called an adult "sex camp." I was about to begin writing a book on this subject, and we wanted to be sure we were not missing something other couples had. So we went to the desert with thirty other couples who were there for many different reasons. Some had not had sex in more than a year, and some were having great sex and wanted it to be even greater.

The wives of many of these couples were average-looking women—not knockouts or beauty queens, but well-dressed women who paid attention to how they looked. Over the course of the four-day workshop Misty and I got to know the other couples well. When the men were with me separately, I got to hear them talk about their wives. And to my astonishment, each spoke as if he was married to the most beautiful, sexiest woman on the planet. These husbands spoke of their love and passion for their wives, and their admiration just oozed out in every discussion session. During those four days, as the couples connected on new and deeper levels, the men's admiration for their wives grew even stronger.

As a result of listening to their husbands talk, I began to see the women differently. I began to see beauty in them that I would never have seen passing them in an airport or shopping mall. I began to see why each man was so in love with his wife. Even though these women were of average beauty, their husbands were drawn to them on multiple levels. What I heard were real men describing their love for their wives based on much more than just physical appearance.

I came away from the workshop with a new appreciation not only for my own wife's multiple dimensions of beauty, but also for the depth of love demonstrated by this random cross section of American men. I believe any woman who isn't able to replicate the physical appearance she had ten, twenty, or thirty years ago can still become the most beautiful woman in the world to her husband if she explores the different levels of beauty available to her. And just as encouraging is the fact that men can indeed look beneath the surface in their quest for beauty.

CONCLUSION

FROM SECRETS TO SOLUTIONS

You have gathered from reading this book that I am a Christian. But I hope you haven't concluded that my faith is a marginal part of my life based on the scarcity of Bible verses in the book and my nonpolemical style of writing. That conclusion would be wrong. My entire life and vocational pursuits are based on a firm faith in Jesus Christ as the Son of God and Savior of mankind.

So why the low-key approach to faith in this book? Two reasons: first, secrets are human realities, not Christian. Before any man becomes a Christian he is first a human. That's why we surveyed both Christians and non-Christians in the research that this book is based on, and why we weren't surprised to find that in the vast majority of cases, Christian men and non-Christian men keep similar secrets.

Second, the book was intended to be a mirror. Granted, in the "New Directions" and "New Connections" sections of each chapter, I donned my counselor hat and dispensed some recommendations and advice. But even then, the advice was usually as equally applicable to those who are evangelical about life as to those who are evangelical about faith. My goal in writing this book was to raise the discussion level among men and their female counterparts—mostly wives, but also girlfriends, mothers, or sisters—about the secrets men keep. That which is kept in the dark can't be talked about, and what can't be talked about can't be helped.

Having discussed secrets, I want to conclude this book by addressing some of their solutions, and to do that I have to turn to the Bible. Whether one believes, as I do, that the Bible is a trustworthy guide to faith and practice for all of life, or that it is a collection of wise teachings of wise men through the ages, but not necessarily truth from God, there is value in what it says about secrets and solutions. As a man who has encountered many difficulties in his life—some of my own doing, many not—I can attest that the truth and wisdom of Scripture have always remained valid guides for whatever I faced. The counseling and therapy I have received varied greatly; the Bible has not.

WHAT GOD WANTS

One of the most well-known stories in the Bible is that of King David's adultery with Bathsheba and his arrangements to have her husband, Uriah, one of his most faithful military men, killed. (The complete story is told in 2 Samuel 11–12.) David seems to have struggled with lies and deceit for most of his life. His public career began notably when he bravely faced down the Philistine giant Goliath and dispatched him with a single sling-shot to the head. Still a teenager when this happened, he was catapulted into the public eye as a "war hero." Unbeknownst to the public, David had also been anointed shortly before this event as the new king of Israel, in due course to succeed the disgraced Saul who was to be removed from the throne for failure to keep God's laws.

When Saul began to understand that his successor was a teenager who had already managed to win the hearts of the populace by his bravery, he became insanely jealous and spent the next couple of years trying to murder David. Rather than standing securely in God's promises and protection, David lapsed into a life of insecurity, trying to convince the paranoid, mentally unstable Saul that he was wasting his time chasing David all over the Judean wilderness. When that didn't work, he began to live a deceitful life in order to win protection from others—he used lies and hubris to protect himself from Saul. The drama of this story is as profound as anything in ancient history.

When Saul was finally killed in a battle, David became king at age thirty. He seemed to have learned some valuable lessons during his teens and twenties, but his tendencies toward deceit still haunted him. He even wrote about it in a backhanded way in Psalm 139, in which he talks about how God knows his every move in life—that there is no escaping God's presence.

These tendencies overcame him when he saw Bathsheba, the beautiful wife of Uriah, and wanted her for himself. This wasn't just a garden-variety case of lust. David's armies were at war, and he should have been with them. Instead, he was at home in his palace. Using his kingly prerogatives of power, he summoned Bathsheba and committed adultery with her (David was also married at the time). When Bathsheba became pregnant, David conspired (again, using lies and deceit) to have her husband killed. To his credit, after Uriah was killed, David brought Bathsheba into his palace and made her one of his wives so that she and his child would be provided for.

Yet here was deceitful David, the king of Judah, living with the secrets of being a selfish schemer, an adulterer, and an accomplice to murder. *And he lived with these secrets for almost a year.* To the public, it appeared that Uriah was killed in battle (he was, by David's arrangement), and that David had married his widow and conceived a child—a seemingly natural chain of events.

But then things went awry. For nine or more months, David lived with his conscience-searing secrets. After his son was born, a prophet named Nathan came to him and rebuked him for his parts in the whole tawdry affair. God had revealed the details of David's sins to Nathan, *and Nathan exposed to the light what David had kept in the dark for almost a year.* The result was that David moved from secrets to solutions in his life.

These solutions were not painless, however. David could have been put to death as an adulterer, but he was spared. Instead, his newborn son's life was taken by illness and David's sins were exposed to the nation. He was also told by God, through the prophet, that calamity would come upon him in his remaining years as king, which it certainly did:

> *This is what the LORD says: "Out of your own household I am going to bring calamity upon you. Before your very eyes I will take your wives and give them to one who is close to you, and he will lie with your wives in broad daylight. You did it in secret, but I will do this thing in broad daylight before all Israel." (2 Samuel 12:11–12)*

As soon as Nathan finished speaking, David said to the prophet, "I have sinned against the LORD." David was learning yet again that hiding secrets from God wasn't a profitable enterprise. Just when he thought the dust was settling in his life, his secrets were made known. But he did the right thing. He owned his sins and repented of them. He even went public for the sake of posterity. He wrote Psalm 32 (hiding secret sins from God results in a tortured life; confession results in blessedness), Psalm 51 (a psalm of confession and absolution, heartbreaking in its honesty), and Psalm 139 (don't even think about trying to go somewhere where God isn't and do something wrong).

In David's case, we know what God was for: honesty, openness, revelation, confession, repentance, discipline, and restoration. Is God still for those things today?

The late John Wimber was the founder of the association of churches known as Vineyard Christian Fellowships, now numbering more than six hundred congregations in the United States. Wimber was controversial in the evangelical culture because of his advocacy for healing and the gifts of the Spirit as a part of a Christian's daily life. Say what you will, Wimber walked his biblical talk and tried to remain open to listening for God's direction on a moment-by-moment basis.

For instance, he has recounted publicly and in print that, when he was on an airplane flight, he happened to look across the aisle and see something that he had never seen before. The man seated across from him had the word *ADULTERY* written across his forehead. Not physically, of course—but it may as well have been. Wimber saw it as clearly as if someone had taken a bold-tip Sharpie and written it permanently on the man's skin. In addition, the name of a woman he didn't know came to Wimber's mind and he concluded it was the name of the woman with whom the man was committing adultery.

So, in Nathan-like fashion, Wimber leaned across the aisle and asked the man softly (he assumed the woman sitting next to the man was his wife), "Does the name so-and-so mean anything to you?" When the color drained from the man's face Wimber concluded three things: the man was indeed an adulterer; the name was the woman with whom he was sinning; and, based on the fear on the man's face, the woman next to him was his wife. John and the man went to a private part of the plane where John told him in no uncertain terms that God had sent him to tell the man that he needed to repent of this sin or expect God's chastening. The man confessed his sins and accepted Christ as his Savior. He summoned his wife, confessed to her, and she became a Christian as well. All this at 35,000 feet over mid-America.

Apparently, two-and-a-half millennia after God wanted David's secret sins to be revealed, God still wants that today.

I imagine the man John Wimber spoke to had the same reaction as the apostle Paul described in 1 Corinthians 14:24–25:

> *But if an unbeliever or someone who does not understand comes in while everybody is prophesying, he will be convinced by all that he is a sinner and will be judged by all, and the secrets of his heart will be laid bare. So he will fall down and worship God, exclaiming, "God is really among you!"*

It's easy to misread passages like that, to take them out of the larger context of who God is. One could make a case that God is just looking to catch us doing something wrong and wants to expose us for the nasty, covering-up sinners we are. To conclude that would be to miss the point. What God wants is this: for every man to live with a pure heart, free from the encumbrances of guilt and shame. God made us and knows how we function best. Man can no more live at peak performance with dark secrets in his heart than a Ferrari can win a road race with a cup of sugar in the gas tank. God is love, and He loves us. He doesn't want us to deal with secrets in order to embarrass us but to see us grow up before we grow old, to watch us live the abundant life He created for us to enjoy. Many of us walk through life collecting dark secrets like burrs on our socks while walking through a field. We often don't realize it until later, but at some point they need to be removed.

WHAT GOD DOES

Just as every father feels a natural need to know what's going on in his house, so God wants to know what's going on in His. It's a father's job and the Father's as well. What is God's house?

> *The earth is the LORD's, and everything in it, the world, and all who live in it.* (Psalm 24:1)

That means we, and the secrets of our hearts, are God's. It's His business to know them all. Look at these passages from the Bible that speak about what God knows, including those things that we think only we know:

> If we had forgotten the name of our God or spread out our hands to a foreign god, would not God have discovered it, since he knows the secrets of the heart? (Psalm 44:20–21)

> O LORD, you have searched me and you know me. You know when I sit and when I rise; you perceive my thoughts from afar. (Psalm 139:1–2)

> I the LORD search the heart and examine the mind, to reward a man according to his conduct, according to what his deeds deserve. (Jeremiah 17:10)

In this next passage, I've taken the liberty of rearranging the verses to show how we look at our lives, then how God looks at them. We see our lives as seventy or eighty years, but to God, a thousand years is like one day. We see life as a linear series of events, but God sees it as a single event: past, present, and future. Everything we have done, are doing, and will do are revealed "in the light of His presence":

> The length of our days is seventy years—or eighty, if we have the strength; yet their span is but trouble and sorrow, for they quickly pass, and we fly away.

> For a thousand years in your sight are like a day that has just gone by, or like a watch in the night.

> You have set our iniquities before you, our secret sins in the light of your presence. (Psalm 90:10, 4, 8)

> And when you pray, do not be like the hypocrites, for they love to pray standing in the synagogues and on the street corners to be seen by men. I tell you the truth, they have received their reward in full. But when you pray, go into your room, close the door and pray to your Father, who is unseen. Then your Father, who sees what is done in secret, will reward you. (Matthew 6:5–6)

What all those verses mean is that God watches over us like a father watches over his children. He knows the baggage we carry around in our hearts, sinful or not, and wants to free us of it. Again, as a father would sit down with his burdened child and say, "I can tell something's bothering you—would you like to talk about it?" so God wants to say the same to us. It's just what God does.

FROM SECRETS TO SOLUTIONS

Some secrets are sins—adultery, lying, cheating, murder—and some are not: inferiority, fear, insecurity, inadequacy, and the like. Secrets that are sins *will* be brought to light, and secrets that aren't *ought* to be brought to light. Why?

Secrets that are sins act as moral chasms between ourselves and God, and between ourselves and others. Every man knows this is true. It's impossible to relate to God when we are hiding secret sins in our heart. God's solution to secrets that are sins is the cross of Jesus Christ. The Bible says God sent His Son into the world to die for our sins so we wouldn't have to. But to rid our hearts of secret sins, these need to be confessed to God so we can receive His forgiveness (and to those we may have wounded by our sins, where appropriate). These secrets will be revealed. We can either reveal them now or God will reveal them later, when forgiveness is no longer an option:

> *This will take place on the day when God will judge men's secrets through Jesus Christ, as my gospel declares.* (Romans 2:16)

Secrets that are not sins are chasms of another sort—emotional chasms that stand between us and ourselves, and us and other people. We cannot become the men God created us to be when we are separated from our true selves by fear, doubt, feelings of inadequacy, and fear. Nor can we be wholly honest and intimate with others. God's solution to secrets that are not sins is the *character* of Christ. Man's basic problem is the lack of a model, a template, to live by. All of us were raised by imperfect templates; our fathers were men who, to one degree or another, fell short of the glory of God (Romans 3:23). So how could we possibly grow up whole? We turned out like a finely-machined gear that was cut on a lathe that was itself out of spec. Therefore, we have to look to Christ to see what a whole man is supposed to look like. And the Bible says plainly that He is the model:

> *For those God foreknew he also predestined to be conformed to the likeness of his Son, that he might be the firstborn among many brothers.* (Romans 8:29)

God intends for Christ to be the solution for every man's secrets. His cross is the remedy for secrets that are sins, and His character is the answer for our secrets that are not.

Dealing with the secrets in a man's heart is a lifelong process. Even when we receive God's forgiveness for sins committed in the past, there will be new sins tomorrow. And it takes time to learn to live secret-free. I've read where the control of adult elephants begins when they are young. Keepers chain baby elephants to a stake in the ground that they aren't strong enough to pull up. By the time the elephants are mature, when they could easily pull the stake out of the ground, they've become convinced the stake is immovable.

A secret in the heart of a man is like that stake. Even when it is removed, or we are told we no longer have to be submitted to it, it takes time to break away. But it can happen. Unfortunately, we are not as good at forgiving ourselves as God is.

My hope for every man and woman who reads this book is that they will take advantage, individually or as a couple, of the intimacy that comes with the sharing of secrets. Jesus told His disciples secrets that He didn't tell the general public, and it bound them together as a band of brothers:

> *He said, "The knowledge of the secrets of the kingdom of God has been given to you, but to others I speak in parables, so that, 'though seeing, they may not see; though hearing, they may not understand.'"* (Luke 8:10)

When men reveal their secrets to one another, or a husband shares his secrets with his wife, a bond is created that is a sacred trust:

A gossip betrays a confidence, but a trustworthy man keeps a secret. (Proverbs 11:13)

May God grant freedom, propriety, courage, and grace to you as you move from secrets to solutions in your life.

APPENDIX

"MEN'S LIFE SATISFACTION" SURVEY

		Number of Responses	Response Ratio
1. Are you married?			
Yes		1982	55%
No		1616	45%
	Total	3598	100%

		Number of Responses	Response Ratio
2. How old are you?			
30-35		526	15%
36-40		467	13%
41-45		515	14%
46-50		681	19%
51-55		803	22%
56-60		606	17%
	Total	3598	100%

		Number of Responses	Response Ratio
3. Are you a Christian?			
Yes		2649	74%
No		949	26%
	Total	3598	100%

		Number of Responses	Response Ratio
4. Men are disappointed about what they have achieved in their careers.			
Never		46	1%
Rarely		211	6%
Sometimes		2379	66%
Often		919	26%
Always		43	1%
	Total	3598	100%

5. Men are concerned that physical problems may lead to early death.

		Number of Responses	Response Ratio
Never		29	1%
Rarely		415	12%
Sometimes		1915	53%
Often		1135	32%
Always		104	3%
	Total	3598	100%

6. Men are bored by the idea of church and church activities.

		Number of Responses	Response Ratio
Never		84	2%
Rarely		377	10%
Sometimes		1910	53%
Often		1049	29%
Always		178	5%
	Total	3598	100%

7. Men need to be more respected by women.

		Number of Responses	Response Ratio
Never		65	2%
Rarely		467	13%
Sometimes		1885	52%
Often		896	25%
Always		285	8%
	Total	3598	100%

8. Men wish they had married someone
   other than their wife.

	Number of Responses	Response Ratio
Never	217	6%
Rarely	754	21%
Sometimes	2113	59%
Often	463	13%
Always	51	1%
Total	3598	100%

9. Men are fearful about financial security
   with growing families or in retirement.

	Number of Responses	Response Ratio
Never	24	1%
Rarely	97	3%
Sometimes	1019	28%
Often	1912	53%
Always	546	15%
Total	3598	100%

10. Men have frequent and intense
    sexual fantasies.

	Number of Responses	Response Ratio
Never	17	0%
Rarely	155	4%
Sometimes	1386	39%
Often	1492	41%
Always	548	15%
Total	3598	100

11. Men feel frustrated trying to communicate with women.

	Number of Responses	Response Ratio
Never	28	1%
Rarely	174	5%
Sometimes	1694	47%
Often	1405	39%
Always	297	8%
Total	3598	100%

12. Men find it difficult to talk about their feelings.

	Number of Responses	Response Ratio
Never	24	1%
Rarely	147	4%
Sometimes	1531	43%
Often	1634	45%
Always	262	7%
Total	3598	100%

13. Men have a fragile ego in the bedroom.

	Number of Responses	Response Ratio
Never	67	2%
Rarely	421	12%
Sometimes	1917	53%
Often	999	28%
Always	194	5%
Total	3598	100%

14. Men are frustrated that women are not more aggressive sexually.

		Number of Responses	Response Ratio
Never		46	1%
Rarely		313	9%
Sometimes		1838	51%
Often		1121	31%
Always		280	8%
	Total	3598	100%

15. Men wish they had more private time away from their families.

		Number of Responses	Response Ratio
Never		83	2%
Rarely		584	16%
Sometimes		2143	60%
Often		667	19%
Always		121	3%
	Total	3598	100%

16. Men feel they don't measure up to women spiritually.

		Number of Responses	Response Ratio
Never		203	6%
Rarely		919	26%
Sometimes		1908	53%
Often		515	14%
Always		53	1%
	Total	3598	100%

17. Men are uncomfortable with the notion of total commitment.

	Number of Responses	Response Ratio
Never	138	4%
Rarely	699	19%
Sometimes	2086	58%
Often	600	17%
Always	75	2%
Total	3598	100%

18. Men are threatened by the idea of their wife being the primary breadwinner.

	Number of Responses	Response Ratio
Never	208	6%
Rarely	702	20%
Sometimes	1813	50%
Often	769	21%
Always	106	3%
Total	3598	100%

19. Men are intimidated by successful women.

	Number of Responses	Response Ratio
Never	213	6%
Rarely	681	19%
Sometimes	1938	54%
Often	692	19%
Always	74	2%
Total	3598	100%

20. Men are afraid of close, self-disclosing relationships with other men.

	Number of Responses	Response Ratio
Never	93	3%
Rarely	510	14%
Sometimes	1669	46%
Often	1139	32%
Always	187	5%
Total	3598	100%

21. Men have a deep-seated fear of not living up to their parents' expectations.

	Number of Responses	Response Ratio
Never	136	4%
Rarely	701	19%
Sometimes	1852	51%
Often	771	21%
Always	138	4%
Total	3598	100

22. Men place a high level of value on the physical appearance of women.

	Number of Responses	Response Ratio
Never	29	1%
Rarely	128	4%
Sometimes	1136	32%
Often	1881	52%
Always	424	12%
Total	3598	100%

23. Men need to feel more intensely adored and cherished by their wives.

		Number of Responses	Response Ratio
Never		58	2%
Rarely		365	10%
Sometimes		1902	53%
Often		1051	29%
Always		222	6%
	Total	3598	100%

24. Men are bored or impatient with their role as a parent.

		Number of Responses	Response Ratio
Never		203	6%
Rarely		981	27%
Sometimes		2027	56%
Often		348	10%
Always		39	1%
	Total	3598	100%

25. Men are drawn to pornography in movies, magazines, or on the web.

		Number of Responses	Response Ratio
Never		72	2%
Rarely		370	10%
Sometimes		1711	48%
Often		1188	33%
Always		257	7%
	Total	3598	100%

26. Men are disappointed by the lack of romance and excitement in their lives.

	Number of Responses	Response Ratio
Never	50	1%
Rarely	381	11%
Sometimes	2110	59%
Often	928	26%
Always	129	4%
Total	3598	100%

27. Men feel inadequate in meeting women's needs (emotional, spiritual, or sexual).

	Number of Responses	Response Ratio
Never	82	2%
Rarely	548	15%
Sometimes	2144	60%
Often	739	21%
Always	85	2%
Total	3598	100%

28. Men feel awkward about being spiritual leaders in the family.

	Number of Responses	Response Ratio
Never	180	5%
Rarely	754	21%
Sometimes	2014	56%
Often	585	16%
Always	65	2%
Total	3598	100%

NATIONAL SURVEY OF 3600 MEN

Numbers of Surveys Conducted
  3,600   All Men
  2,651   Xn Men
  949   Other Men

1. Men are fearful about financial security now and in retirement.
   68.3%   All Men
   69.1%   Xn Men
   66.2%   Other Men

2. Men place a high level of value on the physical appearance of women.
   64.0%   All Men
   63.1%   Xn Men
   66.9%   Other Men

3. Men have frequent and intense sexual fantasies.
   56.7%   All Men
   54.1%   Xn Men
   64.2%   Other Men

4. Men find it difficult to talk about their feelings.
   52.7%   All Men
   53.5%   Xn Men
   50.4%   Other Men

5. Men feel frustrated trying to communicate with women.
   47.3%   All Men
   46.1%   Xn Men
   50.6%   Other Men

6. Men are drawn to pornography in movies, magazines, or on the web.
   40.1%   All Men
   39.0%   Xn Men
   46.6%   Other Men

7. Men are frustrated that women are not more aggressive sexually.
   38.9%   All Men
   38.6%   Xn Men
   40.0%   Other Men

8. Men are afraid of close, self-disclosing relationships with other men.
   36.8%   All Men
   37.3%   Xn Men
   35.6%   Other Men

9. Men need to feel more intensely adored and cherished by their wives.
   35.4%   All Men
   36.9%   Xn Men
   31.1%   Other Men

10. Men are concerned that physical problems may lead to early death.
   34.4%   All Men
   35.9%   Xn Men
   30.2%   Other Men

11. Men are bored by the idea of church and church activities.
   34.1%   All Men
   27.9%   Xn Men
   51.3%   Other Men

12. Men have a fragile ego in the bedroom.
   33.1%   All Men
   33.3%   Xn Men
   32.6%   Other Men

13. Men need to be more greatly respected by women.
   32.8%   All Men
   34.3%   Xn Men
   28.7%   Other Men

14. Men are disappointed by the lack of romance and excitement in their lives.
   29.4%   All Men
   30.6%   Xn Men
   26.9%   Other Men

15. Men are disappointed about what they have achieved in their careers.
   26.7%   All Men
   27.1 %   Xn Men
   25.6%   Other Men

16. Men have a deep-seated fear of not living up to their parents' expectations.
   25.3%   All Men
   26.1%   Xn Men
   22.9%   Other Men

17. Men are threatened by the idea of their wife being the primary bread winner.
    24.3%   All Men
    24.6%   Xn Men
    23.6%   Other Men

18. Men feel inadequate in meeting women's needs.
    22.9%   All Men
    23.7%   Xn Men
    18.5%   Other Men

19. Men wish they had more private time *away* from their family.
    21.9%   All Men
    21.1%   Xn Men
    24.0%   Other Men

20. Men are intimidated by successful women.
    21.3%   All Men
    21.1%   Xn Men
    21.8%   Other Men

21. Men are uncomfortable with the notion of total commitment.
    18.8%   All Men
    17.5%   Xn Men
    22.2 %   Other Men

22. Men feel awkward about being spiritual leaders in the family.
    18.1%   All Men
    18.0%   Xn Men
    16.2%   Other Men

23. Men feel they don't measure up to women spiritually.
    15.8%   All Men
    17.1%   Xn Men
    12.1%   Other Men

24. Men wish they had married someone other than their wife.
    14.3%   All Men
    12.9%   Xn Men
    18.1%   Other Men

25. Men are bored or impatient with their role as a parent.
    10.8%   All Men
     9.7%   Xn Men
    12.3%   Other Men

NOTES

Introduction

1. David McCasland, *Oswald Chambers: Abandoned to God—The Life Story of the Author of* My Utmost for His Highest (Grand Rapids: Discovery House Publishers, 1993), 177.

Chapter 1

1. http://moneycentral.msn.com/content/savinganddebt/p102297.asp.
2. Alan Eisenstock, "Home Court," chap. 1 in *Ten on Sunday: The Secret Life of Men* (New York: Atria Books, 2003).
3. http://www.Kiplinger.com/personalfinance/apnews/XmlStoryResult. php?storyid=153744.
4. http://www.aetna.com/presscenter/kit/plan_your_health/retirement_exec_summary.html.
5. http://www.ml.com/index.asp?id=7695_7696_8149_46028_46503_46635.

Chapter 2

1. Bob Buford, foreword to *Stuck in Halftime* (Grand Rapids: Zondervan Publishing House, 2001), 9.
2. Robert Morison, Tamara Erickson, Ken Dychtwald, "Managing Middlescence," *Harvard Business Review*, March 2006. For a good summary of the article, see http://pubs.acs.org/chemjobs/employer/chemhr/MarApr06/midcareer.html.
3. Buford, 39. This book is the third of Buford's on the subject of moving from success to significance, the other two being *Halftime: Changing Your Game Plan from Success to Significance* (Zondervan, 1994) and *Game Plan: Winning Strategies for the Second Half of Your Life* (Zondervan, 1997).
4. Eisenstock, *Ten on Sunday* 89–90.
5. *The Family Man*, directed by Brett Ratner (Hollywood: Universal Pictures, 2000).

Chapter 3

1. Susan Schmidt and James V. Grimaldi, "The Fast Rise and Steep Fall of Jack Abramoff: How a Well-Connected Lobbyist Became the Center of a Far-Reaching Corruption Scandal," *The Washington Post*, 29 December 2005, A01(N).
2. Gordon MacDonald, *When Men Think Private Thoughts: Exploring the Issues That Captivate the Minds of Men* (Nashville: Thomas Nelson, 1996, 1997), 59–60.
3. Patrick A. Means, *Men's Secret Wars* (Grand Rapids,: Revell Books, 1996, 1999), 53–54.
4. MacDonald, *When Men Think Private Thoughts*, 69–71, 73–74.
5. Leanne Payne, *Crisis in Masculinity* (Grand Rapids: Baker Books, 1985, 1995), 79.
6. Leanne Payne, *Restoring the Christian Soul: Overcoming Barriers to Completion in Christ Through Healing Prayer* (Grand Rapids.: Baker Books, 1991), 31.
7. Means, *Men's Secret Wars* 60–61.
8. Ibid., 59–60.

Chapter 4

1. http://magazines.ivillage.com/redbook/sex/happy/articles/0,,284445_669656-5,00.html.
2. Ibid.
3. http://www.infoplease.com/ipa/A0193820.html.
4. http://www.infoplease.com/ipa/A0763170.html.
5. http://www.cnn.com/2004/US/Careers/10/22/equal.pay/.
6. Pat Regnier and Amanda Gengler, "Men, Women . . . and Money," *Money*, April 2006, http://money.cnn.com/2006/03/10/pf/marriage_short_moneymag_0604/index.htm.
7. Christy Casamassima, "Battle of the Bucks," *Psychology Today*, March/April 1995, http://www.psychologytoday.com/articles/pto-1356.html.
8. Anne E. Winkler, "Earnings of Husbands and Wives in Dual-Earner Families," *Monthly Labor Review* 121, no. 4 (1998), http://www.bls.gov/opub/mlr/1998/04/art4exc.htm.
9. http://magazines.ivillage.com/redbook/sex/happy/articles/0,,284445_669656-5,00.html.
10. Ibid., Casamassima.

Chapter 5

1. http://archives.cnn.com/2001/CAREER/trends/08/30/ilo.study/.
2. http://www.nclnet.org/stress/summary.htm.
3. http://www.breakingtravelnews.com/article/20051209021145135.
4. Patrick Morley, *Understanding Your Man in the Mirror* (Grand Rapids: Zondervan, 1998), 68–79.
5. Scott Haltzman, *The Secrets of Happily Married Men: Eight Ways to Win Your Wife's Heart Forever* (San Francisco: Jossey-Bass, 2006), 118.
6. Sam Keen, *Fire in the Belly: On Being a Man* (New York: Bantam Books, 1991), 244–245.

Chapter 6

1. http://www.fatherhood.org/fatherfacts_t10.asp.
2. Weldon Hardenbrook, "Where's Dad? A Call for Fathers with the Spirit of Elijah," chap. 23 in John Piper and Wayne Grudem, eds., *Recovering Biblical Manhood and Womanhood: A Response to Evangelical Feminism* (Wheaton, Ill.: Crossway Books, 1991), 392.

Chapter 7

1. MacDonald, 42–43.
2. David C. Bentall, *The Company You Keep: The Transforming Power of Male Friendship* (Minneapolis: Augsburg Books, 2004), 56.
3. H. Norman Wright, *The Key to Your Man's Heart* (Ventura, Calif.: Regal, 2004), 45–51.
4. Bentall, 58–59.
5. Ibid., 62.
6. Emerson Eggerichs, *Love & Respect* (Nashville: Integrity; Colorado Springs, Colo.: Focus on the Family, 2004), 141.
7. Larry Crabb, "He Was There and He Was Silent," chap. 7 in *The Silence of Adam: Becoming Men of Courage in a World of Chaos* (Grand Rapids: Zondervan, 1995).
8. Bentall, 57.

Chapter 8

1. I have heard this quote a number of times over the years, but have yet to track down its source. Authentic or not, it's a great story. Cited in *Today in the Word*, November 1996, 27.
2. Crabb, 160.
3. Morley, 118–119.

4. Warren Farrell, *Why Men Are the Way They Are* (New York: Berkley Books, 1986), 6–7.

5. Gail Sheehy, *Understanding Men's Passages: Discovering the New Map of Men's Lives* (New York: Ballentine Books, 1998, 1999), 169.

6. MacDonald, 10–11.

7. Bentall, 7.

8. Ibid., 171.

9. Crabb, 165.

10. Bentall, 177.

Chapter 9

1. http://en.wikipedia.org/wiki/Life_expectancy.

2. http://www.cdc.gov/nchs/data/hus/hus05.pdf#073.

3. http://www.cdc.gov/nchs/data/hus/hus05.pdf#063.

4. http://www.jr2.ox.ac.uk/bandolier/band112/b112-6.html.

5. Barbara Starfield, M.D., "Is US Health Really the Best in the World?" *Journal of the American Medical Association*, 284 (2000): 483–485.

6. Ibid.

7. http://www.kaiseredu.org/topics_im.asp?imID=1&parentid=61&id=358.

8. http://www.prostatecancerfoundation.org/site/c.itIWK2OSG/b.189965/k.743F/FAQs_About_Prostate_Cancer.htm.

Chapter 10

1. Heidi H. Sung et al., "Definition of Adventure Travel: Conceptual Framework for Empirical Application from the Providers' Perspective" (paper presented in the 1996 Annual Society of Travel and Tourism Educators Conference, Ottawa, Canada, October 1996), http://www.hotel-online.com/Neo/Trends/AsiaPacificJournal/AdventureTravel.html.

2. Christina Heyniger, "Industry Demands Credible Adventure Travel Research," *Adventure Travel News* (June 2005), http://www.adventuretravel.biz/research_atn_0605.asp.

3. Ibid.

4. John Eldredge, *Wild at Heart: Discovering the Secret of a Man's Soul* (Nashville: Thomas Nelson, 2001), 7.

5. http://www.dedelen.com/2004/12/lord-of-bored.html.

6. Zig Ziglar, *Better than Good: Creating a Life You Can't Wait to Live* (Nashville: Integrity Publishers, 2005).

7. Ibid., 166–167.

8. Sam Keen, *Fire in the Belly: On Being a Man* (New York: Bantam Books, 1991).

Chapter 11

1. *The State of Our Unions 2002: The Social Health of Marriage in America* (Piscataway, N.J.: Rutgers, 2002), 3. See http://marriage.rutgers.edu.

2. Ibid., 19–20.

3. Ibid., 20.

4. Ibid., 7.

5. Farrell, 150.

6. Scott M. Stanley, "What Is It with Men and Commitment, Anyway?" (keynote address to the 6th Annual Smart Marriages Conference, Washington, D.C., July 9–16, 2002), http://www.smartmarriages.com/stanley.men.anyway.html.

7. http://www.romanceopedia.com/E-TheCommitment.html.

Chapter 12

1. From David Murrow's *Church for Men* Web site, http://www.churchformen.com/allmen.php.
2. The Barna Group, "Commitment to Christianity Depends on How It Is Measured," 8 November 2005, http://www.barna.org/FlexPage.aspx?Page=BarnaUpdate&BarnaUpdateID=203.
3. David Murrow, *Why Men Hate Going to Church* (Nashville: Thomas Nelson, 2005), 228.
4. "I Still Haven't Found What I'm Looking For," from U2, *The Joshua Tree*. ©1987 Chappell Music/US (ASCAP).
5. But no less a respected theologian than Eugene Peterson, author of *The Message* Bible translation, believes Bono to be filling the role of a modern-day prophet (see http://www.atu2.com/news/article.src?ID=4232).
6. Murrow, 228.
7. http://www.newcanaansociety.org. NBC reporter David Bloom, who died while covering the march of American forces to Baghdad, was part of the New Canaan Society. There are few stories of men's love and sorrow for one another more touching than that reported of Bloom's death by one of the Society's leaders (http://www.newcanaansociety.org/index.php?id=180).
8. Ibid.
9. Charles Colson with Anne Morse, "Soothing Ourselves to Death," *Christianity Today*, April 2006, 116.
10. For example, Leon J. Podles, *The Church Impotent: The Feminization of Christianity* (Dallas, Texas: Spence Publishing Company, 1999).
11. Murrow, 23–24.
12. Tim Stafford, "Good Morning, Evangelicals!" *Christianity Today*, November 2005, 41.
13. Steve Sonderman, *How to Build a Life-Changing Men's Ministry: Bringing the Fire Home to Your Church* (Minneapolis: Bethany House, 1996), 215–216.
14. http://www.touchstonemag.com/archives/article.php?id=16-05-024-v.
15. Murrow, 14.

Chapter 13

1. "The Demographic Characteristics of the Linguistic and Religious Groups in Switzerland," by Werner Haug and Phillipe Warner of the Federal Statistical Office, Neuchatel, Switzerland. It appears in Volume 2 of *Population Studies No. 31*, a book titled *The Demographic Characteristics of National Minorities in Certain European States*, edited by Werner Haug and others, published by the Council of Europe Directorate General III, Social Cohesion, Strasbourg, January 2000. See http://www.touchstonemag.com/docs/issues/16.5docs/16-5pg24.html.
2. Robbie Lowe (vicar in the Church of England), "The Truth about Men & Church," a paper summarizing the implications of the Swiss study, available at http://www.touchstonemag.com/docs/issues/16.5docs/16-5pg24.html.
3. Ibid.
4. Keen, 226.
5. Willard F. Harley Jr., *His Needs, Her Needs: Building an Affair-Proof Marriage* (Grand Rapids: Revell Books, 1986, 1994, 2001), 146.
6. Jim Conway, *Men in Midlife Crisis* (Colorado Springs: Cook Communications, 1978, 1997), 266–267.
7. Keen, 223–224.
8. Bentall, 114.

9. Thomas J. Peters and Robert H. Waterman Jr., *In Search of Excellence* (New York: Warner Books, 1982).
10. Keen, 185.

Chapter 14
1. http://www.abcnews.go.com/sections/us/DailyNews/church_poll020301.html.
2. Crabb, 97.
3. Textual notes on Genesis 3:16 in *The Expositor's Bible Commentary* (Grand Rapids: Zondervan, 1979).
4. http://www.medicinenet.com/script/main/art.asp?articlekey=35176.

Chapter 15
1. Shaunti Feldhahn, *For Women Only: What You Need to Know About the Inner Lives of Men* (Sisters, Ore.: Multnomah Publishers, 2004), 178–180.
2. Ibid.
3. http://magazines.ivillage.com/redbook/print/0,,289119,00.html.
4. http://www.thehomeschoolmagazine.com/reviews/reviews.php?rid=144.
5. Wright, 58.
6. Lou Cannon, "Why Reagan Was the 'Great Communicator,'" *USA Today*, 6 June 2004, http://www.usatoday.com/news/opinion/editorials/2004-06-06-cannon_x.htm.
7. Haltzman, 163–164.
8. Ibid., 172.
9. Barbara De Angelis, *Secrets About Men Every Woman Should Know* (New York: Dell Publishing, 1990), 286–307.
10. Morley, 140.

Chapter 16
1. Gary Chapman, *The Five Love Languages, Men's Edition: How to Express Heartfelt Commitment to Your Mate* (Chicago: Northfield Publishing, 1992, 1995, 2004), 41.
2. Eggerichs, 57.
3. Morley, 124.
4. Gary and Barbara Rosberg, *The 5 Love Needs of Men & Women* (Wheaton, Ill.: Tyndale House Publishers, 2000), 147–148.
5. Chapman, 42–43.
6. John Gray, *Men Are from Mars, Women Are from Venus: The Classic Guide to Understanding the Opposite Sex* (New York: HarperCollins Publishers, 1992), 148.

Chapter 17
1. Feldhahn, 21–23.
2. Eggerichs, 58. (See the results in Feldhahn, p. 25.)
3. In Titus 2:4, Paul says older women are to "train the younger women to love their husbands and children." But here he uses a different Greek word for love than the word used when he tells husbands to love their wives in Ephesians. There, the word is *agapao*, the classic word for sacrificial, unconditional love. In Titus, the root word is *phileo* which means brotherly love. In that passage, Paul means for the younger women to be devoted to their husbands and children—to be domestically oriented in their faithfulness to God so that no one will "malign the word of God" (v. 5).

4. Eggerichs, 68–69.
5. Ibid., 17–18.
6. Ibid., 60.
7. Harley, 155–156.

Chapter 18

1. MacDonald, 129–130.
2. http://lawgeek.typepad.com/lawgeek/2006/02/index.html.
3. http://www.ssc.wisc.edu/nsfh/.
4. http://www.physorg.com/news11319.html%20%20main%20link%20to%20study. The study, "What's Love Got to Do With It? Equality, Equity, Commitment and Women's Marital Quality," appeared in *Social Forces* (March 2006), a respected academic journal of sociology (online access restricted to subscribing academic libraries).
5. *Network*, directed by Sidney Lumet (Hollywood: Metro-Goldwyn-Mayer, 1976).
6. Gray, 146–150.

Chapter 19

1. Sylvia Ann Hewlett, *Creating a Life: What Every Woman Needs to Know about Having a Baby and a Career* (New York: Miramax Books, 2004).
2. http://www.management-issues.com/display_page.asp?section=research&id=714.
3. The study is summarized at http://www.thisislondon.co.uk/londoncuts/articles/16934878?source=Daily%20Mail. The complete study can be found at http://www.sciencedirect.com/science?_ob=ArticleURL&_udi=B6V9F-4F1GRC0-1&_coverDate=05%2F31%2F2005&_alid=403510400&_rdoc=1&_fmt=&_orig=search&_qd=1&_cdi=5897&_sort=d&view=c&_acct=C000050221&_version=1&urlVersion=0&_userid=10&md5=d3935d2031f6acd9fd8d073d5388e614.
4. http://www.umich.edu/news/index.html?Releases/2004/Dec04/r120804.
5. Richard Morin, "Major Changes in Black Family Structure," *Washington Post*, 25 March 1997, A15(N).
6. Eldredge, 151–152.

Chapter 20

1. http://catholica.pontifications.net/?p=1058. See also http://www.natcath.com/NCR_Online/archives/062102/062102e.htm.
2. http://www.faithworks.com/archives/stay_married.htm.
3. http://www.marriagesavers.com/MarriageSaversOverview.htm.
4. Ibid.
5. http://www.marriagesavers.com/Marriage%20Savers%20Proven%20Strategies%202004.htm.
6. http://www.utahmarriage.org/index.cfm?id=MORE13.
7. Zig Ziglar, *Courtship After Marriage: Romance Can Last a Lifetime* (Nashville: Thomas Nelson, 2001), 11.
8. http://www.americanvalues.org/html/r-unhappy_ii.html. See also Karen S. Peterson, "Unhappily Wed? Put Off Getting That Divorce: Study Finds That Waiting, Working It Out Can Pay Off," *USA Today*, 11 July 2002, 1D, http://www.usatoday.com/usatonline/20020711/4263891s.htm.
9. These findings were summarized by Mike McManus of Marriage Savers from the book by Linda Waite and Maggie Gallagher, *The Case for Marriage: Why Married People Are Happier,*

Healthier, and Better Off Financially (New York: Broadway, 2001). See http://www.marriage-savers.com/public/the_case_for_marriage.htm.
10. http://catholica.pontifications.net/?p=1058.
11. http://www.utahmarriage.org/index.cfm?id=INDEX01.
Even after reading this chapter, any man (or woman) still considering the possibility that they married the wrong person should read the pamphlet by Dr. Brent A. Barlow, *Crossroads: Why Divorce Is Often Not the Best Option.* It's online at http://www.utahmarriage.org/index.cfm?id=MORE13.
12. http://en.thinkexist.com/quotes/tom_mullen/.
13. http://www.smartmarriages.com/continued.html.
14. Thornton Wilder, *The Skin of Our Teeth: A Play* (New York: Harper Perennial Modern Classics, 2003).

Chapter 21

1. Alon Gratch. *If Men Could Talk . . . Translating the Secret Language of Men* (Boston, New York, and London: Little, Brown, and Company, 2001), 95–96.
2. Alex Berenson, "Sales of Impotence Drugs Fall, Defying Expectations," *The New York Times*, 4 December 2005.

Chapter 22

1. Gary Langer et al, "A Peek Beneath the Sheets," ABC News *Primetime Live* Poll: American Sex Survey, http://www.abcnews.com, 21 October 2004.
2. John Ayto, *Dictionary of Word Origins* (New York: Arcade Publishing, 1990), 219.
3. *The Oxford English Dictionary*, 2d ed., s.v. "fantasy."
4. *The American Heritage Dictionary of the English Language*, 4th ed., s.v. "fantasy."
5. http://www.wikipedia.com.
6. New Life Ministries (http://www.newlife.com). Stephen Arterburn, Fred Stoeker, and Mike Yorkey, *Every Man's Battle* (Colorado Springs: WaterBrook Press, 2000).
7. Francis Brown, Samuel R. Driver, and Charles A. Briggs, eds., *A Hebrew and English Lexicon of the Old Testament* (Oxford: Clarendon Press, 1952).
8. MacDonald, chapters 3–4.
9. Ibid., 35.
10. Ibid., 53.

Chapter 23

1. Richard Corliss, "That Old Feeling: When Porno Was Chic," http://www.time.com, 29 March 2005.
2. Lisa Takeuchi Cullen, "Sex in the Syllabus," *Time*, 26 March 2006, http://www.time.com/time/archive/preview/0,10987,1176976,00.html.
3. Nancy Ten Kate, "Keep on Trucking: Americans Are Indulging Their Love for Vehicles with Carrying Capacity," *American Demographics*, March 1996. See http://www.findarticles.com/p/articles/mi_m4021/is_n3_v18/ai_18056289.
4. For a large collection of statistics on the spread and impact of pornography, especially Internet pornography, visit http://www.protectkids.com/dangers/stats.htm#broken.
5. *Christianity Today* Leadership Survey, December 2001.

6. Jacobellis v. Ohio, 378 U.S. 184, 197 (1964)
http://library.findlaw.com/2003/May/15/132747.html#edn1.
7. Payne, *Crisis in Masculinity*, 17.
8. Gordon Dalbey, *Healing the Masculine Soul* (Nashville: W Publishing Group, 1988, 2003), 80–81.
9. Ibid.
10. Ibid., Corliss.
11. Testimony of Jill Manning, M.S., *The Impact of Internet Pornography on Marriage and the Family*, "Hearing on Pornography's Impact on Marriage and the Family," (11/10/05), 13–20, http://new.heritage.org/Research/Family/loader.cfm?url =/commonspot/security/getfile.cfm&PageID=85273.

Chapter 24
1. Cathryn Conroy, "What Women Want Most in a Man," Leger Marketing-Canadian Press poll, Netscape.com, 10 February 2004, http://channels.netscape.com/ love/package.jsp?name=love/fun/womenwant/womenwant.
2. Morley, 133.
3. http://jmm.aaa.net.au/articles/5202.htm.
4. Feldhahn, 97.
5. Gray, 41.
6. Ibid., 45.
7. Ibid., 56.
8. Harley, 50–52.
9. David Schnarch, *Passionate Marriage: Sex, Love, and Intimacy in Emotionally Committed Relationships.* (New York: W. W. Norton & Co., 1997).
10. Harley, 60.
11. Based on a ten-year study of 2,500 men aged 45-59. Kelly McCarthy, "Want Yet Another Reason to Have Sex?" *Psychology Today*, March–April 2001, http://www.psychologytoday.com/articles/pto-20010301-000015.html.

Chapter 25
1. Shaunti Feldhahn, "The Truth About the Way You Look," in *For Women Only: What You Need to Know About the Inner Lives of Men* (Sisters, Ore.: Multnomah Publishers, 2004).
2. http://www.seinfeldscripts.com.
3. Morley, 176.
4. Shmuley Boteach, "Are Husbands to Blame for Their Wives Becoming Fat?" http://www.worldnetdaily.com, 4 December 2003.
5. Feldhahn, 173

Tired of That Old Yo-Yo
Weight Loss/Weight Gain Cycle?
Lose It for Life!

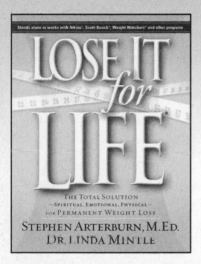

Most weight-loss plans will help you drop a few pounds, but for how long? You deserve better. You deserve *Lose It for Life*, a uniquely balanced program that deals with the physical, emotional, and even spiritual elements that lead to permanent weight loss.

Even if you have already experienced some success on another weight-loss program, this book will give you the information and motivation you need to achieve a permanent "state of weightlessness," which is *the* secret to lasting results.

Lose It for Life was developed by best-selling author and radio personality Stephen Arterburn who lost 60 pounds 20 years ago and has kept it off. In this revolutionary book, he and Dr. Linda Mintle, who is known for her clinical work regarding weight issues, will help you accomplish what you desire most: permanent results.

A refreshing approach
to addiction and
temptation that offers
hope for anyone
whose life has spun
out of control.

We've all known someone who just can't seem to break free of a cycle of self-defeating and destructive behavior. Or perhaps we've suffered the consequences, large or small, of addictive behavior in our own lives. Stephen Arterburn offers insight and hope for anyone whose life has spun out of control due to addictions. His revolutionary and refreshing approach to recovery positively recognizes and affirms that our capacity to enjoy and savor life is a gift from God that must be fed for us to be healthy. From there, he helps readers identify and understand what needs they are really seeking to fulfill through their problematic behaviors, and lays out a proven step-by-step plan that enables them to reclaim control of their relationships, career, personal happiness—and life.

Available wherever books are sold
ISBN 1-59145-478-6